NEWMAN'S LIVES OF THE ENGLISH SAINTS

ENGLISH SAINTS

VOL. V.

MANSUETI HÆREDITABUNT TERRAM

ET DELECTABUNTUR

IN MULTITUDINE PACIS

From a Photograph by

Elliott & Fry

The Very Rev.ᵈ Richard William Church.
Dean of St. Pauls.
Wadham Col. Oxford B.A. 1836. M.A. 1839.
Fellow of Oriel Col. 1838 - 54.

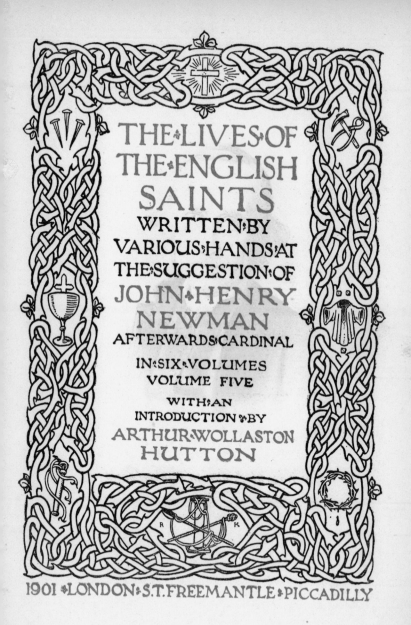

THE LIVES OF
THE ENGLISH
SAINTS
WRITTEN BY
VARIOUS HANDS AT
THE SUGGESTION OF
JOHN HENRY
NEWMAN
AFTERWARDS CARDINAL

IN SIX VOLUMES
VOLUME FIVE

WITH AN
INTRODUCTION BY
ARTHUR WOLLASTON
HUTTON

1901 LONDON S.T. FREEMANTLE PICCADILLY

CONTENTS

ST. WULSTAN

ST. AELRED

ST. NINIAN

CONTENTS

ST. WALTHEOF AND ST. ROBERT OF NEWMINSTER

LIFE OF

ST. WULSTAN,

BISHOP OF WORCESTER, CIRC. A.D. 1008–1095.

LIFE OF
ST. WULSTAN

BISHOP OF WORCESTER, CIRC. A.D. 1008-1095.

ST. WULSTAN'S history has many points of interest.
He was the last Saint of the Anglo-Saxon Church.
His name closed the roll of that company so excellent
and numerous, which gained for England the title of
the Isle of Saints. He was the link between the old
English Church and hierarchy and the Norman; he
saw the ruin of his people, but was spared himself.
And he was a type and representative, as complete
perhaps as could be found, of the religious character
of the Anglo-Saxon Church; plain, homely, and
simple-hearted, cherishing a popular and domestic
piety, rather dwelling on the great broad truths of the
gospel, than following them into their results; scrup-
ulous and earnest in devotion; without the refinement, learning, and keen thought of the Normans,
yet full of fresh and genuine feeling. Wulstan was
a monk indeed, and an ascetic, but his vocation lay
not in the learned school or meditative cloister, but
among the people of the market-place and the village,
—his rough, yet hearty and affectionate countrymen.

The following account of him pretends not to be

a critical history; it aims merely at giving the idea of St. Wulstan which was impressed on the minds of those who had seen him and lived with him. They certainly believed that they saw in him the tokens of saintliness—more than common humbleness and faith in God—and so they portrayed him; an image which moved them to greater self-control and self-devotion, and gave them courage and hope in their dark times, by assuring them that religion was still a reality.[1]

Wulstan was born in the early years of the eleventh century, in the days of the second Ethelred; the time when the greatness of Alfred and Ethelstan was ending in unspeakable desolation. They were as dreary and disastrous days as ever were seen in England. The terrible idolaters of the north could be kept off no longer, and were now working their will upon the land, rendered tenfold more merciless and savage by the massacre of St. Brice's day. Year after year the scourge continued :—before the inland country had heard that "the fleet" had been descried, their grim and raging troops mounted on horses,

[1] Et veterum quidem gestis pro antiquitatis assurgunt reverentia; sed alacriori capiuntur dulcedine, si alicujus Sancti, qui nuperrime fuit, vita producatur in medium, in quâ sicut è speculo conspicentur, ut ita dictum sit, vivum religionis simulachrum. Accedit enim jocundæ relationi novitas; ne aliquis desperet a se per Dei gratiam fieri posse, quod audit ab alio de proximo factum fuisse. . . . Quapropter benigno lectori grande paciscor commodum; ut quamquam B. Wulstanum non minus quam priscos pro miraculorum gloria suscipiat familiaritas, tamen pro recenti ætate mores ejus æmulo exercitii pede sequi contendat.— Will. Malm. Prolog. in Vit. Wulstani. ap. Wharton, Angl. Sac. vol. ii. p. 243.

were sweeping like wolves, over moor and hill, through plain and valley, burning town and hamlet, and leaving those who had given them hospitality, murdered on their own hearths. The visitation seemed to be too frightful to resist; there was no help for the "miserable people" in the king and his chiefs; on all sides was treachery, cowardice, or hopeless imbecility and weakness; all that the great men found to do, was to plunder also, in order to bribe the Danes; meanwhile, as long as they might, they feasted and revelled.

"Over midsummer," writes the contemporary chronicler, in 1006, "came the Danish fleet to Sandwich, and did as they were wont; they harried, and burned, and slew, as they went. Then the king called out all the people of the West Saxons and Mercians, and they lay out all the harvest in arms against the Host; but it availed nought more than it had often done before; but for all this the Host went as they themselves would; and the armed gathering did the country folk all the harm, that foeman's host from within or from abroad, could do. About midwinter, the Host went out to their ready store, through Hampshire into Berkshire, to Reading. And there they did after their old wont; they lighted their camp-beacons as they went. . . . And at Kennet they came to battle, and put the English folk to flight, and then carried the prey of their Host to the sea. There might the Winchester folk see the proud and restless Host, as they passed by their gates to the sea, and fetched food and treasures more than fifty miles from the sea. Then was the king gone over the Thames, into Shropshire,

and he took up his abode there in midwinter-tide.
Then was there so great fear of the Host, that no
man might think or devise how men should drive
them out of the land, or hold his land against them :
for they had roughly marked every shire in the
West Saxons with burning and harrying. Then
began the king in earnest to consult with his Witan,
what to all of them seemed the best counsel for to
defend this land, before it was utterly undone. Then
resolved the king and his Witan, for the behoof of
all the people, though they were all loth, that they
must needs pay tribute to the Host. Then the
king sent to the Host, and bade tell them that he
desired that there should be peace between them,
and that men should give tribute and food to them :
and they agreed to all these things, and men fed
them throughout England." [1]

Such were the reports brought year by year to
the Minsters of Peterborough and Worcester, and
recorded by their anxious inmates in their homely
but forcible style. The sickening tale came over
and over again—how navies were built at a great
charge, how some of the ships were wrecked or
burned, and how the king and the " Ealdormen," and
the " High Witan," lightly deserted the rest and went
home, and "let all the labour of the people perish
thus lightly, and the fear was not lessened, as all
England hoped,"—how "the Host" came again to
the Wight, to Sussex, and Hampshire and Berkshire ;
—to Kent and London—through Chiltern to Oxford ;
northward to Bedford, eastward to the wild fens of
the East Angles, westward to Wiltshire,—how accord-

[1] Saxon Chron. a. 1006.

ing to their wont, they were harrying and burning
for months together, "slaying both men and cattle";
—how when the king's army should have gone out
to meet them, they went home; and "when they
were in the East, men kept the king's army in the
West, and when in the South, our army was in the
North";—how "whatever was advised stood not a
month,"—how at length there was no chief who
would collect an army, but each was flying as he
could—how there was not a single shire that would
stand by another:—till at last the frightful news
came, that in spite of the tribute and the peace, they
had beset "Canterbury, and entered therein through
treachery; for Elfman delivered the city to them,
whose life Archbishop Elfege had formerly saved."

This was the climax of horrors. The Danes
"returned to their ships, and led the Archbishop
with them, and they kept him with them till they
martyred him." This happened soon after. The
following Easter, says the chronicle, the great men
of England paid their tribute — eight and forty
thousand pounds—but the Archbishop would pay
nothing, for to satisfy the Danes, he must plunder
his tenantry. "Then on the Saturday was the
Host sore stirred against the Bishop; because he
would not promise them any fee, and forbade that
any man should give any thing for him. They
were also very drunken, for there was wine brought
them from the South. Then took they the Bishop,
and led him to their 'hustings,' on the eve of the
Sunday after Easter, and there they shamefully
killed him. They overwhelmed him with bones
and horns of oxen; and one of them smote him

with an axe-iron on the head, so that he sunk with the blow; and his holy blood fell on the earth, and his holy soul was sent to the kingdom of God."[1]

Such were the scenes rife in England, in Wulstan's early years; he first knew it under a cloud. The first he saw of it, showed it him as a land under the scourge of strangers; its name was associated in his earliest impressions, not as now, with security and greatness, but with dishonour and misery; from the first, the idea was made familiar to him, that he lived among a people under God's judgment. As he grew up, the prospect cleared for a while, but the tokens and sights of his youth returned in his old age. He lived nearly through the century; he saw it begin with the Danish harryings, and end with the Norman conquest.

He was born at Long Itchington,[2] a village in Warwickshire, where his family had long been settled, and where his parents, Athelstan and Wulfgeva, were probably the chief people. He was educated at the monasteries of Evesham and Peterborough, the latter one of the richest houses and most famous schools in England. Here, in the "Golden Burgh,"[3] with the children, the "infantes" of the convent, some of them already vowed to religion, others preparing for the world without, he enjoyed what education a Saxon monastery could give; he was broken in to a life of hardship and self-discipline; taught to rise before day, and to take a special part in the sacred service; in the morning he chanted, in the afternoon he was taught

---

[1] Saxon Chron. a. 1012.
[2] Icentune.   [3] Sax. Chr. 1066.

to write, to illuminate and bind books, or he learnt
Latin from interlinear translations, or from conning
over the pages of the Psalters and Sacramentaries
which were produced in the writing room of the
convent. The rod which punished the offences of
the grown - up brethren, was not spared to the
children. "Hast thou been flogged to-day?"[1] asks
the imaginary master, in Ælfric's Latin and Saxon
Dialogue; to which the boy answers, as if it was
an exception, "No, for I behaved myself warily";
but he will not answer for his companions. "Why
do you ask me? I must not tell you our secrets.
Each one knows whether he was whipt or not."
The same book, perhaps composed for Peterborough,
and from which Wulstan may have learnt his Latin,
gives an account how the children spent their day.
"To-day," says the boy in the Dialogue, "I have
done many things; this night, when I heard the
knell, I arose from my bed, and went to Church,
and sang night-song with the brethren; and after
that, we sang the service of All Saints, and the
morning lauds; then Prime, and the Seven Psalms
with the Litanies, and the first mass; then Tierce,
and the mass of the day; then we sang the mid-
day hour; and we ate, and drank, and went to sleep,
and rose again, and sang Nones. And now we are
here before thee, ready to hear what thou wilt say
to us." They were allowed to eat meat, because
"they were still children under the rod"; they drank
ale if they could get it, else water; but wine "they
were not rich enough to buy, and besides, it was
not the drink of children and foolish persons, but

[1] In Thorpe's Analecta, pp. 116, 117.

of old men and wise." "Who awakens you," says the Master, "to night-song?" "Sometimes I hear the knell, and rise, sometimes the master wakes me roughly with his rod." School is the same at all times.

Under this discipline, Wulstan made good progress. He was thoughtful above his years; he voluntarily submitted to exercises and self-denials from which the children were excused, and formed a habit of continually applying examples of excellence which were brought before him, whether living or departed, to his own improvement.

From the minster schools at Peterborough, Wulstan returned home, to live in the country, in his father's hall, a Thane's son, who might one day be a Thane himself, among his father's dependants, and friends, and enemies, with such amusements and such business as Thanes' sons followed. He was beautiful in face, and of a well-formed person; active and dexterous, of free and engaging manners, and he entered with zest into the society and sports of his companions. The life of ease and idleness is a dangerous life at all times; and it was especially so then. Besides the temptations of birth and rank and freedom and personal attractions, the disorders of the times left all men very much to their own ways; yet the young Thane's son fell not.

At length came one of those events which give a turn to a man's character for life. A young woman of the neighbourhood became his temptress. Her wiles, often repeated, were in vain. But on a day, when in a crowded field, he had won the prize in some trial of speed or strength, in the excitement of victory and exertion, she approached him. He had never before felt the allurements of her presence, but now he wavered. It was a sharp struggle, but he was true, and it was a short one. He rushed from the scene of mirth and sport, and threw himself down in a solitary place, among brushwood and furze, and there he wept over the thought of sin which he had indulged. He lay there long, and fell asleep. When he awoke, his soul was clear and fresh, and from that time he was never again tempted. His friends said that he had spoken of a miracle—of a bright cloud descending and enveloping him, and of the dew of heaven, which quenched in him for ever the fires of sin; and that this cloud was beheld by his companions. But whether or not they understood him aright, the trial itself, the victory and the reward, formed an epoch in his life.

Time went on; and his father and mother, who had grown old, came down in the world. They went to Worcester; and there, by mutual consent, they both took the religious habit, and passed the rest of their days in monasteries. Wulstan accompanied them, and entered the service of Brihtege, the Bishop, that he might devote himself to the service of the Church. The Bishop took him into favour, and soon ordained him, though against his will, to the priesthood.[1]

"A layman in his garb, a monk in his way of life"—this is the description of him while a secular priest. But having adopted the strictness, he wished also for the helps and advantages of the monastic life—the great refuge of religious minds in those

[1] A.D. 1033-38.

days, from a state of society where it was hard to live pure and in peace. He declined, therefore, the preferment which the bishop pressed upon him, and obtained his permission to enter a monastic congregation, where he continued for above twenty-five years,[1] rising through various offices, till he became the Prior, or as it was then called, the "Præpositus" of the monastery.[2]

They were years to him without much change or eventfulness; years of noiseless duty, and hidden self-discipline. Wulstan, the holy monk of Worcester, was heard of, indeed, in many parts of England, and the proud Earl Harold was known on one occasion to go thirty miles out of his way, to make his confession to him, and beg his prayers.[3] But little was seen or felt of him beyond Worcester and its neighbourhood. There, those who lived about him saw a man of kind yet blunt and homely speech, of frank and unpretending demeanour, who had a word for every one, and always the right word; who was at at every one's service, and was never wearied of his work; a man of not much learning, but who had all that was within his reach; who had made the Gospels his daily meditation, and knew the Psalms by heart; whose voice, when he preached, seemed to the people to have the dignity, the sweetness, and the awfulness of an apostle's; a man who, humble and cheerful as he was, could be stern in rebuke, and decisive in action, when sin offended him; a man who was always in earnest, in the minutest details of life. There was

---

[1] Until 1062.   [2] Will. Malms. Vit. S. Wulstani, p. 247, c. v.
[3] Will. Malms. Vit. S. Wulstani, p. 248, c. vii.

no mistaking in him the man of God. In those days, indeed, character expressed itself, and was noticed, with a grotesque simplicity, at which, so that we do not sneer, we may be pardoned for smiling, for our times are different; but we must be more blind than men were then, if in the plain rough-hewn Anglo-Saxon monk, we cannot discern, as they did, high goodness and faith, and a genuine English heart.

"The devotional duties," says his biographer, "which we in our laziness count a great punishment, he reckoned among his greatest pleasures. Every day at each verse of the Seven Psalms, he bent the knee, and the same at the 119th Psalm at night. In the west porch of the Church, where was the Altar of All Saints, with the trophy of the Lord's banner, he would lock himself in, and there call upon Christ with tears and cries. His sleep was snatched as it were by stealth; his bed was the church floor or a narrow board—a book or the altar steps, his pillow. Every day he visited the eighteen altars that were in the old Church, bowing seven times before each." Often in the evening, he used to retire from the crowd and noise of the city, and the companionship of the convent, to some solitary spot in the outskirts — the graves of the dead, or the empty silent village church, whose stillness was only broken by his chant and prayers. In these lonely hours, when other men trembled, he walked without fear; and it was told how that the spirit of darkness had once assaulted him, while kneeling before the altar, and how Wulstan had boldly wrestled with him, and though he felt his fiery breath, had thrice overthrown him.

Day and night he served God in the temple with fasting and prayers, yet none the less did he serve his brethren. The common people especially looked upon him as their friend. He often finished his daily devotions very early in the morning, and then gave up the rest of the day till noon or evening, to the wants and business of the poor. He used to sit at the Church door, accessible to all who came; listening to complaints, redressing wrongs, helping those who were in trouble, giving advice spiritual and temporal. In the troubles of the times, great abuses had sprung up among the rude Clergy, who served in the country parishes; they scarcely ever preached, and they are accused of the terrible practice of refusing baptism to the children of the poor who could not pay for it. Wulstan did his best to remedy this evil. From all parts of the neighbouring country the peasants brought their children to Wulstan to be baptized, and the same became a fashion even among the rich. He also took up the neglected work of preaching with zeal and ability. Every Sunday and great Festival, he preached to the people. "His words," says his biographer, "as he uttered them to the people from on high in the pulpit, seemed to be the voice of thunder, issuing from the shrine of a prophet or evangelist; they lighted like bolts upon the wicked; they fell like showers upon the elect." And speaking of a later period, he says, "All his life, he so drew the common people to him by the fame of his preaching, that ye might see them flocking together in crowds, wherever it was reported that he was to dedicate a Church. He also so chose

his subjects, that he was ever sounding forth
Christ's name, ever setting Christ forth to his
hearers, ever, if I may so speak, drawing Christ
by violence to his side." The offence which his
zeal gave did not stop him; and a story went
about how a monk who was displeased with his un-
wonted energy, and who reproved him for taking on
him a duty that did not belong to him, was punished
in a vision for his interference and ill nature.

Thus did Wulstan labour on year after year,
zealously and earnestly, though very likely we
should be surprised if we knew all that he did and
said. For he was not the religious man of a
romance, but of the plain-speaking, plain-dealing
eleventh century; and we should no doubt find
his religion not confining itself to what at a distance at least looks high and great—enlightening
the ignorant, comforting the unhappy, defending
the unprotected — but running on into a number
of subjects with which sentiment has little to do.
We should find him combating pride and self-will
and love of pleasure in great detail, and in a very
matter-of-fact and unequivocal way. We should
find, for instance, that he thought that greediness
was a common fault even among grown-up men
and women;—certainly in his day they did not
care to disguise from themselves that they found
considerable pleasure in eating and drinking:—and
that he looked on it rather seriously and severely.
He was not above confessing that a savoury roast
goose which was preparing for his dinner had once
so taken up his thoughts, that he could not attend
to the service he was performing, and that he had

punished himself for it, and given up the use of meat in consequence. And the summary and practical measure which he dealt out to himself, he could extend on occasion to others. Short words and a rough buffet were all the courtesy he extended to sin and impudence, even in a woman of rank and wealth.

At length, about the year 1062, two Roman Cardinals, Hermenfred, Bishop of Sion, and another, came to Worcester, with Aldred the late Bishop, who had been made Archbishop of York, and who with some reluctance had just resigned his former charge, which had often of late been held together with York. They were entertained at the Cathedral monastery, where Wulstan was Prior, and there they spent the whole of Lent. This time was kept by Wulstan with special severity. As a courteous host, he left nothing undone which was due to his guests from English hospitality and bounty; but he himself adhered rigorously to his accustomed rules; he omitted none of his prayers, and relaxed none of his abstinence. All night long he continued in prayer, even after the night Psalms were ended. Three times in the week he tasted nothing day or night, and during this time never broke silence; the other three days his food was bread and common vegetables, and on Sunday he added some fish and wine, "out of reverence for the Festival." Every day he received and ministered to three poor men, supplying to them their daily bread and washing their feet. When Easter came, the Cardinals returned to King Edward's court, and when the question arose, who was to be the new Bishop of Worcester, they mentioned with high admiration the name of the austere and hard-working Prior, of whose way of life they had lately been daily witnesses. Their recommendation was taken up and seconded by the great English Lords at Court,—Earls Harold and Elfgar, Archbishop Stigand of Canterbury, and after some hesitation between Wulstan and another, by Aldred, the late Bishop. The popular voice at Worcester itself, was allowed by King Edward to express itself, and was equally strong in his favour ; and his election being confirmed by the king, Wulstan was summoned to Court, to be invested with the Bishopric. He heard of his election with sorrow and vexation, and strongly resisted, declaring with an oath, that he would rather lose his head than be made Bishop. His friends long argued with him in vain ; but he was cowed at last by the words of an old hermit named Wulfsy, who had lived in solitude for forty years. Wulfsy rebuked him sternly for his obstinacy, and his dis-obedience to the will of those around him, and threatened him with God's wrath if he still made opposition. Then he yielded. He received the pastoral staff from the hands of the Confessor, and on the feast of St. Mary's Nativity, he was con-secrated [1] by Archbishop Aldred. [2] His prognostic verse, the supposed omen of his future administration, was "Behold an Israelite indeed, in whom is no guile"; and his career as a Bishop fulfilled it. The Normans when they came in, thought him, like his Church, old-fashioned, homely, and unrefined ;

[1] September 8, 1062.

[2] Stigand, the Primate, was under interdict. "But Wulstan," says Florence of Worcester, "made his Canonical profession to the Arch-bishop of Canterbury, Stigand, not to Aldred his ordainer."

but even they were obliged to admire, though in an Englishman, his unworldliness and activity, and the freshness and heartiness of his character; and their literature has preserved his memorial.

His life as a monk had not been, as in the case of the great strangers who were soon to take charge of the English Church, that of a man of study and thoughtful retirement. His work had always been of an active and popular kind; ministering to the common people, supplying the deficiencies of the parochial Clergy, and preaching. And his Episcopate was of the same character. His care for his diocese, and his constant personal oversight of it were the points which struck his contemporaries. His practice seems to have been to be continually visiting some part or other of it. He travelled about on horseback with his retinue of clerks and monks. As they rode along, he repeated the Psalter, the Litanies, and the office for the dead, the attendants taking up the responses, or aiding his memory when it failed. His chamberlain always had a purse ready, and "no one ever begged of Wulstan in vain." He never passed a Church or Oratory, however hurried he might be, without stopping to pray there; and when he reached his halting place for the night, before he retired to rest his first care was to go and "salute the Church." In these progresses, he came into personal contact with all his flock, high and low—with the rude crowds, beggars and serfs, craftsmen and labourers, as well as with priests and nobles. When the Archdeacon gave notice of the Bishop's approach, the people poured out to meet him, to look on him, to ask his aid or counsel. They confessed their sins to him, for men would open their hearts to him who would do so to no one else: they flocked to hear him preach, for no one in England so touched the hearts of the common people, and "he never sent them away without saying mass and preaching." He pleaded the cause of the poor; he reconciled those who were at variance, and it was believed that terrible judgments fell on those who despised his mediation.

The "chiefest" in his diocese, he made himself the "servant of all";—his time, his exertions, his personal presence, were denied to none who claimed them; all who came to him he saw; and wherever he was called he went, "so that he seemed not so much to travel as to fly from one part of his diocese to another." But to him the most touching claim and the most sacred duty was when children came to him to be confirmed. To this every thing else gave way; business was to be broken off—retirement, rest, devotion given up, to attend at once on Christ's little ones; and from sunrise to sunset, on a long summer's day, he would go on without tasting food, giving the sacramental seal and his benediction to batch after batch, as they came and knelt before him, till his attendants and clerks were fairly wearied out; while he himself seemed proof against fatigue.

He was a great Church builder: he took care that on each of his own manors there should be a Church, and was very urgent with other Lords to follow his example. The Cathedral of his See, which he rebuilt, and the old ruined Church of Westbury, which he restored, and made the seat of a monastic congregation, are especially mentioned as instances of his zeal. But he cared little about ornament or beauty in his churches. The Saxons generally had no taste either in their domestic or public buildings for that architectural grandeur of which the Normans had formed so magnificent an idea, and of which they were so passionately fond. And when the vast Cathedrals and Abbeys of the Norman Prelates were rising throughout England, those who kept up the old feelings of the days of King Edward saw little to admire in them.[1] Wulstan, who was thoroughly a man of the old English school, looked with dislike and contempt on what he considered a mere taste and fashion of the day, ministering chiefly to human pride and vain glory. When his new Cathedral was ready for use, the old one which had been built by St. Oswald was to be demolished. Wulstan stood in the churchyard, and looked on sadly and silently, while the workmen began to unroof it. At last he burst into tears. The monks were surprised at his being downcast on such a day; he ought, they said, to rejoice, at the honour and grace which God had vouchsafed to the Church. "Nay, it is not so"; he said, "we, poor creatures that we are, are destroying the work of Saints, and think in our pride that we improve upon it. Those blessed men knew not how to build fine

[1] Vide W. Malm. de G. Pontif. p. 256, of Osbern, Bishop of Exeter, "unde in victualibus et cæteris rebus ad Anglicos mores pronior, Normannorum pompam suspiciebat, consuetudines Domini sui R. Edwardi efferens, et cum per alios exhiberentur cum assidentibus manu et gestu aggaudens. Ita pro more antiquorum præsulum veteribus contentus ædificiis," etc.

churches, but they knew how to sacrifice themselves
to God whatever roof might be over them, and to
draw their flocks after them. But all we think of
is to rear up piles of stones, while we care not
for souls."

Yet with a life of pastoral activity, Wulstan still
retained the devotional habits of the cloister, and
its simple and severe mode of life. "Whether he
lay down, or rose up, whether he were walking or
sitting, a psalm was in his mouth, and Christ in
his heart." His first words on awaking were a
psalm; the last words which he heard before going
to sleep, were from some homily or legend, which
was read to him while he was lying down to rest.
He attended the same services to which he had
been bound when in the monastery, and all his
manor-houses had a little chapel attached to them,
where he used to lock himself in, when business,
or the public service, did not call him. His attendants remembered how earnest, as well as frequent,
he was in prayer; and how, when he came to a
verse in the Psalter, which expressed strong feeling
towards God, such as the verse, "Bow down thine
ear, O Lord, and hear me, for I am poor and in
misery," he would repeat it two or three times
over, with up-lifted eyes. And he was very strict
in requiring from his monks and those about him
an exact performance of that regular worship for
which monasteries were founded. If one of the
brethren was absent from the night-service, he
took no notice at the time, but when the others
had retired to their beds to wait for morning, he
used quietly to wake the absentee, and make him

go through the appointed office, himself remaining with him, and making the responses.

His warmth and scrupulousness were not always to the taste of his attendants : his monks often thought him very tiresome. When they were chanting the Psalter with him on horseback, on their journeys, he used often to put them out, by his habit, mentioned above, of repeating over and over again, the "prayer verses," "to the weariness of his fellow chanters."[1]

His biographer tells a story which shews the trials to which he used to expose his clerics' patience, and the way in which they sometimes revenged themselves. It is characteristic of both parties. "He always went to Church, to chant matins," says the biographer, "however far off it might be; whether it was snowing or raining, through muddy roads or fog, to Church he must go; he cared for nothing, so that he got there; and truly he might say to Almighty God, ' Lord, I have loved the habitation of thy house.' Once, when he was staying at Marlow,[2] on his way to court at Christmas tide, according to his wont he told his attendants that he was going early to the Church. The Church was a long way off; the deep mire of the road might have deterred a walker, even by daylight, and there was besides, a sleety drizzle falling. His clerics mentioned these inconveniences, but he was determined; he would go, even if no one went with him, only would

[1] "Orationales versus, usque ad fastidium concantantis."—De Gest. Pontif. 280.

[2] Marlow was a manor of Earl Algar, afterwards given to Queen Matilda.—Doomsday, Bucks. lii.

they show him the way. The clerics were obliged to yield, and concealed their annoyance. But one of them, named Frewen, a hot-tempered fellow, to make matters worse, took hold of the Bishop's hand, and guided him where the swamp was deepest, and the road roughest. The bishop sank up to his knees in the mud, and lost one of his shoes; but he said nothing, for the object of the clerics had been to make the bishop give up his resolution. The day was far advanced when he returned to his lodgings, his limbs half dead with the cold, and not till then did he mention his own suffering and the cleric's offence. Yet, he merely ordered them to go and look for the shoe; he spoke no word of reproach to the offender, but put a cheerful face on the matter, and carried off the insult with a cheerful countenance. For the bishop was a man of great patience; nothing put him out of temper, whether annoyance or impertinence; for people there were, who often made game of him, even to his face. But neither these, nor other vexations of the world, disturbed him. Not that I mean to say that his spirit was never moved; for religion cannot extinguish feelings; it may restrain them for a time, but cannot altogether root them out."

Monks and priests were not the only persons to whom his straightforward conscientiousness made him an inconvenient companion. At King Harold's court his neighbourhood was especially dangerous to the long flowing tresses with which it was the fashion of the Anglo-Saxon gallants to adorn themselves, and to which Wulstan had taken a special dislike, as being a mark of effeminacy.

Wulstan had very little notion of ceremony, where he thought that right and wrong were concerned; and he was not without relish for a practical joke at times. "Accordingly," says his biographer, "if any of them placed their heads within his reach, he would with his own hands crop their wanton locks. He had for this a little knife, wherewith he was wont to pare his nails, and scrape dirt off books. With this he cut off the first fruits of their curls, enjoining them on their obedience, to have the rest cut even with it. If they resisted, then he loudly chode them for their softness, and openly threatened them with evil."

But troublesome as his strictness was to those about him, they admired and loved him warmly; the poor simple Saxon monks especially, who in the desolation and shame of their race, sought comfort in the cloister, long remembered their good and noble bishop, his kindness and humbleness among them, the hearty interest he took in their welfare, how gladly he visited them, and how, when he came among them, he took his turn with them in the duties of the Choir and Chapter house; how, when in Church, he saw the boys' vestments disordered, he would bend over and smooth them down; how, when some one said to him that such condescension did not become a bishop, he silenced the objector with the words of the gospel, "He that is greatest among you, shall be your servant."

It was Wulstan's lot to see the long line of his native kings come to an end, and the "dear kingdom of England" pass to a foreign lord. He was the last Bishop who received his pastoral staff from the hands of a Saxon king; and when he died, he was the last representative on the English thrones, of the Church of Bede and Cuthbert. He was the link between it and the Church of Lanfranc and Anselm, and this gives peculiar interest to his history.

He had fallen on days when the noble Anglo-Saxon race, out of which so many Saints and heroic kings had sprung, had sunk into degeneracy and corruption; and he was appointed to see and share their punishment. His people had become coarse, debauched, and effeminate. Their natural temper was free, and blithe, and affectionate; delighting in home, and kindred, and companionship; in the loaded board, and the warm, glad hearth, and the hearty, brimful, noisy merriment of the crowded hall;—the "joy of life,"—they knew it well, and loved it too dearly. Self-indulgence, in its various forms of sloth and pleasure, overcame them. Clergy forgot their learning, and monks their rule. The morning mass was hurried over in the bed-chamber, where the great man had not yet risen from his couch; the drinking bout of the afternoon was prolonged through the night. The very kindliness of their character was giving way. The women servants of their households, mothers of their own children, and those children yet unborn, it was their horrid custom to sell to foreign slavery, or a yet worse fate. A noble people were wasting and decaying in sluggishness, or gross and rude voluptuousness; purpose, and conduct, and enterprise—the wise lawgiver, the loyal soldier had failed among them; they were still brave and high-spirited, but theirs was a fitful and desultory gallantry, headstrong, and without endurance. They had lost all taste for what was great and severe, and cost exertion ; the arts in which they excelled, were those only which ministered to personal vanity—the petty skill of the embroiderer and goldsmith ; and the vein of melancholy and dreamy sentiment which ran through their character only enfeebled it the more.

They had not been left without warning. Judgment had followed judgment ; the Dane had fulfilled his mission, yet there was no improvement. They had seen too among them, with all the stern holiness and fiery zeal of an ancient prophet, startling and terrible as the Danes themselves, Dunstan, the Archbishop, who had dragged a king from his chamber of shame. Yet they would not rouse themselves ; the wine-cup was too sweet, the couch too soft ; the "joys of the hall," the story, the song, the "glee-beams" of the harp, these gladdened their days ; and to these, in spite of the Danes and St. Dunstan, they clung faster and faster. The dream went on ; the lethargy became heavier.

Yet there was in many a vague feeling of uneasiness and misgiving ;[1] a dim foreboding that mischief was not far off. The king had no children. What would become of England when he was gone? Was the royal line of Alfred and Athelstan really ending ? So indeed had a vision boded, which had been seen by an English bishop before Edward was king. In a dream, he had seen Edward crowned by St. Peter ; and when Edward complained that he had no son to succeed him, the stern answer of the apostle was, " The kingdom of the English is

[1] V. Thierry, vol. i. p. 287.

God's ; after thee, he has provided a king according to his own pleasure."[1]

At last the stroke came ; more terrible in its reality than the most anxious had imagined. It was not merely a change of kings or families ; not even an invasion or ordinary conquest ; it was a rooting and tearing up, a wild overthrow of all that was established and familiar in England.

There were seeds of good, of high and rare excellence in the Saxons ; so they were to be chastised, not destroyed. Those who saw the Norman triumph, and the steady, crushing strength of its progress, who saw English feelings, English customs, English rights, trampled on, mocked at, swept away, little thought that the Norman, the "Francigena," was to have no abiding name in the land of his conquest ; that his language was to be swallowed up and lost in that of the Saxon ; that it was for the glory and final exaltation of the English race, that he was commissioned to school them thus sternly. So indeed it was. But on that generation the judgment fell, as bitter as it was unexpected ; it was in their eyes vengeance unrelenting and final ; it seemed as if God had finally cast them off, and given them over without hope of respite or release, to the tormentors.

On the very verge of these days, Wulstan was made Bishop. But vengeance was stayed awhile, till the saintly spirit of the last Saxon king was ready for its crown. He built his burying-place, and then departed.[2] "About midwinter," says the old English Chronicle, "King Edward came to

---

[1] Will. Malms. G. R. lib. 2, p. 374.   [2] Christmas, 1065.

Westminster, and had the Minster there consecrated, which he had himself built to the honour of
God, and St. Peter and all the Saints of God. This
Church-hallowing was on Childermas-day. And on
the eve of Twelfth-day, he departed. And he was
buried on Twelfth-day in the same Minster." [1]

It was believed that in spirit he saw the evils
from which he was taken. On his death-bed, he
dreamed of what was to come, and prayed that if
it was a true message, he might recover his speech
to relate it. His power of speech returned, and he
told it. He had seen two monks, whom he had
known years ago in Normandy, and who had long
been dead. They brought a message—" Since the
great men of England, the chiefs, the bishops, the
abbots, are not the servants of God but of the devil,
God hath delivered this realm after thy death, for a
year and a day into the hands of the enemy, and
devils shall roam over all this land." The king
prayed that he might show this to his people, and
they would repent like the Ninevites. The messengers answered, " Neither will they repent, nor
will God ever have mercy upon them." And when
he asked them when these woes should end—" *Then*,
when the green trees shall be lopped in half, and
the parts be separated by the space of three furlongs,
and shall of themselves come together again, and
bear blossoms and fruit—*then* shall these woes cease."
Those who stood round him listened with fear ;—all
but Stigand the Archbishop. He laughed—it was,
he said, the wandering fancy of the sick.[2]

Then came the short wild reign of Harold, with

[1] Jan. 5, 1066.   [2] Will. Malms. p. 381.

its portents and unnatural strifes, the blazing "long-haired star" in the sky, brother warring with brother to the death, and calling down on him the pirates of the North ; license and riot let loose,—no longer held back by the example of the austere Confessor. Wulstan raised his voice in rebuke and warning. He had been Harold's friend, and Harold valued him ; he called on the king earnestly to correct the evil ; but he was not heard—the time allowed it not—Harold had to defend his realm. One victory he was allowed—he overcame and slew his brother : but it had scarcely been gained, before the Norman fleet was descried from the cliffs of Sussex, bearing with it the curse of the Church against him. In the whole of William's proceedings, from Harold's oath on the relics, up to the prayers and litanies on the eve of battle, there appeared the solemnity of a religious mission ; he was come under God's protection and visible guidance with calm and settled purpose, to do His will in England. But to the last, in the presence of the Avenger, the Saxons clung to their national sin ; they awoke after a night of reckless and noisy revelry, to the day of Hastings.

How the Saxons were humbled and punished, how they fiercely rebelled against their doom and made it heavier, need not be detailed. Wulstan, the prophet who had warned them, did not escape their judgment ; yet in the overthrow of his people and Church, he found mercy, and by degrees won favour and esteem even with King William, and his stern Archbishop, little sympathy as either of them had with any thing English.

Among the native Clergy, the more impatient and

daring, of whom there were many, plunged desper-
ately into the intrigues and partizan warfare of their
countrymen, and shared the dreary fate which over-
took most of William's antagonists. Others among
them, "discreet and wary," yielded to the time and
served him. Wulstan belonged to neither of these.
With the leading men in England, he acknowledged
William ; and then he remained quiet in his diocese,
doing what temporal duties he was bound to, and
keeping aloof from the turmoil round him, despised
and neglected by the Normans. Possibly he may
have been once induced by the fiery and resolute
Abbot of St. Albans, to join an association, which
is said to have extorted from the king an oath on
the relics of St. Alban's Church, to observe the old
laws of England :[1] but his general line was submission. To this his naturally unworldly temper
would prompt him : and the signal and terrible way
in which he saw his own forebodings and warnings
realised, would both support and calm him in trouble.
"It is the scourge of God that ye are suffering,"
was his language to his countrymen ; and when
they bitterly retorted, that the Normans were far
worse than ever they had been, he answered, "God
is using their wickedness to punish your evil deserts,
as the devil, of his own evil will, yet by God's
righteous will, punishes those with whom he suffers.
Do ye, when ye are angry, care what becomes of
the staff with which ye strike?"[2]

Among the stray fragments of those days, has
come down to us the copy of a religious bond

[1] Matth. Paris, Vit. Frideric. Abb. S. Alban, pp. 47, 48.
[2] Knyghton, p. 2366.

entered into after the Conquest, by Wulstan and
the Abbots and brethren of seven monasteries, still
for the most part English. The monks promise to
be true to Wulstan " for God and for the world " ;
and he and they together bind themselves to obedience and to unity among themselves, to be, "as
if the seven minsters were one minster"—"quasi
cor unum et anima una," to obedience to their
worldly Lord, King William, and the Lady
Matilda ;—and besides, to various offices of mutual
intercession, and charity to the poor.[1] Different
men have different offices ; Wulstan's was not to
reform, or build up, or resist, but amid the wild
storm of passions which surrounded him, to be the
witness and minister of peace.

Thus he preserved his evenness of mind in spite
of the change of times. In his dealings with the
Normans, in matters relating to his office, he went
about his work with a kind of straightforward unconscious simplicity, as if he was still in the days
of King Edward, and his position not more precarious and suspected than it had been then.

At the hostile council of Winchester,[2] which gave
such ominous warning to the Anglo-Saxon Clergy,
after several of them had been deposed, Wulstan
stood up among his cowed and silent colleagues,
without embarrassment, as if unconscious that he
was a barbarian, an "idiota,"[3] in the eyes of most
around him, and in bold blunt words called upon
the king, though his officers had just plundered the

---

[1] Probably between 1074-1077. It is given in Hickes's Thesaur.
vol. ii. Dissert. Epist. pp. 19, 20.

[2] After Easter, 1070. Florence of Worcester.

[3] Mat. Paris, Vit. Abb. S. Alb. p. 49.

Church and Monastery of Worcester, to restore some lands to the See, which had been kept back from it by Archbishop Aldred, and had now on his death fallen into William's hands. When the question was put off, he prosecuted it in the same spirit. Thomas, Aldred's Norman successor, met Wulstan with a claim of jurisdiction over Worcester, and Wulstan had to plead his cause before a yet more formidable assembly than the synod of Winchester. The question now touched deeper interests than Wulstan's; — it became one between the two parties who shared power under the Conqueror, the Church party of Lanfranc, and that of the Earl - Bishop Odo, the king's half-brother— Bishop of Bayeux and Earl of Kent, who had led the Norman chivalry at Hastings, and was now the most potent Lord in England. In a court composed of all the great men of the realm, Wulstan the Saxon, with his bad French, meagre show of learning, and uncourtly ways, had to state his case against the Archbishop of York's subtlety and skill, and Odo's power. He was no more disconcerted than he had been at Winchester. The account, derived from a Norman bishop who was present, states that he fell asleep during his opponent's argument; and spent the time given him to think over his reply, in singing the service of the hour, in spite of his companions' horror of the ridicule it would bring on them. "Know ye not," he answered, "that the Lord hath said, 'When ye stand before kings and rulers, take no thought what ye shall speak; for it shall be given in that hour what ye shall speak?' The same, our Maker and Lord, Jesus Christ, who said this, can give me speech to-day, to defend my right, and overthrow their might." And he had been reading, he said, the lives of his canonized predecessors, Dunstan and Oswald, and he had seen them guarding with their prayers the cause of their Church, which would prevail without any eloquence or wisdom of his. And his statement of his case, backed no doubt by Lanfranc's influence, carried the day.[1]

Lanfranc is said on this occasion to have committed to him the visitation of the turbulent Diocese of Chester, which was unsafe for the Norman bishops. But Wulstan and Lanfranc were men of such different characters, that it is not surprising that it was not at once that the Archbishop really understood the genuine but homely excellence of his Saxon suffragan. The popular legend, which represented Lanfranc as wishing to depose Wulstan, on the ground of incapacity and ignorance, at all events points to something of this kind. The legend itself, a most touching and beautiful one, has become indeed the characteristic story of Wulstan's life. It was the subject of his emblem.

"Lanfranc," says the legend, "who like the prophet had been set by God to root out and to pull down, and to destroy, and to build, and to plant, relying on his authority as legate, sought to recall the English Church to a new order. What called

[1] "Hujus narrationis Colemannus testem citat Walchelinum Winton. Episcopum, in virtutibus tunc temporis Lanfranco, sed longo intervallo, proximum. Eum siquidem plusquam semel narrantem audivi, quomodo vir Sanctus pene solus tot optimatibus, et ipsis magno elimatis acumine obnitentibus victor abierit."—W. Malms. Vit. S. Wulst. p. 256.

for correction he corrected ; what was fit to be decreed he established ; and to the clergy and the monks he laid down a more worthy rule of life. Wulstan, the man of God, was accused before him of weakness and incapacity, and with the king's consent or injunction, his deposal resolved upon, as being an ignorant and unlearned man. In a synod therefore which was held at Westminster in the king's presence, Lanfranc called upon him to deliver up his pastoral staff and ring.[1] Upon this the old man rose, and holding the crosier firmly in his hand, replied, 'Of a truth, my Lord Archbishop, of a truth I know, that I am not worthy of this dignity, nor sufficient for its duties. I knew it when the clergy elected, when the prelates compelled, when my master King Edward summoned me to the office. He, by authority of the Apostolic See, laid this burthen upon my shoulders, and with this staff ordered me to be invested with the episcopal degree. You now require from me the pastoral staff which you did not deliver, and take from me the office which you did not confer : and I who am not ignorant of my own insufficiency, obeying the decree of this holy synod, resign them,— not to you, but to him by whose authority I received them.' So saying, he advanced to the tomb of King Edward, and addressed himself to the dead,—'Master,' said he, 'thou knowest how unwillingly I took upon myself this office, forced to it by thee ! for though neither the choice of the brethren, nor the desire of the people, nor the con-

---

[1] Mr. Southey's translation, in his Book of the Church, has been used as far as it goes, with a few changes.

sent of the prelates, nor the favour of the nobles was wanting, thy pleasure predominated more than all, and especially compelled me. Behold a new king, a new law, a new primate! they decree new rights, and promulgate new statutes. Thee they accuse of error in having so commanded: me of presumption in having obeyed. Then indeed thou wast liable to error, being mortal; but now being with God thou canst not err. Not therefore to these who require what they did not give, and who as men may deceive and be deceived, but to thee who hast given, and who art beyond the reach of error or ignorance, I render up my staff; to thee I resign the care of those whom thou hast committed to my charge; to thee I entrust them with confidence, whose merits I know full sure.'

"With these words, he raised his hand a little, and drove the crosier into the stone which covered the sacred body; 'Take this, my master,' he said, 'and deliver it to whom thou will'; and descending from the altar, he laid aside his pontifical dress, and took his seat, a simple monk, among the monks.

"But the staff, to the wonder of all, remained fast imbedded in the stone. They tried to draw it out, but it was immovable. A murmur ran through the throng; they crowded round the spot in astonishment, and you might see them in their surprise, approaching a little, then stopping, stretching out their hands and withdrawing them, now throwing themselves on the floor, to see how the spike was fastened in the stone, now rising up and gathering into groups to gaze. The news was carried to where the synod was sitting. Lanfranc sent the Bishop of Rochester to the tomb, to bring the staff; but he was unable to withdraw it. The archbishop in wonder, sent for the king, and went with him to the place; and after having prayed, tried to move it, but in vain. The king cried out, and Lanfranc burst into tears, and going up to Wulstan, addressed him; 'Truly the Lord is righteous and loveth righteousness; His countenance will behold the thing that is just; truly He walketh with the simple, and with them is His discourse. We mocked at thy righteous simplicity, my brother, but He hath made thy righteousness to shine as the light, and thy just dealing as the noon-day. We must weep for the darkness which covered us, and made us call evil good, and good evil. We have erred, we have erred, my brother, in our judgment of thee, and God has raised up His spirit in His king, to bring to nought our decree, and to show to all how acceptable thy simplicity is to God. Therefore, by the authority which we exercise, nay, rather by the divine judgment by which we are convinced, the charge of which we inconsiderately deprived thee, we again commit to thee and lay on thee, knowing that a little that the righteous hath is better than great riches of the ungodly; yea, surely much better is a little learning with faith, which in simplicity works by love, than treasures of wisdom and worldly knowledge, which many abuse to the service of vanity or foul lucre. Go, therefore, my brother, go to thy master, yea, to ours; for we believe that that holy hand which has refused the crosier to us, will freely resign it to thee.' On this, the holy bishop, with his usual simplicity,

obeyed the command, and approaching the altar,
'Behold me, my lord Edward,' he said, 'here I
am, who entrusted myself to thy judgment, who
submitted myself to thy decision, who resigned to
thee the staff which thou gavest. What is now thy
pleasure and will? Thou hast in truth guarded
thy honour, and declared my innocence, and shown
thy greatness; if, therefore, thy former judgment
of me stands, restore the crosier; if it is changed,
say to whom it shall be given.' With these words,
he tried with a gentle effort to draw out the staff;
it yielded to his hand and came forth, as if it had
been planted in soft clay.

"The king and the archbishop rushed up to him,
and falling at his feet, begged his forgiveness and
his prayers; but he who had learned from the Lord
Jesus Christ to be meek and lowly of heart, in his
turn threw himself before them, and entreated the
blessing of so great a bishop. Lanfranc and Wulstan
blessed each other, and hand in hand returned to
the synod, amid tears and joy, all together praising
God, who is wonderful in His saints."

So writes Aelred, abbot of Rievaulx, who died
within a century after the Conquest, about the way
in which Lanfranc was reconciled to Wulstan; reconciled he certainly was; and Wulstan lived to a good
old age, reverenced by the stern strangers who so
hated his countrymen; one of the few who, in those
times of anxiety and trial, was vouchsafed a life of
quietness;—quietness at least of heart,—the old,
perhaps too prized blessing of his native church.
For the insight into society, the keen far-reaching
intelligence, which pierces through what is compli-

cated and hidden, the discernment of evil and danger and the power to meet them, the "instantia quotidiana,"[1] the daily burden of one to whom his own times are in a way committed, all that made Lanfranc's and Anselm's task so heavy, though so glorious, all this was spared to Wulstan. He was not meant to see what they saw, what cost them so many a bitter hour.

Still these must have been mournful days for Wulstan. He had made the best of the old English system; he was cast in its mould; it had all his sympathies; and now that he was old, it was rudely broken off, its evil sternly exposed and put to shame, its ways of doing good despised. The strangers had their own feelings, which he could not share; and in all that they valued, he was far behind them. A great and noble man was the archbishop, with his vast learning, his austere religion, his deep plans and unwearied care for the Church, yet he was not like the religious men of Wulstan's youth and manhood. They and the Saints before them, whose memory the Anglo-Saxons cherished with such peculiar affectionateness, were out of date; their venerated names were jeered at by the coarse and rude; held very cheaply by the best.[2] Every thing reminded him that he was out of his place. When he went to court, around him were foreign faces, dark complexioned, and smooth shaven, and in his ears a language which he could not pronounce[3]—

[1] 2 Cor. xi. 28.
[2] V. Wharton, Angl. Sacr. vol. ii. p. 40; and the argument between Lanfranc and Anselm about S. Alphege, in Eadmer, Vit. S. Ans. pp. 10, 11.
[3] Vid. quotations in Thierry, p. 115, note 1. Eng. Transl.

circumstance and ceremony, the old grave state and pomp of the English Council, the old jovial mirth of the English board, all was changed.[1] And at home he had to play the Baron, and go about with his retinue of men-at-arms, mischievous and troublesome attendants, and who, for all that they were in Wulstan's service, ate and drank and quarrelled, like their fellows, and were as grasping and extravagant. But he was obliged to maintain them, for the wise archbishop had so settled it, because the Danes were daily expected;[2] and Wulstan had to head his soldiers more than once, to keep the peace of the country.[3] It was a new position for him to hold; a plain old Saxon monk, with no taste for show or business; but he took it meekly and cheerily, with a sort of unconscious patience. He would not dine in private, but sate down in his public hall, with his boisterous soldiers and retainers; nay, while they sate drinking for hours together after dinner, according to the English fashion, he

---

[1] "Ipso igitur persecutionis tempore, exularunt ab Anglia nobiles tam milites quam prælati; viri sancti, generosi ac dapsiles, (qui more orientalium, et maxime Trojanorum, barbas ac comas nutriebant) . . . Quibus exulantibus, pristina Regni sanctitas ac nobilitas, irremeabiliter exulavit."—M. Paris, vit. Frid. Abb. S. Alb. p. 48. "Conculcabantur spreti ac derisi nobiles Angli, jugum servitutis a tempore Bruti nescientes, et more Normannorum barbas radere, cincinnos tondere cogebantur, projectis cornibus et vasis solitis, et refectionibus et dapsilitatibus novis compulsi sunt legibus subjacere."—Ib. p. 46. vid. Will. Malms. de G. Reg. § 239, 245.

[2] "Pompam militum secum ducens, qui stipendiis annuis quotidianisque cibis immane quantum populabantur."—Will. Malms. de Gest. Pont. lib. iv. 280. de vit. S. Wulst. lib. iii. c. 16.

[3] In the rebellion of Roger, earl of Hereford, 1074 (Flor. of Worc.), and again, in the outbreak against William Rufus, a. 1088. Saxon Chron. and Flor. Worc.

would keep them company to restrain them by his
presence, pledging them when it came to his turn
in a little cup, which he pretended to taste, and
in the midst of the din, "ruminating to himself
on the psalms."[1] Not that he was changed himself;
he was still the blunt, unaffected, good-humoured
Saxon, who avoided all show, either of austerity or
pomp, who kept sturdily, in spite of persons and
proprieties, to his old habits, and had his quaint
repartee for those who made impertinent comments.
He would say his grace before drinking, as the
English always used to do, though he was dining
at the royal table;[2] and he would persist in coming
into the company of great lords in a very ordinary
dress—intruding his common lamb-skin among their
rich furs. The rich and courtly Geoffrey, bishop of
Coutances, once took on him, with patronising kindness, to set the simple Englishman right ; with bland
irony he expostulated with him on the unsuitable-
ness, in a man of his dignity, of his usual appearance ; "He could well afford, and really ought, to
wear something more respectable ; some more costly
fur, sable, or beaver, or fox-skin." But the old
Englishman had some shrewd humour in him.
" The skins of such shifty animals," he said, " might
do for experienced men of the world, but for himself,
he was a plain man, and content with lamb-skin."
" Then at least," said Geoffrey, " you might wear
cat-skin." But Wulstan's grotesque reply silenced
him. " Crede mihi," said he, with his usual affirma-

---

[1] W. Malms. vit. S. Wulst. p. 259, de Gest. Pont. p. 280.

[2] "Benedictiones, quas Angli super potum faciebant."—W. Malms.
de G. Pont. p. 280.

tion; "believe me, my Lord, I have often heard 'Agnus Dei' sung, but never 'Cattus Dei.'"[1]

In the Norman court, however, Wulstan's voice was now become of weight. The king listened to him with respect, and his co-operation was used and valued by Lanfranc. A slave trade chiefly with Ireland had long been carried on at Bristol. The slaves were English peasants and domestic servants, the born thralls of the lords of the land, whom their owners found it convenient to get rid of. Among them were many women servants who had been debauched by their masters, and sold when pregnant. The trade was a profitable one both for the dealers and for King William's revenue. Lanfranc however and Wulstan resolved to attack it. With great difficulty, their united influence induced the king to relinquish his duties and declare against it. But King William's opposition was not the greatest obstacle they had to meet; it was easier to bring over the iron-hearted conqueror, than the wild savage race of slave merchants who had been established at Bristol from time out of mind, and were not men to submit easily to any interference with their authorised and gainful traffic. "The love of God had little power with them," as little had the love or fear of King William. Wulstan however undertook the task of persuading them. He knew their fierce obstinacy; but he was a Saxon like themselves, and they might listen in time to their countrymen, and their own language. Accordingly he used to go down and stay among them for two or three months at a time, and every

---

[1] Id. vit. S. Wulst. p. 259. de G. P. p. 280.

Sunday he preached to them in English. And he did destroy the slave trade at Bristol. He completely won the hearts and enthusiastic reverence of these wild people; the trade was given up and proscribed; and when they found one of their own number still determined to carry it on in spite of the Bishop, they rose in fury upon him, and having turned him out of the city, they tore out his eyes.[1]

Wulstan outlived William and Lanfranc, and was one of the consecrators of St. Anselm; but he was then an old man, and he did not see the great struggle which was at hand. He passed his last Lent with more than usual solemnity. It was always with him a time of great devotion, in which he tempered his increased self-discipline with daily acts of overflowing charity to the poor. But this time, with the presentiment which was so remarkable a feature in his character that he was thought to have the gift of prophecy, he felt that what he did would be for the last time. The Thursday before Easter, the day of our Lord's Supper, he had always literally devoted entire to religious offices. On that day, from midnight to midnight, every thought of the world was excluded from his mind. When matins were over, he proceeded at once to ·an apartment, where he found a number of poor collected, and warm water prepared by his attendants. There with his own hands he washed their feet and their clothes; with his own hand he bestowed his alms, and ministered to each the cup of "charity." Then after the briefest interval of rest, during which the servants laid out the hall,

[1] Id. vit. St. Wulst. p. 258. Gest. Reg. Angl. § 269.

he again waited on his pensioners, supplying them,
as they sate at his table, with shoes and victuals;
and the only answer he gave to the remonstrances
of his attendants, who assured him that he had
done enough, was—"Nay, I have done but little;
I want to fulfil our Lord's command." Then he
returned to meditate in the Church, and later in
the day he reconciled the penitents, who beheld
in his "gracious countenance" the face of an angel
of God; and at night after supper, he washed the
feet of his brethren of the convent. But this last
Maunday was such as had never been seen before.
In the monastery, except at the hours of prayer,
all was stir and busy activity, strangely mingled
with a religious silence and restraint. At its gate
and in its courts was a dense multitude from the
country round, poor and blind and halt and maimed,
pressing in or coming out, or waiting to receive in
their turn those cheap, yet to the poor, rare blessings,
water clean and warm for their swollen and begrimed
limbs, a change of dress, and above all, the personal
attention of those above them; to see their Bishop
before them, to hear his words to them, to feel his
hand. In the afternoon, the Bishop's hall was
filled to the very entrance with people, standing
or sitting as they could, so closely crowded as
scarcely to leave room for the busy attendants
who toiled and hurried about in this great company. The guests were the pauper multitude, the
attendants not only the monks of the convent, but
also the young men of noble birth who were
attached to the Bishop's family. In the midst
sate Wulstan. On former occasions he had taken

his share in waiting on his guests; but this at last had become too much for him. Twice was the hall emptied and filled again, and still there were more applicants. Wulstan had bespoken large supplies of provisions from the bailiffs of his manors, but they began to run short. His clerks were in dismay, and urged him to shut the gates against the remaining crowd; but Wulstan would not hear of it,—on that great day, the last occasion of the kind he should see, none should go away empty. Let the Lord's command be observed, — he was sure that God would enable him to satisfy all who came. Nor was he disappointed. News was almost immediately brought him of the arrival of some presents, which were at once turned into money, and which enabled him to accomplish the day in the style of princely beneficence with which he began it.

On Easter day he again feasted with the poor, to the great discomfiture and indignation of his steward, who had invited a party of men of consequence to keep the festival with the Bishop, and who could not understand how his master could prefer the company of a crowd of paupers, to that of a few persons of name and wealth. At Whitsuntide following, he was taken ill. His only sister had died shortly before, and though he had always believed that his life would be a long one, he had recognised in this a token that his own time was near;—"the plough has come at last to my furrow";—he said, and he now prepared for death. He made his confession to his friend, Robert, Bishop of Hereford, and received the "discipline"; but he lingered through the summer and autumn in a slow fever, till the first day of the new year, when he took to his bed. He was laid so as to have a view of the altar of a chapel; and "sitting rather than lying down," his eyes were continually upon it, while to himself or aloud he followed the Psalms which were sung. On the 19th of January,[1] at midnight, he departed, in the eighty-seventh year of his age, and the thirty-third of his Episcopate.

The point which struck his attendants during his last illness, was the quiet but undoubting confidence with which he looked forward to his salvation. There was no fear, no trouble, no misgiving. With the same simplicity and boldness which he had shown in life, he spoke of his nearer presence to God after death, and comforted his friends with the promise of his prayers, more availing then, because he should be no longer in the body.

Mention has been made of Robert, bishop of Hereford, Wulstan's greatest friend among the English bishops, though a very different man from himself; for Robert was a foreigner from Lorraine, and one of the king's judges; an architect too, a mathematician, an astronomer, and man of science; yet he would spend days together with Wulstan. Robert was at a distance when his friend died. Wulstan expired at midnight, and at that same hour Robert, in a dream, saw him appear, to announce his own departure, and to bid Robert come to Worcester to bury him. Robert immediately made all speed to Worcester, and arrived in time; for contrary to the usual custom, the body, which in death had become most beautiful, had been kept

[1] A.D. 1095.

till the third day, and was laid out, arrayed in the episcopal vestments and crosier, before the high altar, that the people of Worcester might look once more on their bishop. The Sunday after his death, Robert buried him, and returned home.

On the thirtieth day after Wulstan's death, Robert in a dream, again saw his departed friend. But Wulstan now appeared to rebuke him sternly for the carelessness of his way of life, and to warn him that his stay in the flesh would be short; but though he had not long to remain here, he might yet by increased diligence secure his crown, and share with Wulstan the heavenly banquet, in the presence of God. And within six months, Robert followed his friend.[1]

The story, as told by William of Malmesbury, sounds like an improvement on that of Florence. Wulstan, says Malmesbury, appeared to his friend, telling him that if he wished to find him alive, he must come speedily. Robert hastened to Worcester, but the night before he reached it, Wulstan again appeared to him, thanking him for his affection, but telling him that he was now too late to see him. He then announced to Robert that he was soon to follow him, and promised him a sign. "To-morrow," he said, "when thou hast buried my body, which has been for three days waiting thy coming, a present shall be given thee from me, which thou shalt know to be mine." Robert found his dream verified, and he buried Wulstan. He had taken leave of the monks, and was just mounting his horse to depart, when the prior of the convent came to him, and on his knees begged him

[1] Flor. Worc. a. 1095.

to accept a present, as a mark of their regard, and a remembrance of his friend. It was the lambskin cloak which Wulstan used to wear on his journeys. Robert recognised Wulstan's token; he took it with fear, and returning into the monastery, he summoned the monks to the Chapter house, and there, with sighs and tears, told them his dream. So having commended his approaching death to all their prayers, he departed. "Wulstan passed in the middle of January, and Robert did not outlive June."[1]

The monks of Worcester sent letters through England, earnestly entreating that if any revelation were vouchsafed concerning Wulstan's lot, it might be communicated to them; and it was reported and believed that such a revelation was made to two religious persons, who in a vision beheld him glorified. But at Worcester such assurance would be little wanted. It is well known, from the strong censures of St. Anselm and others, how the devotion and love of the Anglo-Saxons clung fondly to the tombs of those whom in life they had seen to be venerable and noble; but towards Wulstan, their countryman and townsman, known among them for more than sixty years as the best and holiest man in Worcester, known also in foreign parts, in France and Italy, and to the Pope himself,—the last bishop given them by the holy king Edward, and the last of their ancient hierarchy,—it is not strange that these feelings should have displayed themselves in the most intense degree. He was first canonized, as most were in early times, by the popular voice, by the instinctive enthusiastic

[1] W. Malms. de Gest. Pont. p. 286.

faith of the multitude in goodness,—in its reward and power. " In truth," says his biographer, speaking of the miracles believed to have been wrought by him, "the ready faith of the men of old time would ere this have exalted him on high, and proclaimed him a Saint. But the slowness of belief of our day, which shields itself under the guard of caution, will put no faith in miracles, though it behold them with its eyes, and touch them with its fingers."[1]

Those, however, who wrote his life, had not these doubts. They looked on him as a Saint, and therefore, as from one moving in a supernatural order of things, they expected miracles and they have recorded many. How far the instances mentioned were really tokens of God's power with him; how far his loving and admiring friends read events by their own feelings, gave them an exaggerated meaning, and invented, without intending it; how far their accounts may have been a customary and traditional way of symbolizing, as it were, men's persuasion that he was God's servant; or how far they may have been fictions, imagined and circulated under shelter of the general belief in supernatural agency for good and evil, we have now little means of ascertaining. The chief authority for them is a monk named Coleman, a friend of Wulstan's, and for fifteen years his chaplain, whose Anglo-Saxon life of him is the groundwork of William of Malmesbury's Latin narrative.[2] But William, him-

---

[1] W. Malms. de G. Pontif. p. 282.

[2] He thus speaks of his authority—" Colemannus, monachus vester, vir nec scientia imperitus, nec sermone patrio infacetus. Scripsit enim Anglice, ne gestorum avolaret memoria, vitam ejusdem Patris; si

self so much of a rhetorician that he cannot bring himself to introduce Saxon names,[1] "lest the barbarous sound of the words should wound the ears of the delicate reader," accuses Coleman, not indeed of falsehood, but of exaggeration and unscrupulous love of ornament; of using other men's materials to trick out his own story.[2] However it would be giving an imperfect representation of Wulstan, as he was looked upon in his own century, as one on whom God had visibly set His seal, and who had obtained more than earthly power to cheer and protect and guide his brethren, if we passed over the belief that his life was a miraculous one.

Some of these miracles have been alluded to in the preceding narrative. In most of the others there is little to distinguish them from the class of miracles usually ascribed to the holy men of the middle ages. They are exhibitions of the same character which was shown in his ordinary actions, — of the spirit of charity and mercy, issuing forth in acts of supernatural power, for the relief of the

attendas ad sensum, lepore gravi, si ad literam, simplicitate rudi. Dignus, cui fides non derogetur in aliquo, quippe qui noverit intime mores magistri, ut discipulus, religionem, ut XV annos Capellanus. Hujus ego, ut voluistis, insistens scriptis, nihil turbavi de rerum ordine, nihil corrupi de veritate. Sane verbis, quæ vel dicta sunt, vel in tempore dici potuerunt, enarrandis supersedi, consulens in omnibus veritati, ne videretur periclitari."—Epist. ad Monach. Wigorn.

[1] Vit. S. Wulst. p. 254.

[2] —"Nec minus alta verba, declamatiunculas quasdam, quas ille ab aliorum Sanctorum gestis assumptas prona devotione inseruit. Sicut enim superius dixi, quisquis rem per se satis eminentem verbis exaltare molitur, ludit operam. Quinimo dum vult laudare, infamat potius et attenuat, quia videatur non posse niti argumento proprio, si fulcatur patrocinio alieno."—W. Malms. de vit. S. Wulst. p. 254, vid. pp. 265 and 258, cap. xvi.

afflicted and poor. They are recorded with considerable particularity of place and person. The subjects of them belong for the most part to the class for whom he always showed such especial kindness—"the miserable people," who were without protector or comforter in the world—mostly his own countrymen, whose very names would have been a temptation to the Norman soldiers to trample them like worms—the Outy Grimkelsons,[1] and Turstan Dubbes, and Gouse Gamelsons, and Spurt Lunsers, of the Saxon farm-house and hamlet. A mad woman of Evesham — a poor wretch from Kent, afflicted with the king's evil, begging at his door at Kemsey—a Gloucestershire serf, possessed with an evil spirit — a foreigner lying sick by the roadside — such were the persons for whom his prayers were offered and accepted. They cured hopeless sickness, they brought rest to the troubled mind, they delivered from the peril of fire, or from sudden accidents, they rescued sailors from shipwreck; or else, still marking his kindly and social temper, they were wrought to cheer and grace the rejoicing of friends. When Egelric the Archdeacon built a Church, and gave a feast at its dedication, Wulstan provided a miraculous supply of mead for his friend's guests.

But whether he did these miracles, or they were only reported of him, so he lived, and so he died, that men readily believed them of him; and along with the great men of old, the Apostles and first Pastors of England, was numbered also among the Saints of the Church, Wulstan, the last of the Anglo-Saxon Bishops.

[1] Vid. names in a Charter given in Ingulph, p. 87.

LIFE OF

ST. AELRED

PREFACE

IT is necessary to say a few words on the sources from which the present Life is derived. The account of St. Aelred's parentage is taken from a manuscript in the Bodleian Library (Laud, 668), in which are several works ascribed to him, and amongst others, one "De Sanctis Ecclesiæ Hagulstadensis et eorum miraculis." Whether this work is by him or not, the author has not sufficient critical judgment to pronounce. It is in some places assigned to him, but one circumstance against it is, that it is principally a Sermon, preached in the Church of Hexham, on the translation of the relics of the old Bishops of Hexham, apparently by the Prior of the Canons. A great part of it, however, from fol. 67 of the manuscript, is a written continuation of the history, and was not preached. If one may be allowed to conjecture, this part might be written by St. Aelred. It is like his style (though it should be said that the Sermon also is like it), and the historical knowledge which it displays also makes it likely to be his. There is nothing in the MS. itself to indicate that the persons of whom it gives an account were St. Aelred's ancestors; this fact is gathered from Richard of Hexham, De statu Hagulstadensis Ecclesiæ, b. 2, c. 9. There is also an incidental proof that St. Aelred's ancestors were persons connected with the Church of Durham, in a letter from Reginald, a monk of Durham, to St. Aelred, in which he thanks him for some collections, taken from documents in the Church of Durham by his ancestors, and communicated by him. This letter is found in a Bodleian manuscript, Fairfax, 6.

The life in Capgrave and the Bollandists has only been partially followed, as it contains various historical inaccuracies. St. Aelred's own works have been on the whole the principal authority made use of. A few notices of the Saint have been inserted in the life of St. Waltheof, to whom they rather belong. The author hoped to have brought the two lives out together, which, however, has been found impossible.

St. Aelred was canonized by Pope Celestine III., A.D. 1191, according to the Peterborough Annals.

Rev. John Dobree (late Bernard) Dalgairns
Priest of the Oratory
Exeter College. Oxford. B.A. 1839. M.A. 1842.

LIFE OF

ST. AELRED

CHAPTER I

INTRODUCTION

It is often said that things look on paper or on canvas very different from what they are in reality; how often is the traveller disappointed, on arriving at a spot of which he had read in poetry, or seen portrayed by a painter. We repeat over and over again to ourselves that it is beautiful, as if to persuade ourselves of it, and yet there is something wanting; after all, we have seen woods as green, and streams as clear, and rocks as wild, and the ruined tower that looks over the stream is but a very poor ruin, as the baron who lived there was probably a very indifferent character. And yet were the poet or the painter so unfaithful as we suppose? They saw it under some particular aspect, when the sun was upon it, or when the woods were coloured by autumn, and they caught it at some moment when one of Nature's endless combinations had made it look more than usually lovely. No two

persons see the same scene under the same aspect;
it will not look to-morrow as it does now, and yet
it is the same sun, and the same trees, and the same
river. And so it is with history; the historian must
colour his work with his own mind; it is his view
of facts, and yet it may nevertheless be true. Nay,
in some respects it is more true than the view which
a contemporary might take of them. Kings and
queens are doubtless very different from the ermine-
covered things which we think them to be, and we
must make them objects of the intellect before we
can judge of them; just as a surgeon must in a
manner forget that he is operating on flesh and
blood, before he can do his duty. Besides which
the ideas that contemporaries have of the men of
their day, are after all only theories; they are but
approximations to the truth; events and actions are
but exponents of the inward life of men and nations,
and none on earth can judge them precisely as they
are. We have in this sense only a *view* of our
dearest friends, and yet it does not follow that we
love an abstraction or an idea. And so it by no
means follows that history is untrue because it is
the view of the historian; it is coloured of course
by his character and his opinions. The facts of
history want an interpretation and are utterly
meaningless, like an unknown language, until they
are viewed in relation to each other and with the
whole period to which they belong. This is what
the historian supplies; his view may be true or false,
but all views are not false, because they are partly
subjective. All views are not true, for that would
in fact be saying that all are false, but some are

right and others are wrong, and that, though the facts related are given with equal honesty; just as in physical science experiments are the same, but the true explanation of them is the simplest formula which will take in all their results.

All this eminently applies to the lives of the blessed Saints, because the view which we have of them is in all cases coloured by the reverence of the Christian world, and yet it is by no means falsified. It is history with the perpetual interpretation of Christendom; the mind of the Church acting upon facts in the life of one of her children. It may be quite true that in many instances false miracles or actions which may be proved never to have taken place, may have been ascribed to them. An unknown monk in some obscure monastery may have written a life of a Saint, merely putting together all the traditions which remained of him, without caring to separate the true from the false; but still the result of the whole may be true; and the general aspect in which Christendom views the Saint may be the right one, though some particular stories may be false. How few in many instances are the facts known about some of the Saints in the Middle Ages. Their parentage is often forgotten, and the history of their early years unknown; or perhaps the names of their parents are preserved with the vague and suspicious addition that they were of very noble birth. Some few great deeds are on record, but the internal struggles which led to them are all forgotten; all at once they appear before us as perfect Saints, as if no discipline had been required to form them. We are left to eke out the scanty materials of their lives with what we know must have happened, from the character of the times and from the manners of the age. And yet perhaps we should hardly regret this; the picture of a Saint with the aureole round his head and the meek expression of joy on his features, may be unlike what he was in his lifetime, and yet it may be the more like what he is in heaven now. And after all, if we had come close to him, a real living Saint, should we have understood him? If we had lived with St. Basil, might we not have been tempted to look upon him as a peevish invalid, to think him an austere man, or over-sensitive, or too methodical, and apt to care about trifles? Many a holy Abbot must have appeared cross to a lazy monk. We cannot enter into God's Saints upon earth; even if we stand by their side, we could only make an approximation to the truth, as we do now. This is the case with Saints in Scripture. How little has it pleased the Holy Spirit to disclose of their hidden life, just as much of course as we can bear, and as was needful for His Church, and yet how little! Which of the Saints is there that we can picture vividly to ourselves? In the case of the blessed Virgin indeed, the Church has marvellously filled up the outline of Scripture; of her we know one fact, that she was the Mother of God, and the delicate sense, so to speak, of the Christian mind, has found out that this must necessarily involve much more than appears on the surface of Scripture. The Church has so long dwelt in love on our ever-blessed Lord in His infancy, that we almost fancy that we can "come into the house and see the young child with Mary His mother." This may also be the case with St. Paul, who has left so completely the impress of his mind on his writings, but it is hardly so with any other Saint. St. Mary may be said to live in Christian doctrine; St. Paul in the Holy Scriptures; but the other great Saints connected with our Lord have their life in Christian tradition. Even St. John we think of, not as the old man with the golden mitre, but as ever young and beautiful as we have been used to see him in ecclesiastical pictures and sculptures.

All this may perhaps reconcile us to much that is disappointing from the paucity of materials in the life of Aelred. And yet his life is such an important one, from his being the Cistercian Saint of England, a sort of English St. Bernard, as he is called by his contemporaries, that he seems to deserve that every effort should be made to put forward the little that is known with due prominence. All that can now be done is to interpret the few facts that remain by making him, what he really was, the representative of the internal system of the Cistercian order in England. Facts taken by themselves prove nothing, and to suppose that any real knowledge of bygone times can be obtained from the bare enumeration of them, is the same error as it would be to suppose that all our knowledge comes to us from experience. Without the light thrown upon them by the Cross, the events of the world are the mere stirrings of the sick and distempered life of humanity; even the lives of Saints are the mere developments of a highly moral man, as the actions of a hero are the development of a great man. If a Christian theory does not interpret the lives of Saints, a Pantheistic one will come in its stead. So we will attempt to show what Aelred was, by showing in what relation the system of which he was the head stood to the world and to the Church of the period. As in the life of St. Stephen the external life of the Cistercians was described, so we will attempt now to show what was their inward life, and to bring it out in contrast, not only with the troubled world around, but with that of the leading ecclesiastics of the time. It will then be seen how the cloister was the remedy provided by God for keeping up the contemplative life amidst the busy and distracting scenes in which ecclesiastics were obliged to take part. It is easy to do this in the case of Aelred, because we have a most complete insight into his religious character from his writings ; and because as he himself is the historian of much that is related, we are only endeavouring to look upon the troubled scene without the cloister as he did himself. And all this it is hoped may reconcile us to the scantiness of facts about himself, and also to the long digressions which such a plan involves ; for it is impossible to give an idea of the work in which he was engaged without pointing out what were the wants of the Church of the period. Besides which we cannot gain a correct view of the Middle Ages from the lives of Saints alone. They had their good and bad points, like other ages ; and in order to understand the twelfth century, the world and the cloister must be shown in opposition. Thus, though the cloister of Rievaux will be the central point of the whole, the reader will not be surprised to find himself sometimes on the banks of the Rhine, or beyond the Alps, or to hear the din of border warfare breaking on the peace of the monastery. Though from the fewness of materials, we only catch glimpses of Aelred at intervals, still we will do our best to draw a truthful picture of him, at once the Saint of England and of Scotland, once well known from the Frith of Forth to the banks of the Tyne and the Tees, the man of peace in the midst of barbarian war.

THE OLD MONASTERY

In the beginning of the reign of Henry I. the ancient monastery of Hexham was in a miserable state. Its three Churches were in ruins, and the vast monastic buildings were desolate; for ever since the Danes had sacked and plundered it, there had been no monks to dwell there.[1] One chaplain alone, a married priest, lived there with his family, a careless and indifferent man, with one strong feeling in his soul, and that was a love of the old royal line of England, and a hatred of the Normans. The circumstances which led to his dwelling thus with his children, in the midst of the ruinous Abbey buildings, make up a long tale of mingled good and evil. He was apparently one of a priestly race; for his grandfather and father were priests before him. His

---

[1] Post desolationem Nordhymbrorum quam, irruentibus in Angliam Danis, miserabiliter incurrit, sicut cætera hujus ecclesiæ, hæc Hagulstadensis, ut verbis propheticis utar, multo tempore sine sacerdote, sine ephod, sine teraphim gemebunda resedit. Quicquid de lignis fuerat, ignis absumpsit, bibliotheca illa nobilissima quam præsul sanctus condiderat tota deperiit. MS. Bodl.

grandfather, Alured, the son of Weston, was a good
and a learned man. He used to go about through
the North, repairing the ancient places which the
devastation caused by the Danes had laid waste.
One day, there came to him a man who dwelt at
Hexham. He told him that an old man dressed in
pontifical garments had appeared to him in a dream,
and had bidden him go to Alured, and command him
to come to Hexham, and search for the relics of the
Saints which were buried there. Alured bethought
himself awhile, whether this dream were worth attending to ; but he looked at the man who had brought
him the news, and felt that they were true. He was
a plain man, one of the inferior nobility of the realm,[1]
and one who had had in his rough life far more to do
with the lance than with the psalter. He thought,
therefore, that he might be trusted, and went with
him to Hexham. They travelled through St. Cuthbert's domain, and came to Tynedale, a wasted and
depopulated country, and when they came to Hexham, the miserable inhabitants of the place gathered
about them, to see what they were doing amongst
the ruins. When they heard their errand, the poor
people caught their enthusiasm, and brought spades,
and set to work to help them. From dawn of day they
searched till mid-day came, and they found nothing ;
they searched as men look for treasure, for the names
of Acca and Eata, the ancient Saints of Hexham,
whose bodies they hoped to find, were known as
household words in the hut of every peasant of
Northumberland. They who have no friends on earth,
naturally look about them for friends in heaven, and

[1] Vir quidam de minoris ordinis proceribus. Ibid.

in the midst of their wasted and depopulated fields, they bethought themselves of those who originally reclaimed the country from heathenism. And now they worked on, for they hoped to see before evening fell, and to touch their sacred relics; but the day was far advanced, and they had found nothing, and in their disappointment they began to laugh at Alured for having come all the way from Durham on a fool's errand. But his enthusiasm did not cool, and he rose up, and taking a mattock, went to the porch of the Church, and struck it deep into the ground, saying that there were the holy Bishops buried. So the people set to work again, and by-and-bye they came to two stone coffins, and there lay the bodies of the Saints, waiting for a blessed resurrection, clad in their pontifical robes, which time had not impaired. And all that night they watched about them with chanting and prayer, and the next day they placed them in a shrine on the south side of the Church, near the sacristy. Time went on, and the Conqueror ruled in England, and another storm of war had depopulated Tynedale. Other lords possessed the land, who had never heard of the holy Bishops of Hexham. But cruel as was the rule of the new possessors of the soil, yet they brought reformation with them. The Norman Bishop of Durham, William of St. Carilefe, loved not the lazy canons, who, without submitting to any rule whatever, lived on the broad lands which stretched from the Tyne to the Tees. They were but poor representatives of St. Cuthbert, those thriftless canons, and it was well to remove them. They had the option of becoming monks if they pleased, and provision was made for them if they chose still to be

secular.[1] One alone, the dean, was persuaded by his
son, a monk, to remain and take the vows ; the others
all remained in the world. There was one among
them who disdained to receive anything at Norman
hands, and this was the son of Alured. The royal
family of England was in exile ; English prelates and
abbots were compelled to make room for foreigners ;
he himself and his brethren were turned out of their
house at Durham, and he disdained to be a pensioner
of the stranger. So he bethought himself of Hexham, the seat of the old Saxon bishops, and went
there to hide his head till better times came. And,
indeed, there were rumours of war in the North, and
the king of Scotland might still make a fight for
St. Edward's line, though Edgar the Atheling had
submitted to the Conqueror, and was soon to assume
the cross under Robert, William's eldest son. So
away went Eillan, for such was his name, to Hexham.
The Bishop, who seems to have been indulgent to
the refractory canons, gave him his sanction, though,
indeed, Eillan need have been in no dread of a rival,
for his new dwelling was a sad scene of desolation.
The country around was still bleeding from the
vengeance of the Conqueror and the Scot, and in the
midst of the deserted fields arose the ruined Abbey

---

[1] Successit Walchero Guillelmus habitu monachus, qui clericos ab
ecclesia Dunelmensi eliminans monachos subrogavit, et aliis quidem
possessiones extra ecclesiam ordinavit, alios id suscipere contemnentes
expellere non cunctavit. Intra quos prædicti Aluredi filius qui cæteris
præerat, cum nihil ab episcopo suscipere dignaretur, adiit venerabilem
archiepiscopum Thomam qui primus Normannorum rexit ecclesiam
Eboracensem rogans ut ei Hagulstudensem ecclesiam daret ædifican-
dam.—It does not appear what "qui præerat" means, for the dean
became a monk of the new monastery. Simeon Dunelm. b. iv. 3.

itself.[1] Its Church was half unroofed, and the rain and the snow forced a ready entrance through the gaps in the tiles; the tesselated pavement was in many places torn up, the windows were dashed in, and the high columns were covered with green moss, and with damp, which was rapidly eating away the frescoes on the walls, and on the arch which divided the nave from the choir.[2] Amidst these ruins lived the family of the Saxon priest; the Abbey lands were amply sufficient for their maintenance, but there were no cornfields around, and no vassals to till them; so they lived on hunting and hawking for two years after their arrival, and in the thick woods around them, many a wild deer was aroused by the horns and the hounds of the Saxons. Not long after they came there, the Abbey lands were given to a Norman, by Gerard, Archbishop of York, and this of course did not make Eillan love the strangers a whit more. He was allowed to continue there as chaplain, and a large part of the proceeds still came to him. After his death, his son, also called Eillan, the priest whom we have seen at Hexham, succeeded his father. He found himself heir to the ruined Abbey, and he inherited, too, the feelings and prejudices of his family, the love for Hexham and its Saints, and for

---

[1] Veniens ad locum homo invenit omnia desolata, muros ecclesiæ sine tegmine sordere feno, silvis supercrescentibus horrere, litura imbribus et tempestate dejecta, nihil pristini retinuisse decoris. Erat autem talis terræ illius desolatio ut fere biennio ex solo venatu et aucupio se sum [sic], que familiam sustineret. So well was the remembrance of the family kept at Hexham, that there was not long ago, and may be still, a street in Hexham called Eilan's Street.

[2] Arcum sanctuarii historiis et imaginibus et variis cælaturarum figuris —decoravit. Richard of Hexham, De Statu Eccl. Hagulst. c. 3.

the old royal line of England, and probably, no great goodwill to the Norman rulers, ecclesiastical or civil. But it is said of him that he was "a sinner, and that he lived as he ought not to have done."[1] What this means is not known, but it is probable that he was of the jovial race of hunting priests, who knew more about the winding of horns and the cheering of hounds than about Gregorian chants; for these unsacerdotal accomplishments were but too common among the Saxon clergy of the time. This was not a promising character for the father of a Saint, and yet Eillan had three sons, one of whom was Aelred,[2] and a daughter, who became a holy recluse.

The present is not the first time in the annals of England that her monastic system has been extinct; at least, it was so in the north at the period of which we write; and in the south the spirit of monks seems to have well-nigh disappeared, though there were still vast Abbeys, flourishing in worldly wealth. But their Abbots were often men frank-hearted and generous, yet with far more of the noble lord about them than of the churchman. A type of them was the high-spirited Abbot of St. Alban's, who disdained to submit to the Conqueror, and left his Abbey for the fastnesses of Ely, where Hereward was still

[1] Qui, licet peccator secus quam oportuit vixerit—ecclesias, tamen Christi renovandas ornandas serviendas devotum se et sollicitum exhibebat.—MS. Bodl. From the same manuscript it appears, in the dedication of his life of St. Bridget, that Lawrence, Abbot of Westminster, knew Eillan, and received from him the original life, which being "semi-barbara," he polished up and made "Latinissima."

[2] The common date for the birth of St. Aelred is 1109. The evidence of this depends on the date assigned for his death in the life of him, given in the Bollandists, which says that he died in 1166, in his fifty-seventh year,

fighting for the old royal line of England. In the North, however, monastic life was fairly extinct, and if by chance a stray monk, in the black Benedictine habit, was seen north of the Humber, men stared at his cowl and shaven crown as they would at the strange dress of a foreigner.[1] Aelred, then, was born amid the very ruins of the ancient monasticism of the North. Instead of the green banks where grew primroses and violets, the first place where his little feet would naturally take him, would be the ruined nave of the old church, with its mysterious side chapels; and there were beautiful faces of Saints peering out upon him, amidst the damp green moss which was struggling with the bright colours of the frescoes. And he would first hear of St. Wilfrid, the founder of Hexham, though his relics were far away at Canterbury, for it was he who traced the pictures on the walls, to instruct the barbarous people whom he had to teach.[2] He would hear, too, of Acca, the successor of St. Wilfrid, the friend of Bede, for though his name was almost forgotten in the ecclesiastical calendar, the peasants knew his shrine, and every little child could tell where the relics of the holy Bishop lay.[3] His first play-ground would be the ruined cloisters of the Abbey, where the crosses still marked the graves of the old monks. And the

[1] Simeon Dunelm. in. ann. 1074.

[2] Verum ubi eam beatissimus præsul Wilfridus, adductis secum ex partibus transmarinis artificibus, miro lapideo tabulatu ut in præsenti-arum cernitis, renovavit, et ad devotionem rudis adhuc plebis concilian-dam picturis et cælaturis multifariam decoravit. MS. Bodl.

[3] Nam ante translationem multis annis cum adhuc puerulus essem Accam, Alchmundum, Fredenbertum, Tilbertum ibi simul requiescere nihil hæsitans populus totus clamabat. Ibid.

stories which he heard were of the good St. Edward,
with tales of King Alfred's wars and of Edmund
Ironside.

He was not many years old when a change took
place at Hexham, which took away some portion
of its desolateness. His father had a brother, a
religious and devout man, who was grieved at seeing
the possessions of the church thus turned into a
family inheritance, and by his persuasion, Eillan
was induced to apply to the Archbishop of York
for some canons to serve as a germ for the future
restoration of the community. Conscious as he
was of his own disorderly life, he still loved the
Abbey, and had done his best to clear away the
rubbish from the Church, and to repair the most
ruined portions. It was probably connected in his
mind with the old glories of England ; there is a
strange connection between loyalty for an exiled
royal family and religion. The devotional feeling
is often merely hereditary as well as the loyalty ;
yet it is true that the party of a dethroned monarch
is generally also that of religion. In this way,
probably, did Eillan love Hexham and wish for its
restoration ; still his disinterestedness did not carry
him so far as to give up one jot of his personal
rights over the Abbey lands. So poor were the
canons that they often found it very hard to live
on the poor remnant of their property ;[1] and yet
Eillan showed no inclination whatever to better
their condition. However the canons were there,

---

[1] Curam parochiæ cum maxima parte beneficiorum—de ipsis canon-
icis longo tempore tenuit.—Richard of Hexham, De Stat. Eccl.
Hag. 2. 8.

and Aelred could not wander about the old Abbey-buildings without seeing them, and hearing them chant the service. Monks and monkish men are always good friends with children, and doubtless the fair-haired Saxon boy soon made their acquaintance. He was a happy boy, running wherever he pleased about the old Church and Abbey; and it may have been the remembrance of his curious old home on the banks of the Tyne, and of his holy childhood, which made him dwell with peculiar joy on the infancy and childhood of our blessed Lord, in after-times, when, after many a hard struggle, he had gained another home, even more peaceful and secluded. Strange, indeed, it is, when by dint of fighting and hard blows we have been moulded into that character which in substance is to be ours for all eternity, to look back upon the time of our malleable and plastic childhood. How little often can we remember of it! A mazy dream of sicknesses and pains, all coloured by the scenes in which our lot was cast, the sounding sea or the watery meadows, or the high mountains.

So small a portion of Aelred's life was spent there, that his chroniclers have forgotten it. An obscure charter found in Richard of Hexham incidentally preserves the memory of it. And yet these years of his childhood had much influence on his future life; the chant of the canons remained as an undersong amidst all the festivities and the tournaments of a king's court; for this is the next scene in which we find him.[1] When he quitted his

[1] "Ab ipsis incunabulis," says Aelred, "cum Henrico vixi." De Gen. Reg. Angl. ap. Twysden, vol. i. 368.

home at Hexham, Aelred became the playmate of a prince's son. David, the brother of Alexander, king of Scotland, and heir-apparent to the throne, took him into his family and brought him up with his son Henry. David had left his country in early life, and had preferred the court of his brother-in-law, Henry I. of England, to the chance of succeeding to the turbulent throne of Scotland. He had married the daughter of earl Waltheof, who had fallen a victim to the resentment of the Conqueror, and who was regarded as a martyr of the Saxon cause. His mother was Saint Margaret, the sister of Edgar Atheling. Add to which, besides the two earldoms which he possessed, Huntingdon and Northampton, he had also a claim upon Northumberland[1] in right of his wife, who was descended from the old earls of the county. He would thus be naturally brought to Hexham, the spiritual capital of Northumberland ; and its staunch old Saxon priest would be sure to attract the notice of a descendant of Saint Margaret. Another circumstance would draw him towards the little Aelred ; his first child had perished in his infancy by a terrible accident,[2] and Henry, his son, was left without a companion, for David never had any other male children. The beauty of the Saxon boy struck him, and he determined to bring him up with his son, for his daughters, Clarice and Hodierna, could be no mates for the high-spirited boy, who in after life was called Henry the heroic.

[1] David claimed Northumberland for his son Henry on this ground. Fordun, v. 42.

[2] Orderic. Vital. Eccl. Hist. 8, in ann. 1092.

Henry was a devout and good prince, and even when he grew older and was a soldier in the camp, was said to be like a young monk. But there was another boy of more congenial tastes to Aelred, and that was Waltheof, the son of David's queen by her former husband; but of him more by-and-bye.

CHAPTER II

THE REFORMATION IN SCOTLAND

Who could have in the whole world better prospects than Aelred? The courts of England and Scotland were opening upon him; a rich heiress with a noble fief, or, if he preferred the church, a mitred abbacy would have been reasonable objects of a laudable ambition. But here we must pause, and while Aelred is growing up in David's family, take a look at the state of politics in the north. The kingdom of Scotland, I had almost said the church, was in process of formation. It was Aelred's destiny to be thrown among the ruins of a state of things passed away; by-and-bye he will assist in the raising up of a new system; but we must first learn what were the wild and unruly elements among which his lot was cast. Alas! for Scotland. How was it ever to become like a Christian kingdom? Its hierarchy was as yet unformed; it had been cast out of the stream of European civilisation, and its communications with the Christian world were but few and far between. The sixth century is a long way off from the twelfth; and it was in that early time that a voice was heard going through the western isles and the wild coasts of Argyle, proclaiming peace on earth, good-will towards men.

The good news spread across to the mainland, from Oban, down by the banks of Loch Awe, even to the wild headland of Cantyre; and the savage people were turned to the faith of Christ. It was then that in the north arose Iona, or Icolmkill, Columba's cell; and the kings of Norway, of Scotland, and of the Isles, chose to lie around the shrine of St. Columba, while in the south among the Picts, St. Ninian had founded Whiterne. Still it is quite true that Christianity never seized upon the hearts of the people as it did in the south; it was a hard task indeed to penetrate through all the wild glens, the winding lakes, and the forests of pine which lie among those savage mountains, but this it did accomplish; what it did not do was to bend the stubborn heart, the rough and disputatious temper of the men. There was something forbidding in the original Scottish monks: they did not seize on the hearts of the people. They never succeeded in extinguishing hatred between rival races, and while England was one kingdom at the Norman Conquest, Scotland had not even a right to one name; it was Pictland as well as Scotland, and there was in the north beyond the Grampians, still the Gael, the wild and untamed savage of the north. Scotland was really only Argyleshire and the Isles; the country beneath, from the two Friths, that is, the Lothians and Strathclyde, belonged to England; while Galloway, with its savage Picts, was a debatable land, ground down between both. Christianity had not drawn together the hearts of the savage chieftains; and what was worse, it had not succeeded in purifying their vices; among no nation, calling itself Christian, was the sanctity of marriage so little respected as among the Picts and Scots.[1]

Alas! for Scotland. By the time of the Norman Conquest, the work of St. Columba and St. Ninian was undone. Whiterne had no bishop; he had long ago been driven away in some of the cruel and constant wars which raged in the country. In Scotland, the bishopric of St. Andrews was still standing. But all was in a miserable state; there too monasticism had disappeared; the far-famed Culdees were a set of degenerate priests; they had given up their original rule, and had wives and children; and it is said of them that they hardly ever celebrated mass at St. Andrew's altar, except when the king came to see them.[2] In this state of things, it was well for Scotland that, by God's will, its kings became feudal vassals of England. Feudalism, instead of being, as has been supposed, the partition of a territory among many lords, was in reality the binding of a number of disjointed communities into one. The independent patriarchal chieftain who did homage to his conqueror and received back his lands from him, was bound, on pain of forfeiting them, to assist his suzerain whenever he required his services; and the feudal head thus became the centre of a number of before disjointed hordes.[3] But feudalism also contained another principle, and that was, that within his

[1] See St. Aelred's Life in the Bollandists.

[2] Pinkerton, Enquiry, Appendix, p. 462.

[3] Those who know Sir Francis Palgrave's great work on the Anglo-Saxon Constitution, will see at once how much the author is indebted to him for pointing out the relation which existed between England and Scotland, and throughout this chapter.

own territory each lord was absolute ; his suzerain could not interfere with his jurisdiction ; infangthief and outfangthief implied a very perfect and intelligible power of hanging and imprisoning as he pleased. This of course varied with the real power of the suzerain : in proportion as he was strong, his vassals were less independent ; thus, for instance, the great vassals of the French king were much more like independent chieftains than an English earl under the Conqueror or Henry II. In the case of Scotland, the king, while he became the vassal of the English crown, strengthened his authority at home. He became himself a feudal superior over his people, instead of a patriarchal chieftain with limited powers. Besides which the English king made him the feudal lord of Cumbria, which included not only the modern shires of Renfrew and Lanark, but "merry Carlisle" also, and the whole of Cumberland, to be held as a fief from himself. And the very dependent relation in which he placed himself was perhaps more useful to himself and his people in another way. It made him a portion of the great European body, and brought them into contact with the rest of Christendom.

The Norman Conquest indirectly still further improved Scotland. Malcolm Canmore, an intelligent and upright prince, was then on the throne. He had been driven into exile by Macbeth, the murderer of his father, and had lived for fourteen years in King Edward's court ; here he had learned a lesson which he did not forget when he returned to his own wild and troubled home in the north. He had learned what was the meaning of a feudal king, not only the

leader in war of a savage horde, with whom he was
the common proprietor of a certain number of streams
and mountains, but the lord of the soil, the dispenser
of justice, according to determinate forms. He had
had before him also a model of devotion, chastity,
and justice in the saintly Edward. He had seen
also there Margaret, a Saxon maiden, then a child
of ten years old, and the niece of the Confessor,
in whose veins flowed the blood of the royal house
of England, and the imperial line of Germany ; [1] and
when he came back to his desolate palace of Dunfermline, surrounded by wars abroad and treachery
within, he still thought of the holy family which
he had seen in his exile at Westminster. After
many years news came to Scotland that St. Edward
was dead, and that Harold had seized on the throne ;
and next that a great battle had been fought, and
that the Normans ruled in England. Malcolm at
once armed his powers in favour of Edgar, and of
the line of St. Edward ; but the Conqueror was too
strong for him, and his country was invaded, and
he himself compelled to submit. What in the
meanwhile was become of Margaret? One day,
Malcolm was sitting in his palace of Dunfermline ;
the wind had been blowing fiercely, and news was
brought him that a large ship had been driven by
stress of weather into the bay. He sent down to

[1] Malcolm was fourteen years in Edward's court ; he left it at the
latter end of the year 1056, the very year in which Margaret came
back from Hungary. Comp. Fordun, lib. v. c. 7, 11, 16. Orderic,
as Sir F. Palgrave has observed, says that St. Edward betrothed
Margaret to Malcolm. This appears inconsistent however with
Turgot's narrative, if Fordun gives it rightly ; for he seems to imply
that Edgar betrothed his sister to Malcolm.

the shore some of his nobles to see where the strange ship had come from; then they brought him word that they had seen a man of princely bearing disembark with two maidens, one taller than the other, and of surpassing beauty. Malcolm sent for them, and found to his joy that they were the exiled family of England, whom God had thus directed to his land. Poor Margaret! she had looked with terror at the high mountains and rugged rocks of the land on which they had been cast, and with still more terror at the wild looks of the nobles, who had come to gaze upon them; but she now thanked God who sent to them a protector who loved the memory of St. Edward. Not long after, Malcolm begged of Edgar to bestow upon him the hand of his sister, and Margaret became queen of Scotland. It was by God's good providence that the line of St. Edward was planted afresh in Scotland; it was providential too that Margaret was chosen at this special time to be queen of Scotland, for it was a turning-point in the history of the country, and Margaret became its reformer.

What could a poor foreign maiden do on such a throne? amidst a court where the utmost depravity prevailed, and the wild nobles swore unchristian oaths in the presence of their queen. The very loneliness, and the distance from her country, was enough to appal the heart of a maiden; and the rude rafters and comfortless halls, and the windy passages of an old northern palace, were in themselves sufficient to weigh down with its gloom the heart of a female, brought up in the palace of Westminster. What then could Margaret do?

with what sceptre could she sway her unruly court?
and yet she did reform Scotland, and that too,
church and state. And if any one asks how she
could do this, I will tell him how another queen
did not do it. There once came to Scotland, from
a foreign court, a queen, like Margaret, of surpassing
beauty, of strong affections, and of a cheerful disposition, loving to make all happy about her. But
with all her advantages, Mary did not win the hearts
of the people, nor reform the wickedness of her
nobles, and her reign ruined all that was left of
the Church. It is only when, after long years of
penitence, she died on the scaffold, confessing her
faith, that we can look with complacency on Mary.
But the strength of Margaret lay in her being a
saint. It is true she was what is called a clever
woman ; she knew Latin, and rejoiced in conversing
with the learned men of the realm. But cleverness
is not enough to effect a reform in a barbarous
nation. She had that indescribable tact by which
saints know how to manage those about them, and
to do almost unconsciously just what they ought.
A cold dignity might have awed, but could not have
won over the nobles of her unruly court. But
Margaret had a well-spring of quiet happiness in
her heart which made her smile on all around her.
Her happy cheerfulness was like the purple light
which throws a warm tint on the cold mountain
snow. In her saintly uprightness she could afford
to be amiable without losing her dignity ; and no
one durst venture before her on an evil jest, for
she had a strange power in her presence which
rendered it impossible. The refractory warriors

who frequented her husband's table would not wait till grace was said, and she won them to submission by sending round a cup of choice wine to be given to those who remained, and it was still in after-times called the grace-cup, or St. Margaret's cup. Her character had so endeared her to her husband, that she possessed an unbounded influence over him. His was no weak and easily compliant mind, and yet she converted him to habits of devotion and piety, which were rare indeed among the wild warriors of the twelfth century. He allowed her as much money as she would to distribute among the poor, and with his own royal hands helped her every day to feed the multitudes whom she served within the palace. With her he washed the feet of the poor; nay, so completely did he allow her to give herself up to the boundless love of Christ's poor ones that continually welled from her heart, that he permitted her to bring impure lepers into their common chamber and kiss their sores. He knew well that it was no weak or fanatical devotion which made her do so, but a love for her Lord, and an intense realisation of His oneness with His suffering members. Sometimes she would pretend to steal from the royal treasury what she distributed to the poor, for she knew well that her playful theft pleased her husband; and Malcolm would take her by the wrist, with her hand thus full of gold, and bring her to her confessor, and ask him if she were not a little thief caught in the very act, who deserved to be well punished. He would take up the books in which she read, and kiss them in fond devotion; sometimes he would

carry them away, and have them beautifully illuminated with figures of saints and golden letters; he
would cover them with gold and jewels, and bring
them back to her with joyful triumph.

Her gentle influence was exerted in improving
the taste, and refining the manners of Scottish
females; the most terrible licentiousness reigned in
the kingdom, but she was like a light from heaven, a
type of all purity to her subjects, and her example
purified the land. She had ever about her a number
of noble maidens, whom she brought up within the
palace, and there wrought rich palls for the altar,
and magnificent vestments of all sorts for the service
of the Church. To purify and refine their taste,
she encouraged merchants to come to the kingdom,
and of them she bought the richest wares, gold
and silver vases, and jewels of price. Into this
her little court where she sat with her maidens at
work, she admitted none of the nobles but those
of whom she had a good opinion; and she was
herself the life and the centre of the circle.

But one thing Margaret did, which Popes and
Councils had found a hard matter, and that was,
to bring the Church to a uniformity with the rest
of Christendom. Strangely indeed had the old
tendencies of the Scotch Church developed. Three
centuries had passed since the monks of Iona had
submitted to be like the rest of Christendom; but
these had been centuries of weakness and of sleep,
and when the voice of St. Gregory VII. called men
out of their sleep, each Church had to consider what
evils it had to reform.[1] Feudalism had created

[1] The Scotch appear never to have been treated as schismatics by

national Churches and striven to cut off the communication between the parts of Christendom, and this even where it falls short of actual schism is sure to weaken the healthy action of the whole. Scotland had had no feudalism, and therefore it had no prince-bishops, no high baronial abbots, and no simony. But the old sour and sullen spirit had come out, and the developments of the nationality of Scotland were curious. They had given up their old way of keeping Easter, but they had taken up a wrong method of keeping Lent. Instead of beginning on Ash-Wednesday, they put off the fast till the Monday after. Besides which, with a sort of northern Jansenism, they excluded sinners from the Holy Communion on Easter-day, even those whom after confession and penitence, the Church would have received. Lastly, they used in the administration of mass, certain superstitious rites, unknown to the Catholic Church.

It was a strange sight, that assembly in which Margaret, with her husband for an interpreter, argued these points with the Scotch, who certainly have ever shown a singular immobility in religious matters, both of practice and of faith. It was hardly the province of a woman, it was private judgment; and yet Margaret had that strange way of arriving at conclusions without premises, that unreasoning logic, by which the female mind arrives at what is right by an unconscious process. She had the Catholic church on her side, and it did not require any deep abstract

the Holy See, notwithstanding their different mode of celebrating Easter, which was not that condemned in the Council of Nice. v. Baronius, in ann. 634.

views to tell her that the Scotch were wrong. The
natural rectitude of a Christian heart would tell her,
when the Lenten fast came round, that it was an
unnatural thing to be keeping carnival when the
brethren in other lands were fasting and mourning.
Brethren and sisters love to be together at Christmas,
and when any member of a family is carried to the
grave, terrible as is the grief, all like to share it together, and to accompany the beloved body to the
tomb. The Christian world is one family, and when
the bells in England rang out an Ash-Wednesday
sound, Margaret would not have them rung with a
merry chime in Scotland; as well might a sister
dance while her brother is in mourning. Thus, the
strangely Catholic instinct of the Christian heart
would alone guide Margaret, without any profound
abstract views of unity and uniformity. Cold and
dead does reasoning fall upon the soul, in comparison
with this yearning for oneness, of the same nature,
as the love of brethren and sisters, though tenfold
stronger. In such cases private judgment may be
safely left to itself, and becomes infallible; and so
Margaret felt that she could not err, though she were
teaching the doctors of the church of her nation.
And so again with respect to Paschal communion,
one who had herself received the Body of her Lord
at Easter would feel it strange that any one who was
not actually excommunicated should be banished
from the altar at that holy time; and when the
Clergy urged those fearful words of St. Paul against
those who receive unworthily, " All are unworthy in
one sense," answered the queen, " but they who for
many days before have done penance after confessing

their sins on Easter-day, coming to the table of the Lord in the Catholic faith, receive the flesh and blood of the immaculate Lamb, not to judgment, but to the remission of sins." Three things more she obtained from the council, the abolition of superstitious rites at the holy sacrifice of the mass, the observance of the Sunday, which had fallen into disuse in the realm, and certain canons against unlawful marriages. The high-spirited Scot, in his enthusiastic love for her goodness, gave up to her gentle persuasion what the authority of their king could not have extorted by force, and what they would never have yielded to the arguments of the Saxon priests.

And now it may well be asked what was the hidden life of Margaret. This cheerful queen, who walked abroad clad in gold and jewels, could hardly have an ascetic air; and yet beneath her gorgeous robes was a body chastised by perpetual fasts, and knees hardened by long prayers. She kept a fast of forty days before Christmas, in addition to the fast before Lent; and during those seasons of penitence she rose before midnight, and spent the hours of darkness in singing psalms. A great part of this time she was often alone in prayer in the Church, and when the clerks came in to sing their office, they found her there ready to join them. As the day dawned she lay down again for a very short time to refresh her weary body; and all this while, during these long and wearing fasts, she was going about doing works of active benevolence. Even before her second brief sleep in the morning, she, with Malcolm's help, had washed the feet of six poor people, and given them alms to relieve their wants. And scarcely had she risen again, when nine orphan infants were brought to her; she stooped down on her knees to feed them; and none of the details of sops and of baby linen were beneath her royal care. During the day three hundred poor were relieved by her own hand and that of the king. She had another care, of which nothing has yet been said, the care of her children, and how she fulfilled this duty the subsequent history of Scotland bears witness. How well she loved them and her royal husband, her death will tell. Neither her austere life and religious exercises, nor what was much more likely to do it, her gold and jewels, and queenly apparel, had seared her woman's heart. Her husband and her elder sons were in England engaged in the siege of Alnwick, and she herself had long been ailing, and was now very ill. One day her attendants observed that she was sad, an unusual thing with her; her heart was thinking on her husband and her sons, who were far away over the border, fighting on English ground, and she said to those about her, "Who knows whether some great evil has not happened to the Scottish realm?" She got daily worse and worse, and her features had already the paleness of death upon them. She had received the last sacrament, and ordered the Black Cross to be brought to her. It was a piece of the true cross, on which was an ivory figure of the Lord crucified, the whole enclosed in a beautiful reliquary of gold.[1] She had brought it over with her from England, and now she wished to die with it in her hands, and when it was found hard to open the case in which it was contained, she

[1] St. Aelred, de Genealog. Twysden, i. 349.

exclaimed, "Ah! wretched sinner! I am not then worthy to look upon the Holy Cross"; and when at length it was brought to her, she kissed it, and wept over it, and glued it to her lips, repeating all the while the fifty-first psalm. At this moment her son Alexander entered the room; she revived on seeing him, and asked him for news about his father and brother. He answered that they were well; the dying queen, however, guessed the truth by his mournful countenance, and conjured him by the Holy Cross, which she held in her hands, to tell her. He then told her the truth; his father and his brother had both been killed. Margaret raised her hands to heaven, and said, "All praise be to Thee, everlasting God, who hast made me suffer such agony in my death, as I hope, to the cleansing of some of the stains of my sins." And soon after this her poor broken heart ceased to beat.

She went to where the wicked cease from troubling, and the weary are at rest; and she left behind her war and desolation in Scotland. Scarcely had the breath passed from her body when it was remarked that a sweet bloom had come over the death-like paleness of her face, and her features assumed a beautiful expression of peace. It contrasted strangely with the wild storm which raged around her sacred relics. A party among the Scots hated the rule of Malcolm, as being a favourer of Sassenaghs and foreigners;[1] the wild Gael loved

[1] Omnes Anglos qui de curia regis extiterunt de Scotia expulerant— Post hac eum regnare permiserunt ea ratione ut amplius in Scotia nec Anglos, nec Normannos introduceret. Simeon Dunelm, in ann. 1093.

not the approach of civilisation, and a party was already in arms prepared to besiege the castle of Edinburgh, where lay her body. Hurriedly by a postern door her sacred remains were conveyed away, and buried in the Abbey of Dunfermline. The rebels succeeded for a time in expelling her son from the throne. For five years war and rapine ravaged Scotland, and usurpers wore its crown, but at length it pleased God to restore Edgar, the eldest surviving son of Margaret, to the throne. He was like his great uncle, St. Edward, a mild and amiable prince, and the weary land had peace in his days. After him came a remarkable prince, Alexander, surnamed the Fierce; and need he had of fierceness, for he had to rule an unruly kingdom, and by main force to keep in awe his rebellious nobles. But fierce as he was to them, he was mild and beneficent to the Clergy, whom he loved for his sainted mother's sake. They were men of enlightened policy, these kings of Scotland; they cherished all the learning and goodness which the Norman invasion had drifted from the south. This, however, might have been merely the effect of circumstances; the Saxon kingdom had stretched to the north as far as the castle of the Maidens, the modern name of which, Edwin's burgh, even now bears witness to the Saxon rule. The policy of the Saxon kings, by giving it to be ruled as a fief by the Scottish king, had converted a dangerous enemy into a friend, and when the Norman conquest came sweeping before it all that was English, it was natural that the Saxons should retire towards the north, and Sassenagh, the name so long applied to the Lowlander by the Gael, bears witness to the extent of the southern importation. It shows also their contempt for their native kings who had adopted the manners and civilisation of the Southron; and this feeling created the party among the native Scottish nobles, which cost so much trouble to Alexander and his brothers. This would naturally incline the king to those of Saxon blood. But it could be nothing but a sound and Christian policy which prompted them to amalgamate their discordant races by the erection of new bishoprics.[1]   St. Andrews, for a long time

[1] Amidst the great confusion attending the ecclesiastical History of Scotland, it is difficult to fix the time of the creation or revival of the sees. The common account given in Buchanan cannot be trusted, for St. Aelred (de Genealog. Twysden, p. 348) expressly says that David found only three or four sees when he came to the throne. The truth probably is that there were great irregularities (as appears from the 43rd canon of the second Council of Chalons) and that the sees were for a long time unfixed. It appears that by an unusual regulation, the Abbot and monks of Iona had, not of course the consecration, as has been supposed, of Bishops, but their appointment and mission, v. Thomassin, 1, 3, 14, 12. The Bishops thus continued to be like Bishops in partibus without fixed sees. It is difficult to fix the precise time when this state of things ceased. It probably did not cease at once, for in David's time there was an irregular election of a Bishop, which looks like a part of the old system, v. William of Newbridge, i. 23; and as late as 1297, the Culdees made an effort to regain the right of election. It seems, however, likely that Alexander effected the real change by taking the jurisdiction out of the hands of the Culdees, and thus fixing the sees. First, the expulsion of the Culdees from St. Andrews, and the revival of Glasgow was in his time. The latter event indeed was executed by David, as appears from the inquisition taken by him in Pinkerton; but it was done before he came to the throne, and while he was ruler of Cumbria under his brother, as was usual with the heir-apparent to the throne, v. Palgrave, p. 441. Secondly, a passage is quoted in the preface to Twysden, from a manuscript in the Cotton

was the only fixed Scottish See, and its Bishop was called the Bishop of the Scots,[1] as the prelate of Whiterne, as successor of St. Ninian, was the Bishop of the Picts. To this see King Alexander added Glasgow and perhaps also Elgin, or at least he revived them ; and took care to appoint to these sees men of learning and piety. But the throne of a Scottish diocese was by no means an easy seat. Turgot, whom Alexander early in his reign appointed to the see of St. Andrews, went back to his cloister of Durham, for his heart sunk within him at the difficulties which surrounded him. Eadmer, too, the companion of St. Anselm, was elected to the same see, but the very next year

library, which, though it contains mistakes, is too remarkable to have been written without authority. Anno. ab. Inc. Domini 1108, ac tempore Regis Malcolmi et S. Margaritæ electus fuit Turgotus, Prior Dunelmensis in Episcopatum St. Andreæ et in diebus illis totum jus Keledeorum per totum regnum Scotiæ transivit in Episcopatum S. Andreæ. Turgot was not made Bishop by Malcolm, but by Alexander ; and so it appears that in Alexander's days the jurisdiction over Scotland was taken away from the Culdees, and transferred to the Bishop of St. Andrews. The actual erection of St. Andrews into a metropolitan see was not effected till long afterwards, owing to the opposition of the Archbishop of York ; but the breaking of the power of the Culdees, is in this passage clearly expressed. It is therefore most likely on the whole that the great change is to be referred to him, and not to Malcolm. Caithness and Elgin may have been revived by Malcolm ; yet it is remarkable that the revolt in consequence of which they are said to have been erected, is probably that said by Fordun to have occurred in Alexander's time. The creation of the greater number of the Scottish Sees is owing to David, as St. Aelred says that on his accession to the throne he found three or four sees, but at his death left nine. Two out of these four are known to have been St. Andrews and Glasgow, the other two were probably Elgin and Caithness.

[1] Pinkerton, Enquiry, Appendix, p. 464.

he came back to Canterbury, for it was better to be a simple monk of St. Benedict than to bear the weary crosier of St. Andrews. Again, John, the new Bishop of Glasgow, fairly ran away to Rome, and from thence to the Holy Land, and could only be brought back but by an express command of the Holy See. One part of their difficulty was doubtless their difference with the Archbishop of York, who claimed canonical jurisdiction over them, but the chief obstacles lay in their unruly Clergy, the degenerate Culdees. Alexander, however, determined to remedy this evil; monasticism was reviving in the north of England, and wherever a new monastery was established, or an old one revived, there were the headquarters of religion, and the monks became the instructors of a people, whom the mere pressure of desolation had stupefied and brutalised. The example of Durham had given him a precedent for the expulsion of the secularised Culdees, and he substituted regular canons for them at St. Andrews. He restored to the prior and canons of St. Andrews the lands which had been taken away from the Church, and the quaint style in which the act of restoration was effected is a specimen of the state of things in Scotland. In the cathedral of St. Andrews all the nobles of the realm were assembled; and with them Robert, the newly-elected Bishop, formerly prior of Scone, and the new canons of the convent, their shaven crowns and ecclesiastical habit mingling strangely with the bright armour of the Lowland nobles, and the waving plaid of the chieftains of the Gael. In the midst of this assembly there was led up to the high altar Alexander's Arabian war horse, saddled and bridled, and spendidly caparisoned, with the king's shield fastened to his back, and a silver lance, which afterwards became the shaft of the crucifix of the Church. By this strange charter the lands were delivered to the monks, and the transaction was duly impressed upon the witnesses. Besides which he built the Abbey of the Holy Trinity at Scone, the ancient seat of Scottish royalty, and the monastery of St. Columba, in the little island of Inchcolm, in the Frith of Forth; and any one who has been on Loch Tay, will remember the green islet where a monastery was erected over the grave of his wife Sibylla.

It was in the year 1124 that Alexander died, shortly after he had conferred the lands on the Church of St. Andrews. His brother David thus found himself in possession of an unenviable throne, for Alexander died childless.[1] He endeavoured to avoid the dangerous honour; and indeed he had few temptations to quit the court of England, where he was honoured as the first of English nobles. Henry had loved him for the cheerful and warm-hearted disposition which he had inherited from his sainted mother. He had been knighted by the king's own hand, and was a general favourite with the whole court. He related to Aelred of himself, in after times, that he used to smile at his sister, the good queen Maud, and at the filthy objects whose wants, in her charity, she would herself relieve. But even in the thoughtlessness of his youth, he was preserved from evil, and was already

---

[1] Scimus enim regnum non appetivisse sed horruisse, says St. Aelred.

distinguished by his zeal for the Church in that part of Scotland which, as heir-apparent to the crown, was his appanage. And now he shuddered at the task which was imposed upon him. He yielded, however, to the persuasion of the Bishops, and was crowned. It was of the utmost consequence to Henry, that in the event of a disputed succession, which was likely, Scotland should be in the hands of one bound to the line of St. Edward by so many ties; and he, too, probably urged David to accept the throne. David did not find his kingdom so hard to rule as he had imagined. What his brother, with all his fierceness, could keep only at the cost of much labour and blood, he ruled in peace by his meekness and charity.[1] He managed to reconcile, at least to keep in order, the two discordant elements of his kingdom, the old patriarchal chieftains of the plaided clans, and the new nobles which were rising up, the earls and barons of the feudal Lowlands. He was the king, in an especial manner, of the Church and of the poor. A novel personage for Scotland, and one which she had not seen for centuries, meets us at the outset of his reign—a legate of the Holy See. He met the King with the Bishops and Clergy at Roxburgh. In the reign of Malcolm, the queen was the leading figure in the council, and though perfectly justified by circumstances, it was not the usual mode of proceeding, as may well be supposed. David's object was to fix the hierarchy, and to erect a native

---

[1] Regnum quod frater laboriorissime tenuit, mox ille sine contradictione susceptum, quaquaversum inclinum sibi et quietum tenuit. —Sim. Dunelm. in ann. 1124. St. Aelred calls him the author of the Scottish polity.

church, instead of depending on English clergy. To effect the first of these purposes, he more than doubled the number of Bishops; and for the latter object, he erected many monasteries of the Cistercian order, and houses of regular canons. How well he succeeded is evident from the fact, that while contemplation was by no means the line of the old Scottish clergy, some of the distinguished members of the mystic school of St. Victor, at Paris, were Scotchmen. He was in some measure a St. Louis in the twelfth century, and the story of his often returning to his palace at the petition of a poor man, when he had already foot in stirrup, and the merry horn was calling him to the chase, reminds one of the oak of Vincennes, under which the good Louis sat to give judgment to all who came to him. His brother Alexander's appetite probably was not spoiled when, in his royal justice he hanged a felon; but David was known to weep on ordering an execution. In another respect was David like the sainted king. The good people, in St. Louis's reign, made jingling rhymes about his love for clerks, and one of David's successors called him a "sair Saint for the crown." And yet James might have had no kingdom to govern, if David had not preceded him; and doubtless the crown was not the worse for the prayers which monks and nuns offered up in the many abbeys founded by David; nor were the Scotch less religious because he left nine bishoprics where he found but four. If it had not been for the unhappy invasion of England, which will be noticed by-and-bye, the parallel with St. Louis would have been complete.

CHAPTER III

THE STRUGGLE

WE left Aelred in his boyhood, the playfellow of
Henry, the son of David, Earl of Huntingdon, and
we must now be content to find him a youth in
the palace of David, king of Scotland. Splendid
was the prospect which opened upon him. In a
new and flourishing kingdom just about to take its
place among the nations of Europe, the favourite
of its king, he might have become the first of its
nobles. Aelred's family is said to have been noble,[1]
though, from the present situation of his father, it
must have been decayed; and even if he had been
base-born, the earldoms and fiefs of this period were
not so restricted to men of noble blood but that a
poor adventurer might hope to obtain them. It is
true, that in most cases the feudal lord would be
coincident with the patriarchal chief; but in England, especially, precedents might be found where
the poor knight became an earl, rich in broad lands
and in vassals.[2] Society was forming itself anew,

---

[1] Joscelin. Vita St. Waltheni. ap. Bolland. Aug. 3.

[2] Speaking of Henry I.'s favourites, the author of Gesta Stephani
says, quique regno nobiliores gloriam eorum et pompam, ægre ferebant,
utpote qui ex imo creati genere se multo nobiliores et divitiis excederent
et dominio superarent. Duchesne. Script. Norm. 932. v. also 966.

and a new nobility was arising in England and
Scotland ; and if Aelred had had the warlike taste
of Henry, his companion, he might have fought his
way to be the head of the Scottish chivalry. But
his gentle and retiring spirit led him to books and
study, and Aelred followed the example of Waltheof,
in preferring his books to tilts and tournaments.
Here, too, if he had but been ambitious, a fine
field lay before him. He was a man of learning
rare in those times. In his boyhood, he had read
Cicero and Terence,[1] and those authors quoted by
chance in his works, are but specimens of his acquirements in classical learning. He knew the Latin
Fathers too, and sundry allusions to genus and
species show in him the rising schoolman, to whom
the mysteries of the trivium and quadrivium were
familiar.[2] He left school at an early age, but he
still continued his studies at court. He might have
led, if he had pleased, the march of intellect, as it
may be called, in Scotland, and it would have been
hard if a mitre and crosier had not fallen to his
share.[3] But never was a soul less ambitious than
Aelred's. From his boyhood, his sole ambition was
concentred in loving and being loved ; his text-book

He also talks of landless nobles, p. 956. As for Scotland, there are
said to have been no earls or barons before Malcolm Canmore's time.

[1] De Spirit. Ami. lib. iii. p. 469, ed. Gibbons.

[2] Post scholas præponere relictas. Joscel. Sed proprio sudore et
ingenii subtilis sibi innati exercitio expolitus supra multos literis
sæcularibus imbutos.—Ibid. Laurence, Abbot of Westminster, in
the preface to the Life of St. Bridget before quoted, speaks of his
cura literarum in curia regis.

[3] Tanto amore a Scotorum Rege complexus est ut ad episcopum eum
promovisset nisi ad Cisterciensem ordinem advolasset.—Vita St. Aelred
ap. Boll.

was Cicero on Friendship, which he read with avidity,
and endeavoured to carry out in real life.[1] He read
romances too, for he knew that story which in after-
days he characterised as "a vain tale concerning
one Arthur."[2] The friendship however of David and
Jonathan in Scripture, affected him more than all
the feats of the Round Table, and the love of Queen
Guenever to boot. In the legends of Christian
Martyrs, he wept with tears of tenderness over the
devoted friendship of the Christian soldier who saved
the virgin of Antioch out of the place of shame,
and afterwards shared her crown of martyrdom.[3]
He went about the world seeking for objects on
which to expend his affection, and feeling pained
if his love met with no return. But this was a case
which could not often happen; for he was too
amiable not to be loved by all the world. He lived
far from his home, and very little is told of his
family; his mother's name is not once mentioned,
but this was made up to him by the love of all
about him. He was one of those who, by the
smiling faces which ever meet them, feel sure that
their presence is always welcome.[4] In the ban-
queting hall, while the merry jest was going round,
his quick wit and ready speech made him an
acquisition, while from his guileless unaffectedness

[1] Cum adhuc puer essem in scholis tota se mea mens dedit effectui
et devovit amori ut mihi nihil dulcius quam amari et amare videretur.—
De Spirit. Ami. Prolog.

[2] Spec. Char. 2. 17.

[3] De Spirit. Ami. i. p. 435.

[4] Erat vir optime morigeratus, facetus, facundus, socialis et jocundus.
Joscelin. Vid. also his account of himself, Spec. Chari. i. 28, where
he seems to point to something of the sort.

no one felt his inferiority. Indeed, his guilelessness almost approached to credulity; and though quick-witted enough to see into the faults of others, yet he seemed to have an universal belief in the goodness of the human heart, which neutralised his cleverness. His high favour raised him enemies; but even these he won over by his meekness. One of the king's knights, an envious man, hated him for his good fortune, as he deemed it, and one day his hatred broke out, even in the king's presence, and he loaded him with reproachful and insulting words. But Aelred remained unmoved, and said, "Thou art right, sir knight, and hast spoken right well; what thou sayest is truth, and I see thou art a true friend of mine." The rude soldier immediately begged his pardon, and swore that he would do his best to serve him. "I am glad of thy penitence," said Aelred, "and I love thee the more because by thy hatred I have advanced in love to God." This sweet temper could not fail to bring him friends, and the king above all loved him. He used to tell him family stories about the courage of his father, King Malcolm, and the goodness of his sister Matilda, the queen of England.[1] He gave him the steward-ship of his household, a high office, which afterwards gave its name to the royal family of England and Scotland, and which, about that time, a clerk, the favourite and minister of King Louis, held in France.[2]

[1] De Genealog. ap Twysden.

[2] St. Aelred is called dapifer regius. In common cases dapifer means simply the Reeve, but in a king's household it is equivalent to senescallus. The dapifer of King Louis is called Major domus regiæ, or maire du palais, in the Chronicle of Morigny, v. Benedictine note to St. Bernard, Ep. 78. Laurence addresses St. Aelred as dispensator

Happy Aelred! what had he to do but to lead a religious and literary life; he was known far and wide for his learning, and an abbot of Westminster dedicated to him a work of his, written "in pure Latin," as being one who "in a king's court cultivated letters." It seems that he went out hunting too with the king;[1] at least he is well acquainted "with the law of hunting, which they call the tryste in vulgar tongue," where all the nobles, with their hounds, were posted in different parts of the wood, so as to surround the quarry; and he knew well the paths and recesses of the forest, for he describes a flowery knoll in the midst of it, where the tired huntsmen lay down to rest after their toils. At this time it is probable that he made those acquisitions of historical lore which afterwards fitted him to become one of the historians of England. He had inherited the hereditary love for the royal line of Cedric, and delighted in the beautiful tales of Alfred and St. Neot, and the battle of Ashdown. He loved to trace their genealogy, and he looked forward with hope to their restoration. If to be loved and honoured, and to pass a life in congenial studies, with no enemies, free from great sin, be happiness, then was Aelred happy; and men, as he passed, pointed him out as a man whose lot was to be envied.

And yet the High Steward of Scotland was not happy. It would be easy to give the reason for this phenomenon in a few words. It was the grace

regius, and he himself talks of his having come de coquinis non de scholis.

[1] De Genealog. ap. Twysden. p. 367.

of God, urging him to his place in Christ's kingdom;
it was the cross casting its shadow on all earthly
joys. This is of course the proper explanation of
it; but it is through our own feelings and tempers
that God leads us, and it is the part of history to
unfold the human side of events, which appear to
us, and are really, as far as we are concerned, various
and successive; while, as the work of God, they are
one. What then was the reason of Aelred's un-
happiness amidst all the gifts of nature and of grace?
The friends about him called it morbid restlessness,
and he tried to believe them and to shake it off;
but it would come back again for all his efforts.
Even his books were tasteless: neither Cicero nor
Horace could satisfy him, and the purest latinity
could not confer happiness; nay, the philosophy
of St. Augustine and St. Anselm was at fault;[1]
and after he had proved to his satisfaction the being
of a God, after having confuted Manichees and
Nominalists, the same void was in his heart, and he
was still restless. No one could blame his studies; it
was a noble scheme to reform the taste and arouse
the understanding of a nation arising from barbarism; but it is not enough that a work should be
blameless, if it be not that which the Lord requires
of us. In itself a literary life is of all others the
most empty and unsatisfactory. Things that belong
exclusively to this sublunary sphere are at least in
their place; they are all of earth, and they gain
the things of earth and men enjoy them as they

---

[1] The sixth chapter of the Spec. Char., lib. i., is evidently taken
from St. Anselm; and the influence of St. Augustine de Trinitate is
also evident throughout the Speculum.

may. But the student aims higher and fails; after he has thought, and judged, and analysed, he has not extended one jot the sphere of human knowledge, because it is human after all. The lowest angel knows at a glance by intuition what is to us a laboured fabric of premise and conclusion, and is at best but the shadow of the truth. After all that is often said about the blamelessness of literary pleasures, they do not satiate the hungry soul a whit the more; chalk and chaff are not food, because they are not poison. So learned Aelred by a bitter experience: but he had still something else to learn, and that was, that the heart as well as the understanding can be filled but by one object alone. It was not wonderful that Aelred found his high notions of friendship sink under him. Was it altogether Christian, this craving for being loved, this insatiable desire of winning human hearts? It was not admiration or honour that he sought—it was love; and is this not only a more subtle form of inordinate affection? There was once an Archbishop whom anyone who knows the works of both, would at once compare with Aelred, like him in his generous devotedness, and his warm affections, the favourite of a king's court, the honoured friend of a king's son. Like Aelred he was of classical taste, consulted by wits and learned men, a lover of St. Augustine, a Christian philosopher. Yet all were nothing to him, rank and honour and wealth; they slid away from his mind as from a polished surface, and had no hold upon it; but there was one thing which he wished and obtained, the affection of those about him. High as was his rank, yet the lowest

did not shrink before the stately figure of the Archbishop of Cambray and the Peer of France. He
was dead to all things but one, and that was human
affection. God in his mercy separated him from
the being whom he loved most on earth, the king's
son, who was his friend and his pupil, and thus was
his whole man crucified. How very much of this
resembles Aelred's case, we shall soon see; but
meanwhile we will quote the words of this saintly
prelate, about this same desire of loving and being
loved, which he himself knew so well.[1]

"After having renounced all that is around us,
and which is not self, we must come to the last
sacrifice, which is that of all which is in us, and is
self. If a man's temper is full of frankness and
disinterestedness, if his disposition leads him to
take pleasure in doing good, and if he has keen
delicacy of feeling, and a taste for fair dealing and
for disinterested friendship, then let him beware lest
he fall in love with himself; let him guard against
a feeling of complacency in these natural gifts.
Every one must at some time or other have come
across some man apparently all for other people,
nothing for himself, caressed by all the good, one
who gives up his own wishes and is forgetful of
self. This same forgetfulness is so great a virtue
that even self-love would fain imitate it, and puts
its greatest glory in appearing to seek for none.
This self-command and renunciation, which would
be the crucifixion of nature if it were real and
effectual, becomes, on the contrary, the very subtle
and viewless instrument of a pride, which disdains

[1] Fénelon, Nécessité du renoncement.

all the ordinary methods of rising, and would trample under foot all the gross subjects of vanity, which puff up other men. Still it is easy to pull the mask from this pride, with all its modesty, though it in no way peeps out as pride, so completely does it seem to have renounced all that allures others. If those whom such a man loves, and assists, do not pay him back with their friendship, esteem, and confidence, he is touched to the quick. Look at him; he is not disinterested, however he strive to appear so. The truth is, he pays himself not with the base coin that others seek; he wants not mawkish praises nor money, nor the proceeds of place and external dignity. Still he has his price too; he thirsts after the esteem of the good; he loves that he may be loved, and that hearts may be touched by his devotedness; he only appears to be forgetful of self, that he may be in the thoughts of all."

Such, or something like this, were the thoughts of Aelred. He saw that his soul was in danger, and that he must fly. He bethought himself of such words as these, " If thy foot offend thee, cut it off; if thy right eye offend thee, pluck it out." And before these solemn words, his glowing thoughts of friendship looked like a dream of romance. He saw that friendship was a negative thing, it might be a virtue, or it might be a vice; in itself it was neither. It is one of those natural feelings, which with the whole of man's moral nature is taken for granted in the Gospel. True it is that our blessed Lord has ennobled it by His wonderful condescension in loving St. John, but in

ennobling it, He has declared that it must be sacri-
ficed, if need be, to God's will. This was the lesson
which Aelred learned; he recognized that he had
made human affection paramount even to the love
of God, and the thought struck him at once that
he must fly. He turned pale and trembled at it.
Oh! how comes it that it is always the most loving
who are called upon to sacrifice their love? why
are the tenderest hearts chosen to be torn? why
are they who love father and mother, and brethren
and sisters, and friends, more intensely than others,
ever singled out to stand forth and give them up?
It is one of the miracles of God's grace, bringing
strength out of weakness. But it is never accomplished without rending of the heart and agony,
which makes it a spiritual martyrdom. And this
Aelred felt to the full. How many things were in
array against him, keen arguments, tender delicacy,
good feelings, to say nothing of pride and the love
of ease! Was the High Steward of Scotland to
take his place as the lowest brother in an obscure
convent? the elegant scholar to take to digging?
the trim courtier to put on the coarse monkish
cowl? It was fanaticism to leave the sphere in
which he had been placed, and where he might do
good. It was ingratitude to leave the good King
David, unfeeling to leave Prince Henry, the companion of his youth. Besides which, he had a
friend whom he loved more than life; he does not
tell us his name, but this was the sorest pain of
all. Nothing but the full conviction that his soul
was in danger where he was, could have enabled
him to break away from so many ties.

And where was he to go, when he once turned himself on the wide world, and had given up the royal palace in which he had lived from childhood. In those days there could be but one answer to the question, he could but be a monk. He might have been a secular priest; but first of all, there were the mitre and crosier in the background, which he dreaded; and secondly, it would not have answered his purpose at all, for it would have left him in the midst of his friends with all the ties, from which it was his very design to break away. They knew the cloister and the world well, who made conversion a synonym for monastic life. It was a turning to God, heart and soul, when one who had dwelt in the world, and partaken of its pleasures, went into the cloister to learn to have no joy, but God alone.

Besides which, becoming a secular priest was by no means giving up the world, in the same sense as entering the cloister. It was not the same thing, and if Aelred was called by God's grace to the one, he was not to the other. It should never be forgotten that the middle-age world was a very bad one; it was better than its neighbours, but alas! the world is the world in every age. The twelfth century was not a period of fantastic youth, like the fifteenth, nor was it the faithless, philosophic, calculating manhood of a period, about which the less, reader, that you and I say, the better; it was rather like boyhood, petulant and quaint, in its waywardness. Its tournaments were the rough plays of grown-up boys, ending it might be, in blood, seldom in ill-will; its very policy was

a very inartificial wiliness; a ready lie, a shutting
of ports against Pope's messengers, are specimens
of it. And the Clergy had their world too, one
which would not have suited Aelred. The cathedral Clergy and the secular canons were in a bad
state; their rich benefices were spent in procuring
the means of a senseless pomp. They were but
little like ecclesiastics, those painted figures, on
prancing horses, with gilded bits, embroidered
saddles, and spurs plated with silver, while the
rider himself with his flowing locks, invisible ton-
sure, and pelisse of various furs, with purple collar
and fringe, like a woman's dress, remind us of the
courtly abbé of later times.[1] As for ecclesiastics
in general, Henry II.[2] would not have had a pre-
text for endeavouring to bring the Clergy into the
secular courts if there had not been among them
many criminals of the worst class; and the decrees
of councils in those times fully bear out the infer-
ence. The only way to reform such a system was
to create an order of men, founded on an entirely
opposite principle, to oppose voluntary poverty to
riches, chastity to licentiousness, and obedience to
insolence. An individual might indeed stay in the
midst of the evil, and do his best to reform it;
but this was not enough, system must be opposed
to system. In the monastic system is contained
the remedial system of the church; and this was
the reason why in the twelfth century, regular
canons so often replaced secular, in cathedral
churches; why the Premonstrants were founded

---

[1] St. Bern. Ep. i. 2.   In Cant. xxxiii. 15.
[2] William of Newbridge, ii. 16.

with a direct bearing on the Clergy, and why the Augustinians were to such an extent reformed. The seculars indeed had their own work too; among them arose almost the only martyr in the century, and that one was St. Thomas. Still the monks were the real reformers of the Church. And this was the reason of St. Bernard's impassioned language, by which he calls upon men to come into the cloister. It was the voice of one crying in the wilderness, "Prepare ye the way of the Lord, make his paths straight; repent, for the kingdom of heaven is at hand." This was the voice which sounded through Aelred's heart, and would not let him rest. So he did not go to Durham, where the monks served the stately cathedral, lately built by William of St. Carilefe; nor did he go southward to Westminster, the Abbot of which was his friend, where was the sacred body of his beloved St. Edward; but he chose out an obscure Cistercian monastery, the name of which was hardly known in the world.

It must have been with a heavy heart that Aelred bade adieu to Henry,[1] "that meek and pious man, of sweet spirit, and heart full of the milk of human kindness, him with whom he had lived from his cradle, his playfellow in boyhood, his companion in youth; the good King David too, now an old man, whom he loved above all men"; and many years afterwards the bitterness of that parting remained fresh in his soul, and he declared that "though he left them in body in order to serve his Lord, his heart

---

[1] St. Aelred, De Genealog. ap. Twysden, 368.

was always with them." It must have been with a
sad heart that he heard for the last time the bells
of the Abbey of Scone, and saw at his feet the
noble Tay winding through a vale, whose steep
sides, clothed with thick woods, opened upon a
plain, where even then rose the towers of the fair
town of Perth, the whole bounded by the blue
outline, and the seamed sides of the Grampians.
With a heavy heart did he quit Dunfermline, and
retrace the still recent steps trodden by St. Margaret,
on her painful way from the shore to the palace, and
which even now after seven centuries of revolutions
and estrangement, are uneffaced from the hearts of
the people. Sadly he must have felt, when he
turned his back on Dunfermline, with its expanse
of sea glancing in the sun before him, and on the
wide-spread plain of Perth, for he was going to a
place where the horizon was very circumscribed.
Even now, we may follow his steps. There is in
the North Riding of York, not far from the borders
of Durham, a nook of surpassing beauty amidst a
perfect labyrinth of vales, formed by ridges of hills,
crossing each other in every direction. The place is
one where three valleys meet, two of them shutting
in a third, which is Rievaux. Along the brow of
the hill which overhangs this vale the traveller
passes, and then goes down the steep side through
hanging woods, from terrace to terrace, till at the
very bottom, from the last ledge of all, he lights
upon a ruined Abbey. Lovely indeed it is in its
calm decay, rising to a stately height from the bosom
of its smooth, grassy lawn, and most beautiful it
must have been in the days of its magnificence, when

the Abbey burst upon the sight, lying at the bottom of its deep dell, folded in from the world. Long before the traveller came upon it as he was winding down the successive steeps, it announced its presence by its sweet bells, and great was the joy of the tired wayfarer when it lay before him with its cloistered quadrangle, and over the long roof of the refectory and dormitory rose the lofty Church, with its light lancet windows towering over all. Beautiful it was in all the graceful and disciplined animation of monastic life; its white monks issuing from its gates in their hooded riding mantles, to go to some distant grange, or working all together in a line on the hanging steeps, while the mill was heard, its wheel turning merrily amidst the splashing waters of the mountain-stream, which dashed along its pebbly bed at the bottom of the dell, where it had just joined a sister stream at the fork where the valleys met. Alas! it is very different now; but we will not mourn over it; there was a time when it was just as unlike the stately pile, still noble in its ruins, and that was on the morning of that day when the Abbey gates opened and closed on Aelred.

Many things there are in the middle ages, which look very beautiful at a distance, and were beautiful in reality, but which required something more than romance to make them tolerable. The crusades were a noble conception, but Blanche of Castile fainted when she saw the cross on St. Louis's shoulder, and Joinville durst not cast a look at his castle as he passed it, lest his heart should fail him, and he should return to his wife and children.

If there had been any portion of fine sentiment in

Aelred's retirement to Rievaux,[1] it would have disappeared now. Not one stone of the noble edifice, now in ruins, had then been raised; not an approach to triple lancet, or rose window, or shaft with capital of twisted foliage. A very few years, probably not more than two, had elapsed, since Walter de Espec had planted in this place a colony of Cistercians, sent by St. Bernard from Clairvaux, under William, their first abbot. Tradition in after times framed a romantic story about the foundation of the noble abbey, that Walter had brought the white monks from across the sea to pray for the soul of his son, a high-spirited boy, who had been thrown from his horse at the foot of a little stone cross, by the road side, and had died on the spot. The truth however is, that Walter had no children, and gave a great part of his lands to the Church.[2] Blackmore was the ominous name of the place, which the Norman monks changed to the sweeter name of St. Mary of Rievaux, from the Rye, a little stream that ran through the valley. It is said to have been a place that made the soul shudder, and a vast wilderness, and Aelred himself in after times called it a very deep dale. It was a place hard to find, amidst the windings of the many valleys, and Aelred, after travelling along the high ridge, plunged down through a path cut in the tangled wood. Down and still further down, he went as though he were leaving the cheerful light

---

[1] Rievaux was founded in 1132. There are no data for ascertaining the precise time when St. Aelred left Scotland. It seems likely however that he did so before the foundation of the first Cistercian Monastery in Scotland, which was Melross, in 1136.

[2] St. Aelred expressly says so in his History of the War of the Standard.

of day. The old and gloomy trees seemed to close about him, and as he approached the bottom of the valley, the leaves were dripping with the damp mists which arose from the ill-drained marshy grounds around the little stream. But when he knocked at the lowly gate of the abbey, and the brother fell down at his feet, as was the wont in Cistercian abbeys, with a "Deo gratias," thanking God for the new-comer, then Aelred felt as if he had at last found a resting-place in this weary world. Then William the abbot, the friend of St. Bernard, welcomed the young Saxon to St. Mary's house; and though their dark features were those of foreigners, and their language was that of enemies of his race, yet he felt that he was among brothers. The struggle for life and death was over, and he had but to go on in the path which God had assigned to him. And now that it is over, we will give the description of it in his own words. It will show how he looked back upon it, when time had enabled him to think calmly about it, when he could lay bare his own mind, as St. Augustine did in his Confessions. "Lo! my sweet Lord, once I sought rest in the world for my wretched soul, but every where I found toil and groans, grief and affliction of spirit. Thou didst cry out to me, Lord, Thou didst cry out, Thou didst call me, frighten me and break through my deafness, Thou didst smite and break down my obstinacy; Thou didst bring sweetness to my bitter heart. I heard, but ah! later than I ought, Thy voice crying to me; for I lay, polluted and rolled in filth, bound, and a captive, in the nest of iniquity, crushed under the weight of inveterate habit. Then I bethought my-

self, who I was, where, and of what nature. I
shuddered, Lord, and shrunk in fear, from my own
lineaments; the foul reflection of my wretched soul
frightened me. I was unpleasing to myself, because
Thou wert pleasing. I fain would have fled from
myself, and to Thee, but the merest trifles, as one
has said before me,[1] the vanity of vanities, which had
seduced my soul, held me back; the chains of vile
bodily habit bound me, the love of flesh and blood
held me in bonds, the graces of social life tightened
them; above all there were the ties of a certain
friendship, sweet to me above all the sweets of life.
And men looking on my smiling outside, and knowing nothing of what was going on within, used to say
of me, Oh! how well is it with him, how well! they
did not know that all was wrong where alone all
ought to be right. For my wound was deep-seated
within, tormenting, scaring me, and filling all within
me with its intolerable corruption; and unless Thou
hadst stretched forth Thy hand, who knows if, intolerable burden as I was to myself, I might not have
had recourse to the worst remedy of despair! I began
then to consider as much as one who had no experience could do, what great sweetness there is in
Thy love, how much peace in that sweetness, how
much security in that peace. By degrees Thou didst
become sweet to my taste, still partially diseased as
it was, and I used to say to myself, O! that I were
healed; and I would raise myself up to Thee, but
again I used to fall back upon myself. Still fleshly
pleasures kept me as a man in chains, by a strange
power of habit, though my soul really loved best that

[1] St. Aug. Conf. 8, 11.

which it could yet only guess at by the power of its intellect. Often did I say to my friends, where are now all our pleasures, all our joys, all our delights? at this moment how much of them do we feel? all that is joyful in them is gone; and all that remains is that part which stings our conscience, which causes us to fear death, which binds us to everlasting punishment. Put side by side with all our riches, our delights, and honours, this one thing which those who are Christ's, possess, the right not to fear death. I loathed myself as I spoke this, and sometimes I wept in the bitter struggle of my soul. I loathed all that I saw, and still the habit of fleshly pleasure held me down. But Thou, who hearest the groans of the captives, who loosest those appointed unto death, Thou didst burst my chains; Thou, who bringest publicans and harlots into Paradise, hast converted me, the chief of sinners, to Thyself. And lo! I breathe again under Thy yoke, I am at rest under Thy burden, for Thy yoke is easy, and Thy burden is light."[1]

[1] Spec. Char. i. 28.

CHAPTER IV

THE BATTLE OF THE STANDARD

IT was fortunate for Aelred that he escaped when he did from the court of Scotland to his quiet home at Rievaux. A very few years, probably hardly two, after he had made his profession, a storm gathered in Scotland, and swept over the north of England, such as would have effectually destroyed his quiet had he not already got into shelter. In 1136, Henry I. died, and then began the stormy reign of Stephen, disastrous for all England, but especially for the north. In this chapter then will come out the difference between the world and the cloister. The contrast is like that picture of the transfiguration, where Peter, James, and John are seen with the Lord in the Mount, round the base of which are heard the howlings of the poor demoniac, torn by the devil, whom even the Apostles cannot cast out, and apparently deserted even by the Lord. We will try to look upon this turmoil as Aelred would have done, nay, as he did, for he himself is the historian, from which the greater part is taken; and in the wildest fits of the storm, we may imagine him looking on quietly and listening with his head enveloped in his cowl in the cloister of Rievaux.

Strange was the scene in England as soon as

King Henry was dead; law and justice in those times depended so much on individuals that the withdrawal of one man was a signal for general riot. Henry's power over his nobles was very much of a personal nature; he had done what in the fifteenth century it cost a king of France a rebellion among his nobles before he could effect; he had abridged their rights of chase in favour of the crown.[1] It was not an empty privilege, that of vert and venison in the broad forests of English oak, which covered the land; besides the joys of the noisy chase, there were the huge branches of the oak to keep up the large fire in the baronial hall, and the substantial banquet of the boar's head and venison for the lord and his retainers. Henry had constituted himself protector-general of woods, forests, deer, wild boars, and game of all sorts.[2] Some men durst not hunt in their own woods, for fear of finding a king's officer at their doors, summoning them to appear at the chief pleas; and if Henry's sharp eye discovered that a wood had been thinned or wasted, he would impose a fine on the offender. Hardly was the king dead than a joint attack on woods and forests took place, and a general onslaught was made on the large herds of deer, which a long reign had preserved, "so that hardly two could any where be seen together." The highway had always belonged to the king, as well as the forest, and all offences committed were punished by his officers,

---

[1] v. Michelet. Histoire de France, xiii. 2.

[2] Stephen swore when he came to the throne quod neminem de silvis propriis implacitaret licet venationem in eisdem caperet, sicut fecerat rex Henricus. Brompton ap. Twysden, p. 1024.

but now the king's peace was broken with impunity, for there was no king to keep it. Every man preyed on his neighbour, and made the best of his time, men wiped off old scores, and revenged themselves on their enemies; rapine and violence of all sorts reigned in England as soon as news came that the old king was dead. The matter was not much mended when Stephen, by the perjury of bishops and barons, was elected to the throne.[1] To do him justice, at the beginning of his reign, he seems certainly to have done his best to re-establish peace, but his title to the throne was defective, and when once the Empress landed, anarchy and confusion took their own course, and it was said emphatically that "there was no justice in Stephen's reign." Then arose a species of men, which feudalism had ever a tendency to create; the petty lords, who, from their dungeon-keeps, ruthlessly wasted and harried the whole country around them. Our notions of feudal barons are ever connected with fair castles and trains of knights, fluttering pennons, and glittering armour. But the fact is that during the reigns of the first Norman kings, very few nobles were allowed to have castles.[2] It was from the lack of fortresses that England fell so soon into the power of the Conqueror; and he built castles every where to keep the country in awe; but then he kept them in his

---

[1] Gesta Steph. 929.

[2] Thus one Turgisius in Stephen's reign, holds a castle, and the country round, but it is said rex ad conservandum magis quam ad possidendum commiserat. Gesta Steph. p. 966. Thus of the castle of Exeter it is said, quod semper regalis juris extiterat. Ibid, 934. The Bishop of Durham asks leave to have a castle (Anglia Sacra, 723), as also the Bishops of Salisbury and Ely in Henry the First's time.

own hands, and his soldiers were only warders not possessors. The manor house, and not the castle was then the characteristic of England; magnificent Umbravilles and Bagots must as yet content themselves with a low moated house, two storeys high, with its staircase outside, and only to rise by-and-bye to the dignity of a castle. But in King Stephen's time,[1] every man did as he pleased, or as he could, and when the day of reckoning came in Henry's time it was found that every knightling possessed not only a castle but a seal, like the king of England himself. Little do they know of these iron-hearted men, who picture to themselves a generous knight-errant, pricking forth in search of adventures. Alas! chivalry is but an ideal, a high and beautiful standard, created by Christianity, but never realised except in individuals; for one St. Louis there were a thousand Bluebeards. The knight of the twelfth century was not the fantastic and often licentious champion of later times; but in King Stephen's time at least he was often a needy adventurer, who roamed about the country, pillaging his neighbours, and looking out for a fief. Exceptions occur which cheer the weary reader of history, for instance that young Christian knight, who, as the beginning of the good deeds to which his vow of knighthood bound him, sheltered in his house a whole convent of forlorn monks, whose new-built monastery had been burnt over their heads.[2]

---

[1] William of Newbridge, i. 22.
[2] Dugdale v. p. 349. Dominus Rogerus de Molbray qui cingulum militare de novo sumpserat, inter initia bonorum operum suorum habitationem providit, etc.

But generally speaking your knight at the time of which we are writing was a very suspicious character. As for the nobles, they were but too often men of brutal licentiousness, great consumers of beef and wine, and great oppressors of the poor.[1]

When such men as these were let loose upon the world by the license of civil war, it was not wonderful that the defenceless Church should suffer. The churches were found to be excellent castles, ready made, without the trouble of building. Thus a certain Geoffrey Talbot seized on the cathedral church of Hereford, expelled the priests, and made it a garrison for his soldiers; in the churchyard fortifications were thrown up, and the dead were torn from their graves, and their bodies thrown about, while a military engine was in full play on the tower, throwing large stones and missiles from the place "whence" says the chronicler, "the sweet and peaceful warnings of the bells were wont to be heard."[2] This is but one specimen of what often occurred; and it will be easily believed that monasteries were not better treated than secular churches. The Abbeys of Ramsay and Coventry were turned into fortresses, and the monks expelled; a nunnery at Winchester was burnt, and even the holy Abbey of St. Ethelreda, at Ely, was plundered by these wicked soldiers.[3] No place was safe from them, and the inmates of every monastery might prepare themselves each night at compline, for the possibility of being expelled from their homes before the bell sounded for matins.

[1] Gesta Steph. 946.   [2] Gesta Steph. 948, 958.
[3] Matt. Par. p. 79, 80.   Gesta Steph. 960, 964.

All this took place south of the Tees, but the
north of England was exposed to the inroads of
a terrible enemy, and the ravages inflicted by these
savages must have been more painful to Aelred,
because they were let loose upon England by his
best friend, David, king of Scotland. The friendship
of David for Henry I., and his love for the family of
his mother, and for his niece, the Empress, all induced
him to take her part against Stephen. Her succession to the throne was looked upon as the restoration
of the line of St. Edward to the English throne.
King David, with all the barons of England, had
sworn to King Henry that he would uphold his
daughter, and he would not perjure himself as the
others had done. Besides which he laid claim to
the earldom of Northumberland for his son Henry.
These motives might be enough to call for his invasion, but still it involved an awful responsibility to
let loose upon the north the savage Picts. David
would have been more like St. Louis had he paused
before he put in motion this uncontrollable power ;
but he was deceived by the Scottish party among
his subjects, who played off his predilection for the
Saxon line to urge him on against the Saxons of the
north of England. But however this was, in the year
1136, not long after Aelred's conversion, news arrived
that the Scottish army was coming over the border.
On came the torrent, the chivalry of the Lowlands
forming its centre, though far out-numbered by the
motley assemblage of half-naked Galwegians, and
men of the Isles. The miseries inflicted by a modern
army, with all its discipline, are horrible enough, and
a feudal army where each man was accounted for,

and knew his banner was a scourge wherever it
went; but all this was nothing to the passage of
a horde of undisciplined savages, most indifferent
Christians at home, and giving loose to every passion
which disgraces human nature abroad. It can only
be paralleled with the miseries inflicted by the mer-
cenary troops of the 16th century,[1] when armies
were no longer modelled on the feudal principle, and
before the modern standing army had been introduced. The commissariat of a Pictish host was
doubtless none of the best, and besides this, they
had all the wanton cruelty with which the savage
loves to torture his victim. It would be wrong to
give the sickening detail of their cruelties; suffice it
say that droves of captive women whom they had
made widows and childless, driven before them with
spears, formed the van of this horrible army. This
mass when once set in motion was beyond the control of him who had called these uncouth beings out
of their native morasses. Churches were burnt and
pillaged, and monasteries sacked, in one case, which
has happened to remain on record, the poor monks
of Calder, in Copeland, were turned out on the wide
world, with their whole property contained in a
wagon, drawn by eight oxen; and this was doubtless not a singular instance. The only alleviation to
this misery was, that David placed a guard of his
own soldiers over Hexham, and all the miserable
inhabitants who had taken refuge there. He also
gave back into the hands of the Prior of Hexham all
that part of the booty of the wretched country which
had fallen to his share. Hexham was Aelred's old

[1] V. Manzoni, Promessi Sposi.

home, and this probably crossed David's mind when he chose it as a place of sanctuary for Northumberland. One other softer feature amidst this scene of horrors is the circumstance that William, Abbot of Rievaux, was chosen to give into the hands of the king of Scotland the town of Wark, which belonged to Walter de Espec, the founder of the monastery. In his white habit he might venture in safety as a messenger of peace through the Scottish army ; and it must have been a strange sight to see the Abbot at the head of the haggard inhabitants of the town, who had been reduced by famine to feed on pickled horse-flesh, issuing from the gates to deliver up the keys to the conqueror.

The stream of invaders was rapidly moving on towards Rievaux, when it was stopped by an event long afterwards celebrated in the annals of border warfare—the battle of the Standard. Aelred's dearest friends, David of Scotland and Henry, were engaged in it, and yet he could not wish them to conquer. Besides, his affections were divided, for on the other side was Walter de Espec, the founder of Rievaux, his new home, and so from the bottom of his deep-hidden valley he prayed with his brethren for the success of the English arms ; and when it was over he became the chronicler of an action which saved Yorkshire with its churches and monasteries from desolation. It was a very crusade, this war of the Standard, for it was apparently a hopeless task to attempt to stop the progress of the countless swarms which David had brought out of Scotland. But the old Archbishop of York implored the nobles and knights of Yorkshire, for the love of God and His

Saints, to venture their lives, to save from desolation the houses of God, and the poor people from all the horrors which were awaiting them. Aelred becomes enthusiastic when he describes the dark hair, broad forehead, and large piercing eyes of Walter de Espec, and details at length the eloquence of the noble soldier when he addressed the soldiers from the foot of the Standard, and promised them victory, in the name of the Saints and of the Lord. Their standard was a long pole, on which floated the banner of St. Cuthbert, and from which was suspended a pix containing the Body of the Lord ; and under this, they swore to conquer or die. Aelred describes on the day of battle, the small compact body of the English, with their armour glittering in the sun, and their pennons floating on their lances, while the priests in their white albs flew from rank to rank to exhort them. The Bishop of the Orkneys blessed and absolved them, and the whole army answered his benediction with a loud Amen. Then the trumpets sounded, and with a wild shriek the Galwegians came on, but their countless host was broken before the serried ranks of the men-at-arms, around which they closed as the waves dash against the rock, which is islanded amongst them. They might at length have broken this little band, but their headlong valour was rendered useless by the incessant clouds of arrows discharged from the bows of the Yorkshire yeomanry. However at the moment that they were yielding, the battle was again rendered doubtful, for with the speed of lightning Henry, prince of Scotland, charged with the chivalry of the Scottish army ; and here Aelred's love for the friend of his youth betrays itself, and he almost seems to cheer them on as they broke through "the lines of the Southrons as they would sweep aside a cobweb," and pursued them off the field.[1] But still poured on the steady ceaseless showers of the English arrows, and when Henry returned from the pursuit he saw the royal standard, the Dragon, moving off the field in full flight, and found that he was left almost alone with a few knights about him. And here again amidst his joy for the victory which God had given to the prayers of His church, Aelred pauses to describe the valour of the friend of his youth, how prince Henry, seeing himself left with a few knights about him, turned with a smile to his companions, bade them mingle in the pursuit, as though they were on the English side, and setting spurs to his horse, rode right through the enemy to rejoin his father. This battle freed the north of England from this horrid scourge, and it must be said for David, that when afterwards Northumberland and Durham were ceded to him, the north was resting in peace, while the south was still suffering all the misery of civil war.[2]

---

[1] De Bello Stand. Twysden, 345.
[2] William of Newbridge, i. 22.

CHAPTER V

THE CISTERCIAN NOVICE

SUCH was the world outside the walls of Rievaux, during the few years after Aelred first became a monk, and such the world in which he must from his connection with the court of Scotland have mingled, had he not taken timely refuge in his monastery. Strangely different indeed was his new mode of life from that which he led in the palace of Scone or of Dunfermline. Certainly the good monks of Citeaux showed no anxiety to sweeten the harshness of the rule for their novices. For four days the new-comer was kept like a stranger in the hospice, and no one took notice of him after his first interview with the Abbot; and then he was introduced into the chapter, where he prostrated himself on the ground before the Abbot, and was saluted by him with an abrupt, "What wouldest thou?" Then was detailed to him the rule in all its rigour, and if he persisted in asking for admission, the Abbot said aloud, "God who hath begun in thee, bring it to the end": then all the convent answered Amen. Still the candidate was led back to the house of the guests, and the same ceremony was repeated in the chapter for three days, and on the third only was he admitted into the number of the novices. Then his secular dress, the soft clothing of the king's house, was taken off him, with the words, " The Lord put off thee the old man with his works." And then the novice's dress was put upon him; it had not even the dignity of the cuculla and scapular of the full-grown monks; it was a short tunic with sleeves, and a white cloak with a cowl.[1] If a nobleman were suddenly to find himself arrayed in the dress of a workhouse, the change could not be more complete. But the Abbot as he put it on the novice said, " The Lord put upon thee the new man, who after God is created in righteousness and true holiness." This reconciled Aelred to the change, for in these words were contained the whole of monastic life, and of this all its outward forms were but symbols. Death to nature and life to God, and the carrying out of the vows of baptism, was the moral of the whole. Without this, fast and vigil, rough labour in the fields or beautiful ritual, with vestment of black, brown, white, or grey, were but quaint devices of fantastic devotion, and "friar's trumpery." Alas! there have been worldly and ambitious hearts, beating beneath the monk's habit, for no outward forms can keep the soul against its will; but Rievaux was not at all a likely place to harbour such monks. And at all events Aelred, with whom alone we are con-cerned, looked upon himself as assuming the cross for a life-long crusade against the world, the flesh, and the devil.

" Let the novice begin and leave off labour, read

[1] Nom. Cist. 218.   Rituale Cist. vi. 1.

and go to bed, with the monks; let him eat the same food, and be clad with the same stuff," says the rule. We therefore know at once what Aelred was about; he plunged without delay into Cistercian discipline; and an exceeding trial it must have been. To any one brought up in a king's palace, the details of husbandry must have been inexpressibly irksome; and not only must the novice dig, but he must dig well, for the livelihood of the monks depends on their own exertions. The delicate and jewelled fingers, accustomed only to turning over the leaves of illuminated manuscripts, must have been sorely galled with the spade and the fork. This, however, together with the whole discipline of fasts and vigils, he must have expected before he came; the man who has fled for his life to the wilderness must not expect to find its wild and sour fruits like the summerfruit in a king's garden; thorns and briers grow in the desert; we must look elsewhere for lilies and roses. But one thing there was from which human nature recoils most of all: he was not at all treated as the late High Steward of Scotland, one who had made a great present to religion by his change. He was only brother Aelred, the lowest of the novices, because the last comer, last in every thing, except in processions, where, with his short tunic and sleeveless cloak, and his flowing locks, he preceded the long line of shaven crowns and scapulars, because the lowest walked first. It is a hard thing for one who has been considered rather as teacher than learner all his life, to find himself, when grown up, at the feet of others;

and the years between twenty and thirty are not always the period when men are most docile. The cell of the novices was a portion of the monastery adjoining the cloister, and here they were trained by the master of the novices, an officer who was to teach them to know the Psalter by heart, and to train them in monastic discipline. Aelred could doubtless have instructed this officer in Cicero and in writing Latin, but he submitted to him with the docility of a child, for he knew well that the science of spiritual things required no learning or intellectual power.

When he had a little recovered from his bewilderment at the novelty of his situation, and found leisure to look about him, he was struck with the wonderful peace of this little cloister-world, the noiseless gliding motion of the brethren, as they bent their heads in silence when they passed each other in the cloisters, and the strange way in which one soul seemed to actuate this vast body. And this was what first struck our novice; it was good hard work in which they were engaged, and yet "with such a placid unruffled countenance, with such a holy noiseless order, did they do all things, that scarce did they seem to move at all." [1] And then their mysterious preternatural silence had something awful about it; for it was very unlike a dogged or sullen silence, and this was evident from the bright beaming countenances of the brethren, and the ready cheerfulness in which they helped one another in their respective works. No man seemed to have a will

[1] Ep. Petri de Roya at the end of St. Bernard's Letters, ed. Ben.

of his own; and Aelred thought that he had seen
at last the realisation of his dreams of friendship.
At first, amongst such a number all seemed to
him very much alike; all had the same white
habit, and even the same cast of countenance;
just as in a foreign country, till the eye gets
accustomed to the type of the new race, all seem
equally dark or equally fair, without much difference. By degrees however he learned to distinguish between the countenances about him, and
one in particular struck him. It was the face of
a man, much younger than those of equal rank
in the monastery with himself, which showed that
he must have been hardly more than a child when
he took the vow. The grave sweetness of his face,
and the depth of the recollection and silence of
the young monk struck Aelred; and he learned
(probably from the master of the novices, whose
business it was at times to converse with his
charge), that the monk's name was Simon, and
that his conversion was a miracle of God's grace.
As a mere boy, God had called him away from
his kindred and his home, to serve Him as a
monk. What the circumstances were are not
known; probably Aelred did not know them himself; he only knew that Simon was of noble blood,
and had left his father's house. Men wondered
what could attract him in monastic life at that
early age; "but He knew, says Aelred,[1] who was
leading thee on, who had set on fire thy yet
tender heart with the flame of His love, and thou
didst run after the odour of His ointments.[2] He

---

[1] Spec. Char. i. 34.   [2] Song of Solomon, i. 3.

went before thee, beautiful in form above the sons of men, anointed with the oil of gladness above His fellows, and thou didst run after the odour of His ointments. He went before thee, that One who was lowly in spirit, over the steeps and over the mountains, sprinkling thy path with the fragrance of myrrh and frankincense, and thou didst run after the odour of His ointments. Before thee a Child went, the Child Jesus, showing thee the manger of His poverty, the couch of His lowliness, the chamber of His love, filled with the flowers of His grace, and sprinkled with the unguent of His consolation, and thou didst run after the odour of His ointments." Such was Aelred's way of accounting for the strange fact that a place like Rievaux possessed attractions for such a child; and now in the beginning of his novitiate, he found it of use to look upon this monk, who was utterly unconscious of the admiration which he was exciting. When his eyes and his thoughts wandered in the choir, one glance at the modest face of Simon chaunting devoutly with his eyes fixed on the ground was enough to recall him to himself. There was no danger in this mute veneration and love, for Cistercian strictness forbade his addressing Simon, and it was of use to him to choose this youthful monk for his model. "The rule of the order," says he, "forbade our speaking, but his countenance spoke to me, his gait spoke, and his very silence spoke. The sight of his humility beat down my pride, this contemplation of his calmness repressed my restless spirit."

After a year of probation, novices were admitted

to make their profession: this was the real farewell
to the world, where was made the vow of obedience,
of stability, and of conversion of life according to
the rule of St. Benedict. For a year before, the
novice had counted the cost, and now he felt sure
that by God's grace he could keep what it was
beyond the strength of the natural man to do. It
was with a chastened and a holy joy that Aelred
now bent before the Abbot to receive his benediction as a monk. And well he might rejoice, for
to him had been given a grace, which but very few
could possess. The world must go on, bad as it
is, till it please God to destroy it, and in its miserable service must toil on even the good till its end.
But Aelred, God had called out of the world, and
had made it lawful for him to quit the distractions
of the painful scene, and to serve Him not indirectly
through actions in themselves indifferent, but like
the angels with perpetual acts of prayer and praise.
The whole was the act of God's grace, and therefore
the hymn for Whitsuntide, Veni Creator Spiritus,
was then always sung by the convent, and the
beautiful ritual everywhere prays to the Holy Spirit,
who alone with the Father and Son is the Giver of
all grace, and without whom nothing is strong and
holy. And then after the long hair which the
novice had till that moment kept, as he would
wear it in the world, had been cut off his head by
the Abbot, and he was dressed in the regular monastic garment, he went round the convent and
humbled himself at the feet of each of his brethren.
After which the Te Deum was entoned, and whilst
it was sung, the newly - made monk knelt behind

the Abbot, his hands crossed on his breast within the sleeves of his habit. From this time forth he took his place in the choir with the other monks.

Henceforth, even during the stormy time which we described in the last chapter, so peaceful was the tenor of his life, that hardly anything is known of Aelred, but all that remains of him is of the same cast as has gone before. He is still the same gentle, loving Aelred, under the white habit, as he had been in the world. When he sat in the Abbey garden, as he says himself, his chief delight was to look about him, and think that each of the mute white figures, walking among the trees, was a brother, and to wonder how it was possible that so many men of different countries, tempers and ages, could dwell together in such perfect peace. If they did not talk, they had no chance of quarrelling, is doubtless a ready answer; and yet Aelred was right, it was a phenomenon. Men will manage to quarrel, if they have a mind; and besides, monks and nuns did find ample opportunities of discord, whenever it suited them; and it was this quarrelsomeness, and not other sins more commonly ascribed to them, which was the besetting sin of convents. Cluny had been not long before split into parties under Abbot Pontius; and even Cistercians, alas! in after times must needs call in the judgments of popes and legates to settle their internal dissensions. It is evident that monks when they lose the spirit of their order must be quarrelsome. The very object of Monasticism is to give a proper outlet to devotional feelings, which are stifled in the world, because it would be fanatical to indulge them; it must therefore be made up to a great extent of external actions. To throw oneself at the feet of another, and call oneself a miserable sinner, in a convent is a part of the rule. But when such actions are done by cold-hearted or discontented men, they become technical and formal; and punctilious persons are ever most disposed to quarrel. Besides, there might be proud brethren even amidst the austerities of Citeaux; and let any one consider the heart-burnings of an ambitious monk, when brother so-and-so was made Prior or Sub-prior over his head, or was sent on a mission, or allowed to accompany the Abbot to the general chapter; it was enough to sour a whole convent. Again, it is not quite true that monks never spoke to each other. A perfect silence is enjoined by the rule at certain times; especially from compline to prime next morning, at refection, in church and in the cloister, not a word was spoken under severe penalties; but this implies that there was a less strict silence at other times. When at work, monks might speak to each other, if it was necessary for what they were about. An awkward monk might be reproved by his fellow, or they might differ in opinion, and any one who has tried, may know how hard it is to yield simply for the sake of peace. Aelred therefore was perfectly right in wondering how a large convent of three hundred monks, for such was the number of the brethren of Rievaux, could hold on its even course without bickerings and quarrels! Sometimes Aelred had a specimen of a slight fit of ill-temper, just to assure him that such things were possible;[1] but if monks would be cross, they had also their own way of smoothing crossness down. One day, he spoke a word which offended one of the brethren, and at once he fell at his feet to beg his pardon, and waited there till the monk raised him up. And this seems to have been the established conventual method of settling a dispute.[2]

Besides which, it appears that license was sometimes given by Abbots to certain of the brethren to converse together;[3] and in this way Aelred at length was allowed to speak to Simon, the young monk, whom he had from the first proposed as his model. It is curious that the Cistercians do not seem to have been so jealous of particular friendships in their communities as were other orders. It was a first principle in monastic life that each individual should devote himself body and mind to the service of his brethren. The monastic system was an expansion of the love of the domestic circle upon a large community; it was a supernatural home raised by Christianity out of man's natural affections, an expansion of the narrowed sphere of usefulness allowed to most men in the world. It was necessary then that all within that circle should share this love alike. In a large family, if not carefully brought up, the eldest often know little of the youngest; they naturally form into knots, and the petty factions quarrel with each other.

---

[1] De Spir. Ami. ii. 453.   [2] Spec. Char. i. 29.
[3] See note to Life of St. Stephen, p. 140; to which add Spec. Char. iii. 40.

And so it would be in a monastery, which is only a very large family, if the father Abbot was not watchful to prevent an evil, which every careful mother would banish from her home. Thus, if brother Ambrose and brother Benedict were to swear a deathless friendship, and to put their black cowls together in recreation-time, and never talk to anyone else, the other brethren might well think themselves aggrieved. And if the same brethren were to proceed also to sit together in cloister, and to nod and wink, when they could not talk, if they were discontented and cross when the Prior set them to work in different parts of the grounds of the monastery, then the father Abbot would have just cause for punishing the refractory brethren. Human love, if not submitted to rules, is a wayward, fantastic, moonstruck thing, flitting from object to object, and never satisfied; or if fixed upon one in a wrong way, overleaping the bounds of law, human and divine. It is like an organ, of which every fool may pull out the trumpet stop, and bring forth a volume of wild discordant sounds; but which, when played by rule, discourses most healthful music. Now in a Cistercian monastery, at least at the period when Aelred entered Rievaux, this same unmanageable element was subjected to such stringent rules that there was little danger of its doing mischief. When there was no regular recreation-time, and where the brethren never conversed but by license from the father Abbot, and those licenses were few and far between, there was no danger that the spirit of exclusiveness should creep into a convent, for the brethren could not possibly form cabals amongst themselves. No ambitious monk could form a party and intrigue to be elected Abbot; no harm could come to monastic discipline by heart-burnings and jealousies, breaking out at length into open rebellion, from being long brooded over, when the cowl was drawn over the head, and none could see the workings of the discontented heart upon the face. Aelred could therefore love Simon without fixing his heart upon him with a merely natural friend-ship. In the painful struggle with himself, before he quitted the world, his affections had been cruci-fied, and they could now revive and flourish again in the cloister. The period of his internal struggles was a long and cheerless winter, during which his heart was "like a tree withered down to its roots. But now that this winter was past, and that all was dead that God would have had die, then came the happy springtide and all revived." That took place in him which we will describe in the words of our old friend the Archbishop of Cambray, for we are not skilled in spiritual matters ourselves. "God then gives back friendship with all his other gifts an hundred-fold. Then revive all the old loves for true friends. A man no longer loves them in himself, and for himself, but in God, and for God, and that with a love, lively, tender, full of sweetness and of feeling, for God can easily purify feeling. It is not feeling but self-love which corrupts friendship." So Aelred gave himself up without scruple to his holy friendship, for it was God, who by the order of His Providence, bound them together, and inspired them with His love; and it was Him whom they loved in each other.[1]

Aelred's talents and his loving disposition did not escape the penetrating eye of Abbot William. The friend of St. Bernard could not but love one whom posterity, by a sort of unconscious judgment, has called "a second Bernard"; so he made him the master of the novices. Next to the Abbot this was the most important officer in the convent. His business, as has been said before, was to train the novices in monastic discipline, that is, not to teach them to chant Gregorian tones, to march in procession, no, nor even to fast, and to rise in the night to sing psalms. All these were but means to an end; his business was to form a character in them. The method of forming a Christian character has now been almost reduced to a science, for the ways of God in His dealings with the souls of His elect, have so much uniformity, with all their variety, that a science of spiritual life has been framed out of the reflections of holy men on their own experience. This science has now spread far and wide, and forms a regular portion of clerical education in most parts of Christendom; but in Aelred's time it was almost confined to the cloister. Very little had been written on the subject till St. Bernard's time, for in early times these Christian writers had been so occupied with the great object of faith itself, that they had comparatively little analysed the dealings of God's grace with the Christian soul. The cloister then was a sort of traditionary system of ascetic discipline, and this was what the Cistercians had

[1] Fénelon, Utilité des peines et des délaissements, 23.

revived through the influence of St. Bernard. Aelred's duty was thoroughly to learn the character of the novice, to support him in heaviness of spirits, to temper his enthusiasm, to judge of his vocation, and if he saw that God had called him to that state of life, to present him at the end of his year of probation to the Abbot. The whole of Aelred's teaching consisted in patience and resignation to the will of God. When first the young novice came into the monastery full of fervour, he was delighted and edified with all he saw. Even the rough bed and coarse food, and the bell bidding him start up when his sleep was sweetest, were all but child's play to him ; the awful silence did not frighten him, and though he could but speak to three men, the Abbot, the prior, and the master, all seemed natural and easy to him.[1] Everything struck him with admiration, but above all, the wonderful concord of the brethren. "Such unity is there among the brethren," said a wondering novice to Aelred, "that each thing belongs to all, and all things to each. And what marvellously pleases me, there is no acceptation of persons, no account of high birth. How wonderful is it too that the will of one man should be the law to about three hundred men, so that what once he has spoken, is kept by all, as if they had come to precisely that determination themselves, or had heard it from the mouth of God Himself." This was the first stage of feeling in the novices, and the prudent master of the novices was obliged with a smile to tell him,[2]

[1] Tribus solum hominibus et hoc rarissime et vix de necessariis loquimur. Spec. Char. lib. ii. 17.
[2] Spec. Char. Ibid.

"I would have thee be cautious, and not suppose that any profession upon earth is without its hypocrites, lest if thou shouldest see any one transgress in word or deed, thou shouldest disturb thyself, as though something strange had happened to thee." And to this first ecstatic stage of wonderment succeeded generally a great calm, when the soul was conscious of no feeling at all, when there was no sensible pleasure in prayer, no tears in contemplating the Passion, or ecstacy in thinking on the love of God. And then the poor novice wondered why he did not feel now that he was in religion, the same sensible joys that he used to feel when in the world. Then Aelred would tell him that the love of God did not consist in sensible joys, but in the junction of the will to the will of God, in the surrender of the human will so that it consents to wish for nothing but because God wills it. "Pure love is in the will alone, so that it is not a love of feeling, for the imagination has no part in it; it is a love which loves without feeling, as pure faith believes without seeing."[1] He told him that it was a greater sacrifice thus to offer up the will to God, and to remain quietly as long as He would in this want of feeling, than to fast and afflict the body with austerities, and that nothing was so agreeable to God as to remain thus crucified, not seeking for consolation till it was His will to give it. "These sensible consolations were given at the beginning of thy repentance," he would say to the novice, "to draw thee on to Christ; but what wonder if, now their work is done, they are taken away? now is the time for warfare, not

[1] Fénelon sur la secheresse et les distractions, 26.

for rest, but by-and-bye, it may be that the Lord will restore these sensible affections, and thus that devout feeling, which at first roused thee, to save thee from perishing, will console thee in thy labour, lest thou sink under it, till after many victories, the pains by which thou art, now in thy novitiate, harassed, will be entirely lulled, and then, like a soldier, whose warfare is done, thou wilt taste the sweets of repose, and be admitted to that consolation of which the Prophet speaks, 'How great is Thy sweetness, O Lord, which Thou hast laid up for them that fear Thee.'"[1]

This is a specimen which has reached us of Aelred's teaching as master of the novices. Doubtless he had many more unpromising novices to deal with than that one whom he has here recorded. Doubtless he had the presumptuous novice, who thought nothing too high for him, who must needs think the order not half strict enough, and would separate himself from his brethren by fasting and watching when the others did not.[2] To this one he would say that strict obedience was the first condition of being a monk at all. Sometimes however he had still more refractory subjects to deal with, and a story remains, which, though it does not rest on very good authority, yet shows the sort of character which tradition assigned to Aelred. There was a clerk, says the legend, who, when he had been a short time at Rievaux, began to grow tired of the strictness and monotony of the place, and determined to run away and go back to the world. Aelred, however, loved him and begged of

[1] Spec. Char. lib. ii. 19.   [2] St. Bern. Serm. in Cant. 19.

God to give him this soul. So the poor novice came to him, and frankly said, that he was going to run away, but Aelred coolly replied, "Brother, ruin not thyself; nevertheless thou canst not if thou wouldest." Still the man would not listen to reason, and went away from the monastery. He plunged into the woods, and wandered about among the mountain paths from valley to valley, thinking all the while that he was going very far from the Abbey. About sunset, however, he was surprised to find himself close to a convent, which looked marvellously like the Abbey of Rievaux, and sure enough so it was; he had been wandering round and round it all day, and at evening he found himself precisely where he had started. It had been hidden from him by the thick woods about it. This circumstance struck him as so wonderful that he could only see the hand of God in it. So he entered again the monastery which he had quitted, he thought for ever, in the morning. The first person whom he saw was Aelred, who fell on his neck and bursting into tears, kissed him, and said, " Son, why hast thou done so to me? Lo! I have wept for thee with many tears; and I trust in God that as I have asked of the Lord, and as I told thee, thou shalt not perish."

CHAPTER VI

THE SPIRIT OF CITEAUX

AELRED, however, soon had other employment assigned him; he was compelled by his Abbot to turn author.[1] It appears that certain monks of other orders censured the Cistercians as being dry, formal, unspiritual men; devotion they thought was incompatible with so much affliction of the body, hard beds, coarse food and manual labour. Theirs was a more smiling religion, which had all the arts at her command, painting, sculpture, and music; and why should the Cistercians be more strict than their neighbours? Now this accusation could hardly be made in France, where St. Bernard was taken as a type of the Cistercians, for dry and formal were the very last epithets that could be applied to him. No one could read a line of his writings without feeling their unction and sweetness.[2] As for his decisions in casuistry some might have called him lax, so fully does he hold that a really conscientious intention supplies material defects. None could therefore with any face accuse the French Cistercians of an unspiritual

[1] V. Ep. cujusdam prefixed to the Speculum, and Spec. Char. lib. ii. 5.
[2] V. Ep. 69, 603.

harshness. In England, the new order wanted some one to be its type in the same way, and Aelred was chosen as being the very man to set it forth.[1] Much did he pray to be excused; he said that he was ill educated, had left school early, and had come straight from a king's kitchen to the desert, where, like a common peasant, he worked for his daily bread among rocks and mountains with the axe and the mallet, by the sweat of his brow. Nothing however would do, the Abbot only chid his tardiness in obedience, and said that his steward-ship in a king's kitchen was only an anticipation of the time when he was to be a steward of spiritual food to his brethren; and as for rocks and moun-tains, there might come honey from the stony rock, and more was to be learnt under the shade of the trees at midday in the woods about Rievaux than in the schools of worldly philosophy. So write a book he must. It was to be called the Mirror of Charity, in which the form of Christian love was to be reflected as in a glass. Hugh, the Prior, had often heard him talk on such subjects, and knew that he was the very man. So Aelred was deputed to write, and a remarkable book it is, considering the time at which it was brought out, while the Scotch were at the gates of Rievaux, during a civil war, in which an empress lost and won a throne, and a king was in prison. When all the world was in arms, bishops and all; when monasteries were in flames, and cathedrals were turned into castles, this monk was sitting quietly in his cloister, writing on the love of God.

[1] V. Ep. cujusdam.

It was a perfect reflection of the Cistercian spirit this Mirror of Charity, and a good comment upon its code of laws, the Chart of Charity. The aim of the Cistercian reform was to introduce a more spiritual religion into the cloister. Monks had begun to expend their religious feelings in the externals of devotion. The eleventh century had been a time of deadly struggle with the powers of the world; its great men were men of action like St. Gregory, and its good monks were half hermits, like St. Peter Damian. It was a time of travail and of labour, for the old world was gone, and the new middle-age world was in process of formation. Men were just recovering from the wild fright into which the close of the first thousand years of the Christian era had thrown them; their panic had broken out in frantic gestures, so that men and women danced [1] hand in hand over the graves in the church-yard like the dances of death in the fifteenth century. And after their recovery they took to building churches, it was the first sign of revival, the fashionable religion, so to speak, of the day. Men and women formed themselves into companies, and marched together to the building of a new church, with banners carried before them. Knights and nobles yoked themselves to carts to carry stones to the new edifice. The utmost splendour of worship of course was the natural consequence of the erection of these splendid edifices, for lofty naves and beautiful choirs were not built to be left in nakedness like vast sepulchres. Images of saints and angels, in all the warmth of colour and gilding,

[1] Fordun, vii. 26.

peopled them on high,[1] and the long train of splendid vestments moved in glittering order amongst the worshippers. This was all as it should be in secular churches, nay, it was well even in monasteries if this graceful and glowing external life of religion was not too busy for the interior and hidden life of the soul. The two schools need not have clashed, but that they did so is certain, for these ancient monasteries found fault with the new school, which arose amongst them on the grounds that there was a real opposition between an austere life and spiritual joy, and that a splendid external religion was essential to internal devotion. They were perhaps conscious that it was so in themselves, and so they attacked their younger brethren, telling them that joyousness and love were essential to religion, and were incompatible with the great austerities which they practised.

Aelred's Mirror of Charity therefore is intended to reflect an image of the love of God, the conception of which had been so strangely disfigured. "The love of God," he says, "is the Holy Spirit within us." Considered as a habit in our souls, it is a perfect union of our will with that of God, so that we wish for nothing but what He wishes. It is not feeling, it is not intellect, it is not joy, it is not reasoning; it is this ineffable union with God, who is not an idea, but a real living God, the source of all joy and all intellect. As man however has fallen, this love must be raised out of the death of nature, and this was the reason of the Cistercian austerities; they were means to

[1] Quo sanctior eo coloratior St. Bern. Apol. ad Guil.

an end, to set up the cross of Christ within the
soul, and they were useful as far as they procured
the perfect resignation of the will. And how can
this be effected, asks the Cistercian, where all things
tend to dissipate the mind and expend its energies
on external things, when in the cloister are found
picturesque animals to amuse the eyes of the
brethren ; quails and curious birds, tame hares
gambolling about, and stags browsing under the
trees.[1] There is the same dissipation when the
walls of monastic churches are covered with paint-
ings of men and horses fighting, and pagan stories
taken from classic history, when the pavement is
of marble, covered with rich carpets, and the
worship is carried on with a glare of wax lights,
amid the glitter of gold and silver vessels ; or
when again, instead of the grave and masculine
Gregorian chants, languid and effeminate music was
used, or else the loud organ imitated the crash
of thunder to the wonder of the gaping crowd
below. "Meanwhile," says Aelred, "the crowd
stands trembling and astonished, wondering at the
sound of the bellows, the clash of cymbals, the
harmony of pipes, yet when they look at the
contortions of the singers and their imitation of
female voices, they cannot help laughing. You
would fancy that they had come not to an
oratory, but to a theatre, not to pray, but to a
spectacle. They fear not that tremendous majesty
near which they are brought, they have no reverence for that mystic manger, at which they are
ministering, where Christ is mystically wrapt in

[1] Spec. Char. ii. 23, 24.

swaddling - clothes, where His most sacred blood
is poured in the chalice, where the heavens are
opened, and angels are standing near, where
earthly things are joined with heavenly, and men
are the companions of angels."

The love of God consists not in these external
things; it does not consist even in the joys of the
interior life, but in the conformity of the soul with
the passion of Christ, in the crucifixion of the whole
man. The soul must patiently wait upon Him, not
forcing itself to feel joy and sorrow, but resting in
faith upon God, ready to be filled with His joys, when
He wills, and willing to remain in spiritual dryness
as long as He wills. "Nevertheless," says Aelred,[1]
"who so presumptuous as to affirm that communion
with the passion of Christ is incompatible with His
Spirit, and lessens the grace of spiritual sweetness.
He is joined to Christ's passion, who bows himself
beneath the discipline of the cloister, and mortifies
his flesh by fasts, labour, and watchings, who submits
his will to another's judgment," and who, when tried
by internal temptations, which are more severe than
any corporal mortifications, commits himself into the
hands of the Lord to suffer what He wills. He must
not be ever looking out for miracles to prove his
acceptance as was the case with many in those days,
he must wait quietly for consolation from on high.[2]

[3] "But when the soul is in this state, beset with
fear, harassed with grief, cast down by despair, swallowed up by sadness, grieved by spiritual sluggishness, there will come down upon it a drop of

[1] Spec. Char. ii. 6.   [2] Spec. Char. ii. 24.
[3] Spec. Char. ii. 12.

wondrous sweetness, from the unguent of that copious mountain, that high-raised mountain: noiselessly and peacefully it drops down upon the soul. At the brightness of its radiant light, all that cloud of irrational feelings melts away; before its sweet taste, all bitterness disappears, the heart expands, the hungry soul is fed, and it feels within it a strange upward power, which seems to bear it on high. Thus by fear sloth is kept away; and by the taste of heavenly sweetness, fear is tempered. Lest the soul should be content to remain in a low and sluggish state, fear rouses it; but if it faints in its labours, it is sustained by its feeling. By these alternations it is continually schooled, till the whole soul, absorbed by that ineffable love, burning for the long-desired embrace of Him who is fairer than the children of men, begins to wish to be dissolved and to be with Christ.[1] But know well that, if ever the mercy of Thy Creator pour upon thee a single drop of His sweetness, it depends not on thy will, when it should come to thee, nor in what way, nor how much thou canst keep of it. When thou hast tasted this spiritual sweetness, be not straightway sunk down in sloth, for soon there will rise up by thy side a spiritual enemy, and he is not to be conquered by sloth, but by prayers. Then after numberless contests, thou shalt be taken on high to receive thy reward, and thy soul will enter into the glory of God, where thou wilt be fed with the fruit of the promises. The fire of heavenly love will burn up the yoke of earthly concupiscence, and thou shalt rest in the brightness of wisdom, in the sweetness of heavenly contemplation,

[1] Spec. Char. ii. 15.

and know of a truth that the yoke of the Lord is sweet and His burden light."

Such was Aelred's doctrine, and he had soon need enough of resignation to the will of God, for while he was engaged in writing this work, his friend Simon died. So full is he of his grief that he quits his subject, and pours his heart out in expressions of grief. His mirror of charity is a home-book; it was meant for the cloister, and for brethren to read. In one place he tells us that he had offended one of the brethren in the morning, and how the thought of it grieved him. And now that he had lost his friend, it seems to have been a relief to him to put all his thoughts on paper. For eight years Simon had been suffering from ill-health; and for a whole year, foreseeing that his end was approaching, he had withdrawn within himself, and seemed forgetful of all external things, "even of me," says Aelred. It appears that he had been sent away from Rievaux, probably for his health, and Aelred was not with him when he died. His body, however, was brought to his own monastery, and Aelred had just come from his funeral, when he wrote these words, "O grave, where is thy victory? O death, where is thy sting? Where thou seemest to have done him some hurt, there thou hast exalted him. Upon me, then, has all thy venom been expended, and in aiming at him, thou hast inflicted dreadful wounds upon me. It is on me that has fallen all the grief, all the bitterness, all the sorrow; for the guide of my path, the rule of my conversation has been taken from me. But how is it, O my soul, that thou didst so long look upon the funeral of thy sweet friend without tears? Why didst thou let that beloved body go without kissing it? I was in sorrow, and with sobs I drew long sighs from my breast, but I did not weep. The object before me called for such intense grief, that I thought that I did not grieve at all, even when my grief was most violent; at least, so I can tell on looking back. So great was the stupor of my mind that I could not believe that he was dead, even when I saw his body was laid out for burial. But now that stupor has given way to feeling, to grief, and suffering. And are my tears blameable? Why should I be ashamed of them? Am I the only one to weep? Tears, groans, and sobs are all about me. But Thy tears, O Lord Jesus, are the excuse for ours, those tears which Thou didst shed for the death of Thy friend, expressing a human feeling, and proving to us Thy charity. Thou didst put on, O Lord, the feeling of our infirmity, but it was, when Thou wouldest; therefore Thou mightest not have wept. Oh! how sweet are Thy tears, how grateful! how they console me! How they drop with sweetness on my harassed soul! Behold, say they, how He loved him. Yea, behold! how my Simon was loved by all, was embraced by all, was cherished by all."

Truly the white monks were not a hard-hearted race, as appears from this touching picture of a monk's funeral. The world does not so regret its friends, at least, if we may judge from the cold, heartless things that funerals are. But we must now accompany Aelred a little way into this same world to another death-bed. It was one of bitter grief to him, and yet it had its comfort too. We have all this while lost sight of the Saxon priest with whom we began this narrative, Eillan, Aelred's father, the priest of Hexham ; and it is only by accident that a document has been preserved to us, from which it appears that Eillan was taken ill at Durham, and repenting on his death-bed of the unlawful possession which he kept of the property of Hexham, sent for the prior of the canons, and also for Aelred and two other sons, whose names are thus known to have been Samuel and Ethelwold. William, Abbot of Rievaux, also came, and in their presence, and with the consent of his sons, he formally gave up into the hands of the prior all the lands of the Abbey which he had kept ; and in token of this donation, he gave Robert a silver cross, containing part of the relics of the Saints of Hexham. Probably Aelred's consent, with that of his brothers, was necessary to make this transaction legal, and it must have been with joy that by this renunciation, he cleared his family of the guilt of sacrilege, which had so long hung over them. His father, when his illness grew worse, took the monastic habit in the Abbey of Durham. "He lived a few days longer in strict self-examination, contrition of heart, and mourning for his sins, and after having received the body of the Lord to help him in his passage from life to death, he breathed his last."

This glimpse of Aelred on the brink of his father's grave, is the last which we catch of him as a simple monk of Rievaux. It took place in 1138, which was the year of the battle of the Standard. When we meet him again it will be in another capacity.

CHAPTER VII

THE WORLD IN THE CHURCH

AND now we must again quit the cloister and go forth into the world, and this time it will not be the noisy world of knights and barons which was battling outside the walls of Rievaux, but the ecclesiastical world, in which a more deadly war was waged during that part of Aelred's life which remains. It will thus appear what dangers Aelred escaped by taking refuge in the haven of the cloister from the sea of ecclesiastical politics. It will also be seen how necessary to the church was a reform like the Cistercian, of which one of the first principles was to give up the politics of the world, and by which Abbots were forbidden to become judges, and to frequent courts of law, or even, except in particular cases, to hold communication with the court of Rome.[1]

A struggle was now beginning different in character from any which had gone before. In the former contests, there appear Saints on the one side, and the world on the other. But here we

[1] V. Inst. cap. Gen. part i. c. 58, de placitis and 84, Nullus scribat domino Papæ nisi pro propriis causis et co-abbatum suorum et episcoporum, archipiscoporum, regum et principum suorum. No privileges were to be obtained from the Holy See by particular Abbots, c. 31.

have civilians and canonists, men of business and
politicians among churchmen, as well as in the
world. Law comes in instead of broad principle,
or rather principle takes the shape of law. Nearly
at the same time two young monarchs ascended
the thrones of England and of Germany, Henry
and Frederic. Both were remarkable men. Henry
was a good specimen of the Plantagenet race; never
would his restless soul leave his body quiet. All
day long he was on his feet, whatever he was
doing, whether at mass or at council; although his
legs frequently gave him pain from the many kicks
which he received from the fiery chargers which he
bestrode.[1] He hardly ever sat down but on horseback, the saddle was his only throne; from one
part to another of his vast dominions he hurried,
rolling everywhere his dove-like, deceitful eyes.
But if any thing aroused his anger, then it was
terrible to look upon him, for his large round eyes
seemed to shoot fire on all around him. Not so
his imperial majesty; inexorable and inflexible he
was; so that on the very day of coronation at
Aix-la-chapelle, one who had offended him fell at
his feet in the very cathedral, thinking that then
kings' hearts are disposed to mercy, but he turned
away, and would not look at him.[2] When the
clergy of Tortona quitted the beleaguered town with
cross and banner, and came to him in procession
with naked feet to beg for mercy, he was unruffled
and undisturbed, and sent them back with a bitter
smile, to live on horse-flesh or to die of famine.[3]

[1] Peter of Blois, Ep. 66.

[2] Otto, de Gestis Frid. ii. 3.

[3] Otto, ii. 19.

Still he does not seem to have had the terrible fits of passion which burst forth from Henry. He was an indefatigable warrior like Henry; but it is not clad in mail and on horseback that we think of him, it is rather seated on his throne on the plains of Roncaglia, dispensing kingdoms with a sword, and provinces with a banner.[1] The sceptre suits best his imperial hand, as the sword, the large, ungloved hand of Henry.[2] Pride was the besetting sin of the Hohenstauffen, and passion of the Plantagenet.

Yet however different they were, they agreed in this: both were men of law and zealous administrators of justice, and both endeavoured to swallow up the church in their reforms. Henry's aim was to extend justice through his dominions by means of his new division of circuits and judges. Frederic's was rather to centralise justice and to make himself its head across the Alps, as he had done in Germany. His aim was wider than Henry's; it extended through all the intricate details of fiefs and arriere-fiefs: the maxims which he studied were those of the imperial court of Constantinople. They involved a theory broad and comprehensive, taking into its extensive range, not only Germany and Italy, but all the world. Wide as was the theory of Innocent III., that of Frederic Barbarossa was its match without its religiousness. Of the two swords given to St. Peter, he claimed one, as the Head of the Church claimed the other, using the same text,

---

[1] Est consuetudo curiæ ut regna per gladium, provinciæ per vexillum tradantur. Otto, ii. 5.

[2] Nunquam, nisi aves deferat, utitur chirothecis. Peter of Blois, Ep. 66.

without reflecting that he spoiled the illustration,
for he at least could not be the successor of the
Apostle. Frederic claimed his throne as the successor of Charlemagne. The old Roman empire
was by no means supposed to be dead ; it was
considered to be continued in Constantinople, and
Charlemagne claimed it on the ground that the
Imperial line of Constantinople had failed, and it
was time that the empire should return to the West.[1]
When afterwards Frederic passed by Constantinople
on his way to the East, he would not meet the
Greek Emperor, for he was himself the Emperor
of Rome ; his Eastern majesty was but the Emperor
of New Rome. Head of the Holy Roman empire
was his title, and his obsequious prelates were not
afraid of the utmost conclusions, which such a title
would warrant.[2] Sole Emperor of the world is
one of the titles by which the Archbishop of Milan
addresses him in a speech delivered on the Roncaglia. Even kings acknowledged his greatness :
our own Henry says in a letter to him, " let the
will of the Empire be done wherever our dominion
extends."[3] It is true that Henry had a point to
gain, and words, it is well known, cost nothing to
him whom a cardinal legate once called the greatest
liar he had ever known ; still they must have meant
something, not to appear preposterous.

But the great support of Frederic were his legists
of Bologna.[4] One day the emperor was riding on
a fine horse with two great Doctors of law, one on

---

[1] Palgrave's Anglo-Saxon Constitution, pp. 490, 506.
[2] Radevic. Frising. ii. 4.
[3] Radevic. i. 7.   [4] Baronius in ann. 1158.

each side of him, Doctor Bulgarus and Doctor Martin, and he asked them whether he was by right lord of the world. Master Bulgarus answered that he was not, as far as the property of it went; but the cautious Martin said that he was. "Then the lord emperor," says the chronicle, "when he came down from his palfrey, presented it to Martin." Here in the introduction of Doctor Martin and his colleagues we have the characteristic of the whole contest in Germany as well as in England. William Rufus had summary methods of proceeding, rude and simple modes of spoliation; but Henry was a more refined tyrant; he set up for a lover of justice and a reformer of law, and so he was, when it suited him. Besides brute force, for that was not wanting too, he fought with appeals, and sentences of suspension and excommunication. But the times were not ready for so much refinement; it was only the commencement of the new system, and he had to spill the blood of a martyr before he had done. The struggle however between Church and State in England had not reached its height in Aelred's time, and it is not mentioned by him in his writings; while that between Frederic and the Church is known to have occupied his attention. We will therefore cross over to the continent and see how the chief ecclesiastics of the day, the spiritual rulers of Christendom, were employed, while Aelred was serving God in peace at Rievaux.

There was something great about Frederic; when he crossed the Alps, to extend his power over Italy, he declared that he came, not as a conqueror, but as a lawgiver; his speech to the diet was a noble

one,[1] and his attempt to pacify the deadly feuds of the
cities was praiseworthy. He gave a written feudal
law to Italy which it had not known before; but
he committed the same fault as Henry. The church
was to be centralised and drawn within the circle of
the empire; the property of the sees to be treated
like that of the baron as imperial fiefs, inalienable
without the consent of the emperor, the lord of
the soil. And in all this it is remarkable how the
civilian everywhere comes into the contest; instead
of the old and dignified watch-words of the contest,
investiture by ring and sceptre, or by pastoral staff,
there now appears all the jargon of feudal finance,
fodrum,[2] and regalia, fiefs and allodial lands. The
spirit of the struggle was, however, the same, as we
shall see as it goes on. Even in the time of Eugenius
differences arose between the aged pontiff and the
young monarch. Frederic had constituted himself
the arbiter between rival candidates for the see
of Magdeburg, a dispute which an ecclesiastical
tribunal only was competent to decide. Eugenius
died before the matter could be settled, and his
successor Anastasius was weak enough to concede
the point. It was a bad lesson for Frederic; it
destroyed the awe that men had for the inflexibility
of the Holy See in a just cause.

Such was the state of affairs when Anastasius died
after a short pontificate; and Hadrian IV. succeeded
him in the See of St. Peter. It was a joyful day for
England when news came that the cardinal Bishop
of Albano was supreme Pontiff, for he was an

---

[1] Radevic. Frising, ii. 3.
[2] Fodrum means the duty of supporting the Imperial army.

Englishman, of genuine Saxon blood, Nicholas Breakspear. He was the son of a man in a low rank of life, who became a monk of St. Alban's. The boy was brought up in the cloister, but when he became a candidate for the novitiate, the Abbot would not receive him. It was not every one who could be admitted into the lordly Abbey of St. Alban's. Much however could not be said for the discernment of Abbot Robert, for the next meeting which he had with the poor Saxon boy, was when he came to Rome on the business of his Abbey, and found his rejected novice in the chair of St. Peter. The Abbot brought with him a considerable sum of money, with three mitres, and sandals worked by Christina, prioress of Margate. But Pope Adrian would not receive the money; he said with a good-humoured smile, " I will not accept thy gifts, for once on a time thou wouldest not have me for thy monk, when I came to beg the habit of thee in all charity." Since he had left St. Alban's, he had become prior of the canons of St. Rufus, and then as cardinal legate of the Holy See, he had been sent into Norway to form the Church among that newly converted nation. In these ungenial regions, amidst this wild people, he passed many years, and when he came back to Italy he left a church, flourishing with monasteries, and a holy clergy where he had found a wilderness inhabited by a half heathen population. Such was the reputation which he acquired for purity of life and prudence in managing ecclesiastical affairs, that on the death of Anastasius he was raised to preside over the Catholic Church. It was at a dangerous time, when the empire was arousing itself, and the church was on the eve of a contest, at which St. Gregory might have trembled. The times were changed since St. Gregory's death; the world had grown accustomed to the great doctrines which he had vindicated, and they had now thoroughly worked into the feelings of Christendom. In another respect however matters were less favourable; St. Gregory had formed his school about him, and his cardinals co-operated with him; but since then affairs had become matters of precedent and custom at Rome, and the Pope often found himself obliged to act against his judgment, from the preponderance of one party or another in the Sacred College. There was at this time an Imperial party amongst the Cardinals, and Hadrian found himself hampered by them.[1]

Hadrian did not at first come into direct collision with the Emperor. Frederic had yet to receive the imperial crown at his hands, and was on his good behaviour. When he appeared at Rome with his German army, the Pope and the Emperor had a mutual enemy to fear, the turbulent people of Rome, and much blood was shed on Frederic's coronation day. All however passed off happily as far as Hadrian was concerned; the sole thing which tended to disturb their peace, was the hesitation of Frederic

---

[1] Repugnabant enim Cardinales illi qui addicti erant imperatori et non nisi quod ipsi placere scirent probandum putabant: in reliquis autem se adversarios objiciebant. Quod sæpe factum ab eis in maximum Romanæ ecclesiæ detrimentum. See the grave words of Baronius in ann. 1155, 23. If it had not been for the opposition of the German party to the terms offered by the king of Sicily, Hadrian would never have been in the awkward position at Beneventum, which forced him to make concessions to Roger.

to hold the stirrup of the Pope, when he mounted his horse. Hadrian in his grave calm way said, "Since thou hast not paid me the honour which thy predecessors have paid me, I will not receive thee to the kiss of peace."[1] Frederic simply took the matter as one of custom and ceremonial. He went in a business-like way to work, looked into old records, and examined as witnesses those who had been present at the crowning of Lothaire, and finding that Hadrian was right, he complied. It was a piece of ceremony, like the kiss of the Pope's feet, very significant certainly, for it implied that the Head of the Church on earth, was above the Head of the Empire; still it had nothing to do with individuals, and his Imperial majesty did not think himself degraded. But a serious cause of offence soon followed, which arising, as it did, from an apparent trifle, showed that two opposite principles were at work and might break out any day into open war. Hadrian sent to the emperor two legates, cardinals Roland, chancellor of the Holy See, and Bernard, to demand the liberation of a prelate who had been maltreated and detained prisoner by some German noble on his way from Rome. In the course of his letter the Holy Father had reminded Frederic how he had bestowed upon him the Imperial crown, and professed himself to be ready to grant him greater benefits.[2] Now it happened unfortunately that the Latin word for benefit, also signifies benefice or fief; and hardly were the words out of

---

[1] See Life of Hadrian in Muratori. Rer. Ital. Scrip., tom. iii. 443.
[2] It seems absurd to suppose that Hadrian meant to claim the empire as a fief. What greater fiefs were there in the world to bestow?

the mouth of the official who read the letter to the
emperor, when his Imperial majesty took fire, and
all the princes of the empire rose up in anger. Was
then the only emperor in the world, the head of the
feudal hierarchy himself a vassal? Was the Holy
Roman empire itself a fief? The notion was intolerable; and when cardinal Roland innocently
asked, "Who then did bestow the crown on the
emperor?" one of the fierce nobles around drew a
sword, and would have struck him if Frederic had
not interposed. The fact was, that the question was
an awkward one. If Frederic's lofty theory was
true, if he was the imperial Head of the Christian
world, where did he get the title? To one like
Frederic, disposed to make it any thing but an empty
title, and, above all, who professed to reduce it to
theory by his legists, and to draw inferences from
it, the question was one which stared him in the
face. Frederic could only ground his title on the
fact that Charlemagne, some three hundred years
before, had received the Imperial crown from Pope
Leo one Christmas day in St. Peter's. The power
of granting this crown resided in Rome, such was
the theory of the times; so much so that the mock
senate of Rome claimed it, and Frederic had to
choose between the sacred Head of Christendom and
this self-constituted assembly. This theory was
enough to justify the greatest pretensions to rule
over temporal princes that the Pope ever made;
and since that power resided in one who was Christ's
Vicar on earth, we need not wonder that the nations
bowed before it. We may look upon it now calmly
and dispassionately, for the power has passed away

and is not even asserted; and without taking fire like Frederic and his princes, we may say that in as far as it could be carried out, it was true. The fact that it could be exercised was its justification, and it might be well if the nations had Christ's earthly representative to be to them a living impersonation of justice, and to step in when earthly and material power is of no avail.

The idea was therefore by no means so preposterous as might be imagined; besides some kingdoms were acknowledged fiefs of the Holy See. However this may be, Hadrian did not in this case lay claim to this power; he mildly answered Frederic that he was surprised that he should misinterpret his words, and that "beneficium" meant benefit, as well as benefice; so the storm cleared away for the present from the imperial brows. But nothing external would keep the peace between two such elements as the Church and the world. The empire of the Church can hardly be defined; in one sense it has no earthly rule at all, and in another it bears rule wherever there are men who have souls to be saved. Wide therefore is its dominion as is the empire of conscience, and thus in one sense the whole world comes under its jurisdiction. But this kingdom, strong as it is, depends entirely on a conscientious basis; when therefore the conscience is vitiated or misinformed, it at once puts itself in opposition to the Church. In this way then there can never long be peace between two such powers, unless one is recognised to be above the other. All this is true in the abstract; but the battle between the Church and the world is hardly ever fought directly on these grounds; but on a much grosser and more material battle-field. And this was especially the case in the struggle between the Hohenstauffen and the Popes. In process of time the Church acquires rights and property, and these in a certain sense circumscribe, because they serve to define her power. Besides which they make her open to attack, by giving her points to defend, for which she cannot fight without the appearance of ambition. She must needs mingle in worldly policy, and appear externally like one of the powers of the world. Church property looks just like any other property, and if a Bishop possesses land, why should he not do homage for it? If it is recognised and defended by the law, it becomes subject to the law. So reasoned Frederic. And while he was about it, he thought he might as well make laws about ecclesiastical property as any other. The Bishops in Italy were possessed of great power in the cities; they were often temporal princes, and he could not be sure of the fair cities of Lombardy without keeping them under. He therefore required the act of homage and oath of fealty from a Bishop as he would from one of his own nobles. When Hadrian remonstrated with him, he answered with a curious mixture of history and imperial theology, while the legist of Bologna evidently inspires the whole. Hadrian's letter begins with saying that the divine law bids us honour our parents. Frederic answered by quoting, "The law of justice, which gives every man his own. From his ancestors did he get his crown, but what had Silvester in the time of Constantine? Whatever that popedom of theirs possesses, it obtains from the liberality of princes." And then came the text about "rendering unto Cæsar all that is Cæsar's," and an exhortation to humility. At another time, when Hadrian complained about the occupation of Episcopal palaces by himself and his retainers, he answered with a quotation from the digests that the soil was his, and therefore so was all that was built upon it.

All this will at least serve to mark the character of the contest; it was the world's law in its process of formation, striving to draw into itself, and to neutralise the Church. If it had succeeded in merging the jurisdiction of the Church into its own, St. Gregory's work would have been undone. It was not however till after Hadrian's death that the Emperor's designs became apparent; for then broke out one of the most audacious acts of schism that ever attempted to divide the Christian world. In the conclave held for the election of the Pope, a large majority of the Cardinals united in favour of Roland, that same Chancellor of the Holy See who excited Frederic's anger by his untimely question. He had already been robed in the purple mantle in which the new Pontiff was presented to the people of Rome, when Cardinal Octavian, supported by two other Cardinals, pulled the mantle off him. A senator who was present snatched it out of Octavian's hand, who then proceeded to robe himself with another mantle, which he had brought with him for the purpose. Unluckily, however, he put on the hind part of the mantle foremost, so that the hood hung down in front; then the doors were thrown open, and thus accoutred, he

[1] Giesler, i. 52.

presented himself to the people, amidst a band of
armed men, while the Cardinals, with the real successor of St. Peter, fled into the church to hide themselves. The instinct of Christendom saw through
the transaction, and recognised Alexander, for so
Roland was now called; even Henry II.'s good sense
led him right all through the struggle, and though
he threatened great things in the height of his contest with St. Thomas, he remained faithful to Alexander. And now the designs of Frederic became
apparent;[1] he wished to have a German instead of
a Catholic Pope. A Pope there must be, and let him
be infallible too; nay, the more infallible the better,
provided he is but the servant of the empire.
Sovereigns were ready enough to acknowledge the
Papal supremacy to the utmost, when it suited their
purpose, when they had a new kingdom to conquer,
or a weak title to strengthen. It was only when he
came in their way that they wished to be rid of him.
So now Frederic called together a council at Pavia;
it consisted but of the bishops of the empire, and so
he could safely talk of his rights as successor of Constantine, and quote the emperors who had exercised
the right of convoking councils. The upshot was, as
might have been expected, that Victor, for so Octavian had called himself, was judged to be Pope. But
this council was a failure; Alexander was too wise
to submit his cause to any council whatever; he was
Pope and could not be judged; besides which the
Christian world had already decided by sending in
its adherence to Alexander. Frederic saw that he

[1] De amissione imperialis curiæ timebat. Acta Alex. III. Muratori
3. 452.

was foiled, and next tried to entice the good Louis of France to a conference, to decide on the claims of the two claimants. Louis had been so far taken in as to promise to meet the Emperor; but Frederic unhappily asserted in the course of the negotiation, that only the Bishops of the empire had the right of judging a cause respecting the election of a supreme Pontiff, his imperial majesty being the especial defender of the Holy See. But Louis smiled at this novel doctrine, and said, "Does not the Emperor know that our Lord when on earth bade Peter feed His sheep? And are not the French Bishops a part of the flock which the Son of God has committed to Peter?" And so saying, Louis "turned his horse's head disdainfully, and flew to arms with his barons and the rest of his forces"; and back went the Emperor, with all his men, and would not wait to confront the Fleurs-de-Lis. The times were not yet come when the world could take in the idea of a French Pope and a German Pope.

It is not our purpose to follow the struggle to its close, to show how the Lombard league was formed, how the Tuscan league, the army of the Church, joined it, and how after many a hard battle by land and by sea, Frederic at last, in St. Mark's Cathedral at Venice, threw himself prostrate at Alexander's feet, and the Pontiff raised him with tears in his eyes, and the Te Deum was entoned for joy. But the contest lasted for many a long year, during which Alexander had conflicting interests to settle, and a line of policy to pursue; at the commencement of the whole contest he had to embark for France with all his train; and little was the peace that he could enjoy with two contests on his hands, one with Henry of England, the other with the Emperor.

Little indeed was the supreme Pontiff to be envied in his high dignity; and for this conclusion, like John of Salisbury, we have high authority. There remains on record a conversation which took place between two frank-hearted Englishmen, one on the throne of St. Peter, the other brought close to it by his position. Considering that one of the interlocutors was Hadrian, the only Pope who was English-born, the dialogue is unique, and forms a fitting moral to this chapter. "I call to witness," says John, "Lord Hadrian, that no man is more wretched than the Roman Pontiff, no condition more miserable than his. If he had nothing else to vex him, the labour alone would make him sink." He had gone through every office in the Church, from the very lowest, and every step brought an accession of bitterness; and yet all former bitterness was joy compared to what he felt on the thorny chair of St. Peter. Well might the crown and the mitre shine with brilliancy, for they were of fire, and burnt the brow of the wearer. And in another place, John tells us how Pope Hadrian begged of him to tell him what men thought of the Roman curia, and how he bluntly laid bare what was one cause of Hadrian's difficulties, the universal outcry against the exactions and avarice of the court of Rome. Doubtless Hadrian was in part right when, with a smile, he answered his rough monitor by quoting the old fable of the body and its revolted members. The administration of the ecclesiastical offices of Christendom could not be carried on without extensive resources. The whole array of expectatives, mandates, and oblations, might be excused on the ground that it was necessary that the Pope should have a certain number of benefices to give away, just as a prime minister cannot carry on the government without the exercise of patronage. All this is true, and the governed are ever apt to over-rate the faults of their rulers ; but it is also true that the voice of St. Bernard had hardly disappeared from the earth, and he had cried out, "O ambition, the cross of the ambitious, how is it that thou art a torment to all, yet all love Thee ! Ambition rather than devotion wears the pavement of St. Peter's ! Does not the papal palace echo to its voice every day ? Is not the whole laborious discipline of law and canon administered for its gain ? Does not Italian avarice gloat over its spoils with insatiable avidity ? " [1] This of course proves nothing as to the rights of the Holy See, nor did it interfere in St. Bernard's mind with the ideal of the father of Christendom, "the hammer to beat down tyrants, the father of kings, the moderator of laws, the dis-penser of canons." [2] Nor does it prove anything against individuals ; the character of Hadrian him-self has never been impeached, and even John of Salisbury, with his hand on his heart, declares, " Never have I seen more honest clerks than in the Romish church." But it does prove that all the in-conveniences of an extensive system belonged to the Roman See. The Pope must be a man of business ; he must be vexed with the complaints of his subjects, and the evil of his ministers ; and the Cardinals and great men of the church must be men of action and

[1] De Con. iii. 1.　　　[2] De Con. 4 fin.

politicians. And now that we have drawn the moral that we wanted from this narrative, we will go back to where we left Aelred in 1138, and see what he was doing while all this was going on in the great world.

CHAPTER VIII

THE CISTERCIAN ABBOT

SILENTLY and rapidly did the Cistercian order spread in England; first came Waverley, and so retired and solitary was its situation, that its existence was unknown to their brethren in the north, and they were astonished to discover that there were white monks in England besides themselves.[1] Rievaux, Tintern, and Fountains came next, and from them issued communities which spread over the face of the land; and this silent rise of the houses of St. Mary in England, is the only redeeming feature of Stephen's miserable reign. "At that time," says William of Newbridge, "when the whole strength of the regal power was gone, the powerful men of the realm, each, according to his means, continued to build castles, either to defend their own or to overrun their neighbours' estates. At this time then, when evil was rife through the weakness of King Stephen, or rather through the devil's malice, the great King of Heaven by His

[1] Battle of the Standard, ap. Twysden. Waverley was founded in 1128, according to its annals. It never rose to the importance of Rievaux; in 1187 it had but a hundred and twenty lay-brethren and seventy monks, while Rievaux, within ten years after its foundation, had three hundred brethren, though the proportion of the lay-brethren to the monks does not appear.

wisdom and Providence, gloriously stepped forth in a marked way to put down the king of pride, by erecting such castles as befit the King of peace. For, many more monasteries of servants and hand-maids of the Lord are acknowledged to have risen up during the short time of Stephen's reign, or nominal reign, than during the hundred years before."[1] It seemed to be the only sign of religion left among the nobles, and it was a source of great comfort to men of restless habits continu-ally exposed to great dangers, when they thought that their monks were praying for them while they were engaged in their perilous wanderings.[2] William of Albemarle declared that he always slept soundly about cock-crow, whether under his tent or on the wide sea, because he knew that then the bells of his Abbey of Melsa were ringing for matins;[3] and at another time, John Courtenay, when in great peril of shipwreck, bade the sailors be of good cheer, for his Cistercians of Ford were at that moment praying for him. The poor people, too, loved "the hooded folk, who spent a part of their time in prayer and the service of God, and the rest in the labours of the field like rustics."

In the year 1143, William, Earl of Lincoln, came to the Abbot of Rievaux, to beg of him to send a colony of monks to Revesby, one of his estates in Lincolnshire. The Abbot complied, and sent Aelred, with twelve monks, to take possession of the new ground assigned to them; and so he left the valley of Rievaux, about five years after the time when we left him at Durham, standing by his father's

[1] William of Newbridge, 1, 15.   [2] Dugdale, v. 393.   [3] Dugdale, 379.

be eloquent and ready, so as to preach dignified sermons to the people in the church; he must not be too learned or too spiritual, and the men that he loves are not the good, humble monks, but men like himself, who make good officials for the convent. Yet he must be irreproachable in his morals, that none speak evil of the convent. A stately figure he must be, to set off the jewelled mitre, and the curiously wrought dalmatic, and the pastoral staff. In fine, he must be such an one as to please the monks of St. Edmund, whose prayer was, when they wanted a new Abbot, "From good clerks deliver us, good Lord."[1] He would form the very beau-ideal of him whose general rule, on an election, was "that we choose not a very good monk, nor yet an over-wise clerk, neither one too simple nor too weak, for I know that some one has said, 'Medio tutissimus ibis.'"

Aelred belonged to neither of these classes; he was rather the Father Abbot, than the Lord Abbot. The Cistercian idea of a superior was, that he should be the spiritual director of the whole convent. What Aelred had been to the novices, he now was to the three hundred brethren of Rievaux, with the additional accession of a dignity marked rather by its influence, than by the external signs of magnificence common in other orders. His office was a laborious one, and he who was made Abbot was considered, in comparison with the simple monk, to be taking the part of Martha rather than that of Mary. Many a time when he would rather have been on his knees in the Church, had Aelred to listen to the

[1] Cronica Jocelini, p. 11.

detail of the spiritual wants of the brethren. Little
do they know of monastic life who suppose that all
temptation was over as soon as the gates of the
monastery had closed upon the monk, and shut him
out from the world. "Ah! brethren," said Aelred, in
one of his sermons to the convent, one Christmas
season, "of those who are just come from the world,
some are unlearned and simple-minded, others erudite
and subtle, some bound by the habits of vice, others,
though sinners, yet free from all crime, some brought
up in luxury, others worn down by a hardy life, some
slothful, others active, some of such a temper as to
feel scarce any temptations to impurity, others
tempted by the least thing, some of a fiery temper,
others naturally mild. It is necessary then to study
the state and the temper of every one who flies hither
from the world, to know what is hurtful to each, and
to point out to him the best refuge from his enemy.
Some are to be kept away from all external employment, others from the society of this or that man,
others are to find a covert under a strict silence from
the burning heat of anger, others must be taught to
cure their lusts by coarse food, others are to be preserved from a restless spirit and a wandering heart
by labour and watchings, others are to be sheltered
from the attacks of evil spirits, by psalms and
prayers, by meditation and reading. In every case
an Abbot must offer to each vice, by which those
under him are attacked, the proper treatment which
experience tells us, is opposed to it."[1] This was
Aelred's occupation.

They were great schools of spiritual life these

[1] Serm. in Isaiam, 28.

first Cistercian convents, wonderful realisations of the Book of the Imitation of Christ. Aelred knew all the stages of the religious life of the soul, and could classify and arrange them as a physician would states of the body. " The first step," he says, " is, that a man flying from the world and eschewing all vice, should shun all worldliness.[1] Then in all obedience let him submit himself to his superior, and let him purify himself, and in hunger and thirst, in watchings and labours, in poverty and nakedness, take vengeance on himself for all that his memory taxes him with, and so must good habits be set up in the place of bad. Thus in the nest of discipline must he remain, till he be full fledged, and have the wings of virtue wherewith to fly, for never can he rule, who has not first learned to obey. And then purified from vice and adorned with virtue, let him pass on to the study of the Scriptures, and there he will receive illumination and gain wisdom. And when he shall have learned in the Scriptures to refer all his life and knowledge to the love of God and of his neighbour, then on the two wings of wisdom and of love, borne up to the mount of contemplation, let him learn to form this earthly tabernacle after the pattern of the heavenly. The first step then is conversion, the second purification, the third virtue, the fourth knowledge, the fifth contemplation, the sixth charity. And these perchance are the six steps to the throne of Solomon ; if any one strives to sit thereon, without having trodden them, he will mount, not to take his seat there, but to fall headlong." In another

[1] Serm. in Isaiam, 28.

place, by a more accurate division, he mentions three stages, — Conversion, Purification, and Contemplation; and in this last stage, "the soul purified by spiritual exercises, passes on to heavenly contemplation and meditation on the Holy Scriptures. Then does virtue begin to grow sweet to it, vice to be loathsome, and it tastes how sweet the Lord is.[1] In the first of these stages, fear, proceeding from the thought of God's justice, purifies the soul; and when it is purified, wisdom illuminates it; and after this illumination the goodness of God rewards it by the infusion of His sweetness."[2]

Strange is this early germ of the threefold division of the progress of the Christian soul into the Purificative, the Illuminative and the Unitive life, which was drawn much more fully many hundred years after by another Saint. Aelred here shows us the spiritual exercises of the twelfth century. And it was this system of which he was the administrator at Rievaux. Like a good shepherd, with his pastoral staff in his hand, he ruled his flock, bearing the weak ones in his bosom, and helping all with his gentle voice to escape the jaws of the lion, who goes about seeking whom he may devour. How much he loved them appears in every word of his writings. Many slight vestiges there are of his conventual history, scattered up and down in his works, scanty glimpses of struggles and pains which he participated with his spiritual children. How they rejoiced when they could chat with him alone, away from the Philistines who took up his time, as they called the strangers who came to him on

[1] Serm. in Isaiam, 31.   [2] De Jesu puero. 493.

secular matters! How familiarly they talked to him, not fearing to use words of playful raillery with each other in his presence, for it was his maxim that the soul required relaxation at times. They ventured to speak to him of his friends, how one had taken offence at him for some trivial cause, how in times when he was falsely accused, one friend who lived beyond the seas, had remained faithful to him, while even another friend, the Sacristan of Clairvaux, had taken part against him.[1] Each of these slight hints contains a whole history of feelings and affections which has now perished; but one thing we can see, that he was still the same Aelred, always looking out for some one to love, and one young monk was especially beloved by him, called Ivo, and for him probably he wrote that most beautiful treatise of his on Jesus,[2] when a child of twelve years old in the temple. But the Lord would not let him love Ivo too well, for this young monk died before he had been long at Rievaux. But even more than for the bodily death of his disciples did he mourn for their spiritual death; one especially, there was a promising brother, who fell we know not how; nor should we know any thing about him, if Aelred did not hold up the fall of this nameless brother as a warning to the convent in one of his sermons. And his love descended to more minute particulars, for he condoles with his brethren for the loss which they one year sustained by the destruction of a flock of sheep,—a serious loss for the farmer monks, who lived by the sale of the wool.

---

[1] De Spirit. Ami. iii. 453, 460, et passim.
[2] De Jesu puero duodenni.

It must not however be supposed that Aelred's life was altogether as quiet as it might at first sight appear. He was sometimes obliged to be my lord Abbot as well as his neighbours. The late Abbot of Rievaux had been obliged to make a journey across the Alps, and to appear at Rome in favour of St. William's deposition. Aelred's journey did not, however, lead him so far from home. On the death of Henry Murdach, St. William was installed at York, without any opposition from the new Abbot. Aelred had, however, many voyages across the sea to the general Chapter of Citeaux. But even without going to Burgundy, he had matter enough to employ him at home. The Abbot of Rievaux was head of the Cistercian Abbots in England, and sometimes causes came before him judicially. In 1151, he decided a cause in favour of the monks of Byland, who after many troubles had at length obtained a settlement. The poor brethren had been expelled from their convent by the Scots, and had been refused shelter by the Abbey of Furness, their mother house, and had managed to find a home on the other side of the Rye, so near Rievaux that the bells of each convent might be heard from the other. This was, however, contrary to Cistercian discipline, and they again removed to Byland. There they were in a flourishing state, and had not only built themselves a church, but also a parochial chapel in an outlying valley, for the use of which they had generously sent one of the bells of the convent in a waggon.[1] When lo! the Abbot of Furness, after treating

[1] Dugdale, v. 351.

them so inhospitably, claimed jurisdiction over them, and the cause came before Aelred, who decided it in favour of his poor neighbours of Byland. But not only by his own order, but by all the monasteries around him, he was consulted in cases of difficulty. In some of the later years of his life, it cannot precisely be ascertained which, he was called to Watton, to pronounce on the well-known case of an inmate of the convent, who had fallen into sin.[1] The only question which was asked him was, What was to be done with the wretched penitent, under the extraordinary circumstances? Aelred, as appears by his writings,[2] was no friend to monks who were ever on the look-out for miracles, but in this case there was no choice between accusing the nuns of a wicked fraud, or believing the truth of miracle. Aelred found that he had reason to believe that the nuns were holy women, and thought the latter alternative by far the less difficult. He had pity on the wretched sinner, and when the prior wrote to him to ask whether she should be punished any more, he answered, "What God has cleansed call not thou common, and what He has Himself absolved do not thou bind."

In the Lent of 1153, he went on a journey which was ever memorable to him. The business of his order took him into Scotland, and he saw King David for the last time in his life. David had founded no less than four Cistercian Abbeys in Scotland, it is therefore not at all unlikely that Aelred should have often seen him since he became

---

[1] V. Life of St. Gilbert, p. 117.
[2] Spec. Char. ii. 24. And also Serm. 4, p. 37.

Abbot; and it must have been with a fearful joy that he revisited those scenes from which so many years before he had fled as if for his life. Many a change had taken place, both in King David and in himself, since he had left Scotland. And on this, his last visit, he missed a face which had ever welcomed him with beaming eyes. Henry, the heir of the crown of Scotland, the brave soldier, and accomplished prince, had died the year before, to the irreparable loss of Scotland. With his devoted piety and enlightened understanding, he would have been a fitting match for the Henry who was just about to mount the English throne. Aelred had left David in the beginning of his reign, full of schemes for the improvement of a realm, which was flourishing under his care; now he found him a penitent and a mourner, bound down by grief, yet resigned to God's will. He acknowledged that the death of his son was a fitting punishment, sent by God for having let loose the savage Galwegians on the north of England. So poignant had been his grief, that had it not been for the entreaties of his whole realm, bishops and nobles, he would have given up his crown and sceptre, and retired to a convent. When Aelred left him, he seemed to have a presentiment that they should never meet again on this side the grave, and he embraced him fondly and shed tears when they parted. A few months after, at the end of May, shortly before the Ascension, news was brought to Rievaux that David had died as he had lived, a holy death. Aelred mourned for his friend and benefactor with the poignant grief which was natural to him. In

the first burst of his sorrow he wrote a sketch
of the good king's character, and afterwards sent it
to one for whom he then felt a great anxiety and
love, to Henry, who had mounted the throne of
England, David's grand-nephew.

It is interesting to see the light in which the
Abbot views the young king; and truly Henry
might well be an object of solicitude to every
thoughtful man. He was the most powerful prince
in Europe, in the flower of his age, and gifted with
talents and the will to extend his power. Henry
began well; near the place of his landing was a
church, into which he entered to pray, and at mass
he came forward to receive the kiss of peace from
the priest. His policy soon showed that he meant
to restrain the power of the nobles, to show justice
to all, and especially to favour the peasants and
the burghers of the towns. In the very month of
his coronation, the election of Adrian to the papal
throne seemed to promise a happy concord between
the English Church and state. Aelred then might
well look with fondness and hope on the young
king. Henry's vices had not yet developed, and
Aelred, with the sanguine and trusting temper
which made him unable to conceive the possibility
of fraud in the convent of Watton, invested the
young king with all manner of virtues. He looked
upon him as the destined restorer of the old English
line to the throne of England, the line of Edward
the Confessor, which the Abbot had never ceased
to love. He applies to Henry an old prophecy,
ascribed to St. Dunstan, and rejoices "that England
has now a king of English blood, and bishops and

abbots, princes, and good soldiers." He fondly
draws out "from ancient chronology," the genealogy
of Henry, through his English mother and English
kings, "even up to Adam, the father of all mortals";
and he holds up, as a model to him, his great
ancestor Alfred, and David, whose death he was
mourning, "whose pure hands had made him a belted
knight." At the same time, with a keen anticipation of Henry's dangers, he drops various hints
about submission to the Church; "how the blessed
Alfred thought that the great dignity of kings
consisted in having no power in the Church of
Christ, and how he imitated the example of Constantine, who said to the bishops, 'It belongs not
to me to judge of priests.'" Henry's latter days,
troubled as they were with the rebellion of his sons,
and stained with the blood of a martyr, would not
have been so different from his religious landing,
when, high in hopes, he threw himself on his knees
in the little church by the seashore, if he had
attended to Aelred's warning.

A part of the Abbot's exhortation to Henry was,
that he should watch over the interests of the royal
family of Scotland; and this portion of the homily
he neglected, as well as the rest. Henry, when he
was made a knight by David, had sworn to leave
the Scottish king and his heirs in peaceful possession of the domains which they held of the English
crown. He, however, outwitted David's successor,
the young King Malcolm, who was no match for
his unscrupulous suzerain. The young prince was
the son of Henry, the friend of Aelred's youth.
From the simplicity and purity of his character, he

was called the maiden king; and of him St. Godric said, that Malcolm and St. Thomas were more acceptable to God than any men between the north and the Alps.[1] For both these reasons Aelred loved him, and was enabled to do him a service which Henry's armies could never have effected. When Malcolm returned from France, whither, with a boyish ardour for war, he had accompanied his cousin Henry, he found his nobles everywhere in revolt, war in the wild clans of the Highlands, and war in Galloway. His people did not like his intimacy with the English monarch, and Malcolm was almost looked upon as a foreigner. He, however, quelled the rising of the Highlands, and expelled the savage inhabitants of Moray, and substituted for them some of his more peaceable Lowland subjects; he reduced his revolted nobles, and Galloway alone remained. In three pitched battles he beat these turbulent Galwegian clans in one year, and the country was reduced to a precarious state of peace. But the cause of the evil still remained, and unless he could have expelled the people, as he had done those of Moray, it seemed likely to remain. The people were the remnants of the ancient Picts, and resisted all the efforts of the Scottish king to

[1] From the connection which undoubtedly existed between Whiterne, the See of Galloway and St. Aelred, it seems exceedingly likely that he persuaded Fergus to retire, though the writer of the life in Capgrave mixes up two events together. It is certain from Fordun, 8, 4, that Fergus did take the habit of a canon at Holyrood, but the dissensions which took place in his family to which he refers, did not happen till after Aelred's death, in the reign of William. Fordun, 8, 25, 39. The revolt of Fergus occurred soon after Henry's expedition to Toulouse, probably in the year 1160, which is the date given in the Chronicle of Holyrood. Ang. Sac. i. 161.

civilise them. Vice seemed so thoroughly engrained into their character that even Christianity had not expelled it. An Abbot of Rievaux, however, might venture amidst the savage tribes of Galloway; Aelred's name was well known all over the border, and even the vicious chieftains of the country felt awed by his simple dignity. It is not known what special cause took Aelred into Galloway. The old bishopric of Whiterne had just been re-established, and the regular canons, who had been introduced, had a great love and reverence for him. He had certainly visited them, and had written the Life of St. Ninian, the founder of the See. It seems that he even knew the dialect of this wild region, for the original life of the Saint was in their language. At all events, all Scotland had heard of the holy Abbot of Rievaux, who had once been high steward to King David; and Fergus, the chieftain of Galloway, knew very well who he was when he saw the white habit approach this mountain fastness. Aelred negotiated a permanent peace with the dangerous chief. This was a strange diplomacy, but a most successful one. Fergus surrendered himself into the hands of Malcolm, but instead of being put to death for his revolt, he was allowed to take the habit of a canon in the monastery of the Holyrood, at Edinburgh.

This is almost the last of the scanty notices of Aelred's life which have been left on record. In the same year in which he rendered this signal service to Scotland, occurred the council of Pavia, and in his sermons to the brethren in the Advent of that year, he mourns bitterly over the miserable schism which was dividing the Church, and declares

his unshaken adherence to Alexander.   The whole
Cistercian order was interested in the contest, for
their brethren in Germany were suffering persecution at the hands of Frederic for their fidelity to
the rightful successor of St. Peter.   There is a deep
and almost prophetic melancholy about the words
of Aelred to his monks, when he applies the words
of the prophet Isaiah to his own times, " Behold the
day of the Lord cometh, the sun shall be darkened
in his going forth, and the moon shall not cause
her light to shine."   " Ah ! brethren," he says, " the
Lord hath created two great lights in the firmament
of the holy Church, the priesthood and the kingdom.
The greater light is the priesthood to rule the day
—that is, spiritual things ; the lesser light is the
kingdom, to rule the night of worldly things.   It is
an unnatural thing if the sun rule the night, if the
priest should draw over the clear light of his conscience, the night of worldly matters ; or if the moon
should rule the day, the king should meddle with
the administration of the sacraments."   And thus
in words rather of sorrow than of anger, he bids
the bishops of the time remember St. Dunstan and
St. Cuthbert.   The contest between Henry and the
Church had not yet begun ; St. Thomas was not
yet Archbishop ; but in Aelred's mournful words,
in which he asks the courtier prelates of the time,
how they could be martyrs who were ambitious and
ashamed of poverty, it might seem as if he foresaw
how in time of persecution they would fall away, as
indeed they did.   And again, in the same sorrowful
manner he speaks of the kingly power, " Then shall
the moon be turned into blood when the hands

of the prince are full of blood, when they take away the right of the just man, and follow not equity, but their own lusts and anger." Both Henry and the prelate, to whom these sermons are dedicated, Gilbert Foliot, the memorable Bishop of London, might have taken warning by these words.

Aelred, too, in the same discourses, takes a long farewell of his brethren, as he was setting out to the general chapter of the year at Citeaux. He seems to feel that his life was precarious, and he bids his children pray for him, " for it is my wish," he says, " to lay down among you the tabernacle of my flesh, and pour out my spirit in your hands, that you may close the eyes of your father, and my bones may be laid in the grave under your eyes." He wished that his tomb, with his crosier sculptured on it, should catch the eyes of his brethren, that they might say a prayer for Abbot Aelred, as they passed it in chapter. Aelred might well fear when he was going on so long a journey, lest he should never see Rievaux again; for many years before his death, one account says ten, he was afflicted with a terrible chronic disease, apparently the stone. He did, however, return from Citeaux, and lived for six years after this journey; but they were years of pain and of living death. Very little is known of this period of his life except that he suffered, and that he died. He does not appear to have given up his functions, at least in the commencement of his disease, for the journeys both to Galloway and to Burgundy come within the period of his sufferings; and to the last he seems to have been able to celebrate mass, but at times his pains were most acute. One account represents him as sitting on a mat before the fire, with his head between his knees, bowed down with pain ; and during the year before his death, after celebrating mass, he used to remain for a whole hour on his bed, unable to speak or move. Still his spirit rose above his wasted and emaciated body ; he spent his time in constant prayer and meditation on the Holy Scriptures. He had said before, in sermons preached in the beginning of his disorder, "Brethren, I tell you, no misfortune can I suffer, nothing sad or bitter arise, which by the opening of the Holy Scriptures cannot be made to vanish, or be borne with greater ease. How often, sweet Jesus, does my day turn into evening ; how often does intolerable pain, like the darkness of night, succeed to the feeble light of consolation. All things become tasteless ; all that I see is a burthen to me. But I go to meditate in Thy fields, I turn over the sacred page, then does Thy grace, sweet Jesus, drive away the darkness with its light, do away with weariness, and then do tears succeed to groans, and heavenly joy follows tears." St. Augustine's Confessions was also always in his hands ; tears were ever flowing from his eyes, and his thoughts were ever fixed on his Lord, for whom he had given up all things earthly. It was no wonder, that while he thus only held to earth by a body which was a perpetual crucifixion to him, the brethren, as they passed the cell of their father, heard his voice speaking, and other voices answering, which by their sweetness they took to be those of angels. At length, about the feast of the blessed St. Laurence, whose martyrdom he had so long imitated by his patient endurance of excruciating pain, his loving and gentle spirit was released from its sufferings, to the presence of Him whom he had seen on earth, reflected, however darkly, in the glass of love.[1]

When the news of Aelred's death came to the Abbey of Swineshead, in Lincolnshire, Gilbert, the Abbot, was preaching on that verse of the Song of Solomon, " I am come into my garden, my sister, my spouse ; I have gathered my myrrh with my spice ; I have eaten my honeycomb with my honey ; I have drank my wine with my milk." Gilbert was Aelred's friend, and knew him well, and broke forth into these words, " Large and copious is that honeycomb, which in these days has passed to the banquet of the Lord, I mean the lord Abbot of Rievaux, news of whose death has been brought to us, while we are commenting on this passage. Methinks that in him, now that he has been taken away, this garden of ours has been laid bare, and a large bundle of its myrrh has been gathered by the Lord, its husbandman. No such honeycomb is now left in our hive. Who more pure in his life, more wise in his doctrine ? Who more suffering in body, more

---

[1] 1166 is the common date given for St. Aelred's death ; but the Chronicle of Melrose gives 1167 ; and in the account of Byland Abbey, given in Dugdale, it appears that the year 1197 was the thirtieth year after his death. He is commonly said to have died on the 12th of January, but the reason of this is probably because his festival was appointed for that day ; no contemporary authority fixes it to that time, while Gilbert, of Hoyland, in a sermon delivered in the octave of the feast of St. Laurence, says that St. Aelred had died " in these days," and that the news had just reached him. It should be added that in a martyrology put out by Benedict XIV., St. Aelred's feast is appointed to be kept in March.

unwearied in spirit! His mouth, like the honeycomb, poured forth the words of honied wisdom. His flesh was sick with a lingering disease, but his soul within him dwelt with a lingering love on heavenly things. While his flesh, on fire with pain, was burning like myrrh, his soul was on fire with a flame, fed with the precious gum of charity; and both together rose up in a perpetual incense of unwearied love. His body was shrivelled and wasted, but his soul was filled with marrow and fatness; therefore will he ever praise the Lord with joyful lips. His mouth was like an honeycomb, dropping honey, for with his whole soul on his lips he used to pour forth the calm feelings of his heart, with his countenance serene, and his measured gestures indicating inward peace. His intellect was clear, and his speech thoughtful. He was modest in his questions, and more modest in his answers. Patiently did he bear with those who were troublesome, although himself a trouble to none; and while he was acute in seeing what was wrong, he was long before he noticed it, and patient in bearing it. Often have I seen him, when any of those who sat near him broke rudely on his words, suspend what he had to say, till the other had wasted his breath; and then when the rude torrent of wearisome speech was passed, he would take up again his words where he had left them off, with the same calmness as he had waited. He was swift to hear and slow to speak. Not that he could be said to be slow to wrath, for he had no wrath at all. A sweet honeycomb was he of whom I speak, overflowing with the honey which was within. His mind was full of cells, and he dropped his sweetness everywhere, from the comb where he had stored up matter for what he said ; and many men are living still who have tasted of his sweetness. In his doctrine he looked not for that wearisome subtlety which has more to do with disputation than instruction. Moral science was what he studied and put out in elegant words ; he was well versed also in the language of the spiritual life, which he was wont to explain among those who were perfect. His doctrine was milk for the consolation of the simple, with which however, he often mixed the wine of words, which rejoiced the heart. So did his teaching, though simple as milk, carry away the hearts of his hearers as though they were drunk with the wine of spiritual gladness. We must mourn that such a man has been taken from us, but still we may rejoice that we have sent forth such a bundle of myrrh from our poor gardens, to the garden of heaven. There he is now an ornament, who was a help to us upon earth."

This is a portrait of St. Aelred, for so we may now call him, drawn by one who knew him, while the recollection was fresh upon him. It may help us to get a clear idea even of his features, pallid and drawn as they were by sickness ; and at all events it gives a vivid picture of his mind, pouring itself out in little offices of love, notwithstanding his pains of body. Every history and every tradition presents the same idea, and marks him as the holy and loving Abbot, well skilled in healing hearts broken by grief, or wounded by sin. Others come down to us as holy Bishops, Martyrs, or Confessors, but St. Aelred was pre-eminently the Abbot of England.

CHAPTER IX

CISTERCIAN TEACHING

THOUGH we have now gone through the life of St. Aelred, as far as time has spared it, and we may look upon the blessed Saint as having gone to his rest, yet in one sense he still lives to us, not only by his intercessions but in his writings, which have remained to us. He is the great Cistercian writer of England, and in this point of view we have still to look upon not only himself, but the whole intellectual movement of which he was a portion. At first sight, it would seem as if Cistercians had little or nothing to do with literature or philosophy. It was by giving up worldly studies that both St. Bernard and St. Aelred became Cistercians; and philosophy was a portion of the sacrifice which they made to God on assuming the white habit.[1] St. Bernard left the schools of Chatillon to go to Citeaux; he had there been the best poet in the school,[2] and the many quotations from the classics found in his writings, show what he really had given up in sacrificing his taste and intellect to religion; and the same was the case with St. Aelred. The only case in which a Cistercian was allowed

[1] Vit. St. Bern. lib. i. 1.
[2] Berengar. Apol. St. Bernard often quotes Persius.

to pursue regular studies, after becoming a monk, was that of Otto[1] of Frisingen, and he, when he became a princely Bishop, retained much more of the scion of the house of Hohenstauffen, than of the pupil of St. Stephen. It is remarkable, too, that the scholars at Paris at first listened unmoved to St. Bernard's eloquence, and to the rough syllogisms which he propounded to them on their violation of God's holy law; Mount St. Genevieve and Citeaux seem from the first to have been in secret opposition.[2] Still the Cistercian reform seemed likely to go on its own way, without clashing directly with the schools, had not St. Bernard been forced out of his cloister of Clairvaux, to oppose the rationalism which was dominant within them, in the person of Abelard. Europe might have anticipated its history by four centuries had it not been for St. Bernard. Abelard's was not a clear and distinct heresy, which could be put in a tangible shape like the Arian or Nestorian. It was a wide-spreading rationalism, sound only by accident on any point, and claiming exemption from all condemnation, on the ground that it was only one way of putting Christianity. It was no heresy, was its plea, but a bright and dazzling display of intellectual activity. The human mind had just awakened from a long sleep, and had become more

---

[1] Otto never misses an opportunity of bringing in metaphysics in his History of Frederic Barbarossa. He evidently thought that Gilbert de la Porée had been harshly treated. It should be said for him that he died at Morimond, and on his death-bed protested his submission to the Church in all that he had said about Gilbert.

[2] Exord. Mag. b. vii. 13, and Vincent of Beauvais quoted in Manriquez in ann. 1122.

philosophical.   It had learned not only its Horace
and its Virgil, but its Aristotle too, and it must not
be stinted in the use of its newly-found treasures.

Now it was true, to a certain extent, that the
twelfth century was the beginning of a new intellectual era ; things immediately before it had been
dark, not that God had ever suffered His truth to
be darkened in His church, but that it was many
centuries before the barbarians, who had seized on
the Western empire, had leisure to spare for learning, sacred or profane.   The Church had enough
to do to teach them the faith.   She had to fight
hard to prevent herself being merged in the body
politic, into which, with desperate throes, society
was forming itself.   But when once that struggle
was over, and the crosier was clearly separated
from the sceptre, then began a more fearful struggle.
Men had leisure to philosophise upon the faith
which they had learned, and just at that time a
great revival of ancient learning took place.   Aristotle and Plato symbolised for them what had lain
undeveloped in their minds ; here were categories
formed, and genera and species classified.   They
thought that they had got a new organ for the
discovery of truth.   It was a new field, like an unknown world, a crusade into the regions of thought.
The syllogistic form was given, and matter was all
that was to be found.   They were not slow in finding
it ; there was matter enough for dispute in their
new philosophy itself.   Poor human nature ! hardly
had it obtained possession of its new treasure, when
it began to doubt of its reality.   There were genera
and species in plenty ; but how far were they the

real representation of external objects, or only our way of viewing them? It was an important question; it was asking, in fact, whether our idea of external things was the true one; or in the words of modern philosophy, how much was objective, how much subjective truth. But Clairvaux and Rievaux had nothing to do with either Realism or Nominalism, and we pass them by. As long as the schools confined themselves to metaphysics, their din probably did not even reach the Cistercian cloister. But in the middle ages, men were not Realists and Nominalists by halves, many of them pushed their principles into their notions of the Blessed Trinity itself. It was a fearful moment for the church. Here was humanity exulting in the discovery of a class of truths which it had forgotten. It was leaping with somewhat fantastic gestures about its new domain, when it came across it to inquire whether it was quite lawful ground. Certain it was that Nominalism, when applied to the highest Christian doctrine, became a sort of Sabellianism,[1] and Realism took the form of a new and nameless heresy. Here then was truth, as they thought, meeting truth face to face, and the fear or doubt presented itself with which they were to side.

At this juncture, there arose a man who attempted to reconcile, after his fashion, the Church and the intellect of the age. This man was Peter Abelard, who is to be considered as the personification of the bold and restless acuteness of the schools, as well as of the worldly-spirited clerks of the time.[2] This

---

[1] Petavius calls it the heresy of the Nominalists.

[2] Héloise says to him, Quid te Canonicum et Clericum facere oportet. c. vii. Hist. Calam. Tanti quippe tam nominis eram et

novel doctor was a canon of the Church, and at the same time a gay and handsome cavalier, whose love-songs and dialectics were equally in fashion. His first exploit was to banish from the schools the Realism which he found there. All was plain and easy to him; the ideas of the soul were but arbitrary classifications emanating from itself; they were real as conceptions, but nothing more. In this way it would follow, that rationality was no more the essence of man than the power of laughing, and it was only in our way of looking upon it, that either could be the differentia of the class.[1] Abelard gained his point; he completely won the day, and beat his master, William of Champeaux, out of the field; but he did not see that, like all other Rationalism, his system introduced a scepticism far deeper than itself. He did not see, that come what may of it, our ideas are the way in which we view the external world, and if they are merely arbitrary, and not in some way a representation of the truth, then we know nothing of any object beyond ourselves. However, as yet, he was but the bold and successful innovator, the idol of the schools, the triumphant logician; but when he afterwards hid his head in the cloister of St. Denis, when Héloise, with bitter regrets for the world which she was leaving,[2] had

juventutis et formæ gratia preeminebam, ut quamcunque fœminarum nostro dignarer amore, nullam vererer repulsam. c. vi. Quorum etiam carminum plerisque adhuc regionibus decantantur. Ibid.

[1] Abelard seems to say this when he makes each individual to have his own form; for instance, in the language of the times, he makes Socratitas to be the form of Socrates. This is true in one sense, but he seems to deny that humanitas is, in any real sense, his form, and he makes a separate form for each part, rationalitas, bipedalitas, etc.

[2] Tua me ad habitum traxit passio, non Dei dilectio. Ep. 4.

taken the veil at Argenteuil, then the conceited
logician became the dangerous theologian. He
must needs remodel theology! the old school was
worn out.[1] It was founded on faith; Plato and
Aristotle would laugh at such a religion, and Abelard
was ashamed of it. He would have a new religion
founded on irrefragable argument, to suit the philosophic mind.[2] Thus he strove to allay the sudden
recoil of his contemporaries upon themselves, the
fright of humanity balancing between its reason and
its faith. Two great schoolmen made shipwreck
of their faith; this he was not disposed to do, for
with his great and glaring faults, his overweening
conceit, and his whole soul still scarred with sins,
and, as yet, unhealed by his forced repentance, still,
to do him justice, he would have been orthodox if
he could. He therefore wished to make out that
faith and reason were identical. He bade the youthful schoolmen, the men of march of mind, go on
and prosper. There was no cause for alarm. The
Christian was after all the great logician, and faith
only an intellectual opinion about things unseen.[3]
They need have no divided love between Aristotle

[1] He tries to prove by the example of St. Paul that difficulty of faith
is a merit. Cito autem sive facile credit qui indiscrete atque improvide
his quæ scivit prius acquisivit quam hoc in quod persuadetur ignota
ratione quantum valet discutiat an adhibere ei fidem conveniat. Introd.
ad Theol. 1060.

[2] Abelard is continually inconsistent with himself, often using
orthodox language, and protesting that he means nothing against the
faith of the Church, while his words are glaringly opposed to it. On
his inconsistency, see St. Bernard's Letter to Innocent.

[3] Abelard Op. vol. i. 3, 28. Ed. Amb. Verbum Dei quod Græci
λόγον vocant, solum Christum dicimus. Hinc et juxta nominis ety-
mologiam, quicunque huic vero Verbo inherent vere Logici sunt. In

and Christianity. Plato indeed was a Christian, and a much better one than Moses and the Prophets, for he had foreseen and made out for himself the doctrine of the Holy Trinity.[1]

Oh, foolish Abelard! he did not know what he himself was doing. If the human intellect could make out the blessed truth for itself, how knew he that it was not the creator of it? How knew he that the doctrine of the ever-blessed Trinity itself was not an emanation from the mind of man, framing to itself its own conception of the supreme good?[2] If he had looked on a few centuries, he would have seen in the same way a certain philosophy make out that the existence of God might be but the product of the human intellect at play with its own notions. But intellect itself would have told him that such matters were not within its jurisdiction; it can mount up indeed through earth and heaven up to the nature of God Himself; but it can only say that such things as it conceives, may be. To rule that they are, is not its office. And so almost by the force of reason, Abelard was compelled to

another place, Charitas Dei per fidem sive rationis donum infusa. Introd. ad Theol. 1027.

[1] Dum multum sudat quo modo Platoneum faciat Christianum, se probat Ethnicum. St. Bern. de err. Ab. c. iv. v. Martenne Thes. nov. Anecd. 5. p. 1152.

[2] Abelard does seem to say so of the Holy Trinity. Videtur autem nobis suprapositis personarum nominibus summi boni perfectio diligenter esse descripta ; ut cum videlicet prædicatur Deum esse Pater et Filius et Spiritus Sanctus, eum summum bonum atque in omnibus perfectum hac distinctione Trinitatis intelligamus. Introd. 1, 7. It may, however, be said of Abelard, that in other places he neutralises what at first sight seems Sabellianism. The language of a late biographer of St. Bernard, who almost makes Abelard his hero, is more unequivocally wrong.

say that in his Introduction to Theology he did not profess to give the truth, but only his opinion of it. His Theology was a mere intellectual exercise, a keen encounter of wits, like a disputation in the schools. Faith itself he defined to be an *opinion* on things unseen. It happened to Abelard as might have been expected; his reason broke under the gigantic task, like an inapt instrument applied to a work which it was never meant to perform. In the attempt to explain the doctrines of the Church in perfect conformity with human reason, he explained them away.[1] By another natural and almost logical consequence of his attempt, he not only shook the certainty of the faith, but he erred grievously in his exposition of it. And no wonder, authority to the theologian is what axioms and postulates are to the mathematician. It contains the data, without which he cannot stir a step. He then that would enfranchise theology from authority, must enfranchise Christianity from revelation; and freedom from the Church in theology is like freedom from numbers in arithmetic. If Abelard had, on throwing away authority, become a sceptic, he would at least have been consistent; but to throw it away and to expect to do as well without it was folly indeed.

Abelard was half conscious of his inconsistency, and felt it necessary to defend himself. How can we believe, he says, what we do not understand?[2] The Church, by putting its doctrine into

[1] Existimatio non apparentium. Introd. ad Theol. p. 977, 1061. Non tam nos veritatem dicere quam opinionis nostræ sensum quem efflagitant promulgare, p. 974, v. also 1047.

[2] Quid ad doctrinam proficit, si quod loqui volumus exponi non potest ut intelligatur. 985.

words, presents them to our understanding, and
the Holy Fathers have used similes and metaphors,
so as to bring them down to the level of our
thoughts and to confute reasoners. Why then
might not the phraseology and the metaphors be
perfect expressions of what they meant, if they
were to be used at all? And this was what he
attempted to do ; he tried to make ecclesiastical
phraseology more intellectual, under the notion that
unless it was a perfect expression of divine things,
it must be false. And he proceeds to attack St.
Augustine, St. Hilary, and St. Anselm, for using
imperfect metaphors on the subject of the Trinity
and the Incarnation.[1] But the Blessed Saints
knew far better than Abelard, how imperfect were
their words ;[2] but they had to choose between saying that truth was unattainable, or that it was
attainable as far as we can bear. The comparisons
which they used were not mere metaphors, but a
tracing out, in the creation, of shadows and types,
of which God is the reality and the antitype. So
too, human terminology, even though used by the
Church, can but most faintly express the nature
of the Incomprehensible Godhead, which eludes
the grasp of words and ideas. And yet words
are expressions of ideas, and ideas are expressions of the truth. Categories are the laws of

[1] Of St. Anselm he has the impudence to say, St. Anselmi similitudo
suffragatur hæresi. 1085.

[2] Tendebam in Deum et offendi in meipsum. St. Ans. Proslog. 1.
Ego certi scio quam multa figmenta pariat cor humanum, et quid est
cor meum nisi cor humanum. de Trin. 4, i. Jam de iis quæ nec
dicuntur ut cogitantur, nec cogitantur ut sunt, respondere incipiamus.
De Trin. 5, 4.

our thoughts, and every man knows what he means when he uses the terms Substance and Relation. They are our way of viewing things, but they are real though they are ours. Much more when used of the everlasting God are they real and objective. God is a Substance in a higher and truer sense than we can know, and the eternal Relations between the Persons of the adorable Trinity are not mere notions of our minds, but real and true in a transcendent sense surpassing all human thought.

Abelard therefore was wrong in supposing, that because ecclesiastical phraseology was imperfect, that therefore it was false. On the contrary, since God is incomprehensible, Abelard's notion of the divine nature was necessarily false, since it pretended to be perfect. Again, he could never be sure that in adoring God, he was not in reality worshipping his own conception of the Deity, for on his own showing it might be an idea created by his intellect. But St. Augustine and St. Anselm knew that they were adoring the one true and right conception of Almighty God, which they had received from without, from the Holy Church who had embodied it in words. They therefore had a right to reason upon the faith, which Abelard had not; for he had no data on which to philosophise. Their aim was to make the faith of the Church as intellectual as that which is above intellect is capable of being; Abelard tried to reduce it to the perfect level of the intellect, and after having fused it in this earthly crucible, he found that it had become, not the faith of the Church, but something else. But the

Saint of Hippo might be bold, for he had long contemplated and adored the ever-blessed mystery, and he knew by loving faith that his burning heart looked not on an abstraction. The idea which he had received from the Church had grown upon him in beauty and intensity the more he had looked upon it. He therefore knew well what he did, when he answered the opponents of the blessed truth by reasoning. He bade them look on their own souls, and see whether they understood themselves; and after confounding them with their ignorance of their own nature, he bids them not despair.[1] Human nature is indeed a mystery, and yet it is the image of God. It is not a mere simile, but it is a true representation of God; imperfect but not unreal. It contains within itself a trinity, a faint shadow of the everlasting Trinity; yet shadow though it be, it does give us a true insight, as far it goes, of the adorable mystery. And after all his efforts the Saint sinks upon his knees, and confesses his inability to comprehend this mighty Truth. So too St. Anselm;[2] if by reason alone he professed to seek for God, it was because he knew that he had found Him already. To every word that he used he communicated the intensity of his own idea, so that they ceased to be mere words, and received a reality which they did not possess in

---

[1] Cum in his quæ nostris corporalibus objacent sensibus, vel quod nos ipsi in interiore homine sumus, scientia comprehendendis laboremus nec sufficiamus, nec tamen impudenter in illa quæ supra sunt divina et ineffabilia pietas fidelis ardescit. De Trin. 5. 1.

[2] Puto quia ea ipsa ex magna parte, si vel mediocris ingenii est potest ipse sibi saltem sola ratione persuadere.—Monolog. 1. Ratione ejus (Roscellini) error demonstrandus est. De Fide in Trin. 3.

themselves. But Abelard was neither St. Augustine
nor St. Anselm, but only Peter Abelard. He did
not choose to be a Christian doctor, so he became
something very like a heretic; and so he might
have died, had not St. Bernard arisen to save
him from becoming an heresiarch.

The first condemnation of Abelard at Soissons
did not proceed from St. Bernard. It seems to
have come from the teachers of the old school,
whose influence he had destroyed.[1] His accusers
were no match for him in learning, and he con-
victed them of ignorance and mistakes in theology;
and in the end he seems to have been condemned
in an arbitrary way. St. Bernard does not seem
at first to have been unfavourably disposed to
Abelard; he visited the monastery of the Paraclete,
of which Héloise was Abbess, and which was under
Abelard's direction, and the nuns were rejoiced to
see him. He does not appear to have read his
works until they were sent to him by his friend
William of St. Thierry.[2] "Of these things," he says

---

[1] There seems no reason to doubt Abelard's own graphic account of
the council of Soissons, in his Historia Calamitatum. Berengarius's
attack upon the Bishops who were present cannot be trusted in detail,
from its manifest exaggeration, but its tone is that of a man attacking
the love of ease of a high and dry school in authority. Berengarius's
work is curious, as a specimen of a middle-age pamphlet. It is a
flippant and profane attack on St. Bernard, which its author was
obliged to defend in his maturer years by treating as a joke. Si
quid in personam hominis Dei dixi, joco legatur non serio. In the
same place, he excuses himself by saying that Aristotle attacked
Socrates, and St. Jerome attacked St. Augustine. Ep. 18, inter ep.
Abael. vol. i.

[2] It seems as if St. Bernard's attack on Abelard had been placed
rather too early. It is true that Abelard points him out as his opponent before he became Abbot of St. Gildas, but from St. Bernard's

to William, " I have hardly heard anything." It was during Lent that the Abbot's book came to him, and he would not break off the quiet of the season by plunging into Abelard's Introduction to Theology. But when Lent was over, and he had thoroughly examined the question, the whole importance of the matter burst upon him. Abelard's doctrines had spread far and wide ; men from all parts of Europe flocked to his lectures ; his books had crossed the seas, and were read beyond the Alps. There was a dangerous Rationalism infecting the intellectual youth of the rising generation. It had even spread among the cardinals, and Abelard had a party in the sacred college itself. It was high time to oppose the evil ; and none was so able to do so as St. Bernard. None had such an instinctive perception of Christian doctrine, or was more capable of laying his finger precisely on the question at issue. It was not hard, therefore, for a mind like his to see the shallowness of Abelard's principles. Nothing is more certain than that opinion and faith are not the same thing ; it is a mere fact that the Saints are as sure of the reality of their faith as of an object perceived by the senses, while opinion, by its very nature, is not certainty. And this was a fact which Abelard overlooked ;

own letters it is evident that he took no active part against him until his return to France from Brittany. And certain it is, that the same Abelard, apparently before he established himself permanently a second time at the Paraclete, but certainly after his retirement to St. Gildas, writes to St. Bernard about the Charitas qua me præcipue amplecteris. Abael. Op. p. vol. i. p. 224. Again, William of Thierry finds it necessary to exhort St. Bernard strongly not to allow affection to prevent his taking an active part against Abelard.

whether rightly or wrongly, faith is entirely independent of reason. Intellect, indeed, has a certainty
of its own in its own sphere, in matters which are
absolutely true or absolutely false ; but no one
would pretend that such is the case with the
subjects treated of in Christian doctrine, for they
are above intellect.[1] Abelard might, indeed, have
said that truth about the nature of God was unattainable on earth, but to say that it was attainable
by reason alone was manifestly untrue.

This was the moral of all Cistercian teaching, and
the history of their quarrel with the schools ; they
taught men to seek certainty elsewhere. "The
Spirit of God will lead you into all truth. What
means all Truth ?" said a voice, heard one Advent
in the cloister of Rievaux. "It means that one
truth which makes all things true. For in one
sense, all things that are are true ; for whatever
is false is not at all. But that truth into which
the apostles were brought, was that in which all
things are, and which is in all things, in which
there is nothing false, nothing ambiguous, nothing
deceptive ; and this Truth is seen by the heart,
not by the flesh." And that this line of teaching
was the right one to save the age from Rationalism,
was proved by the event. Abelard's influence
melted before St. Bernard. He challenged the
Saint to dispute with him at the Council of
Soissons. St. Bernard at first refused to dispute
with one who had been trained to disputation
from his youth ; besides it was a question of

[1] Quod intellexisti non est de eo quod ultra quæras, aut si est non
intellexisti. De Cons. 5, 3.

authority, not of disputation. At length, however, when he found that the truth was likely to suffer from his refusal, he consented, at the instance of his friends, with tears in his eyes, determined, according to our Lord's rule, not to think beforehand what he should say. When the day came, the town of Soissons was crowded with men from all parts of France. The king and the Bishops were there, and on the other hand the noisy and tumultuous men of the schools, the partisans of Abelard. All the world was there to witness the encounter between the two first men of the age, the representatives of opposite principles. To the surprise of all, after St. Bernard had given an account of the opinion to be canvassed, Abelard, instead of replying, appealed to the Pope. Abelard had himself given the challenge, and was not a man wont to be intimidated. Besides, St. Bernard, who once stopped a persecution raised against the Jews, was not a likely man to allow any violence to be used against Abelard's person, either by king or populace. One account, however, says that he appealed to Rome, from dread of a popular tumult. Another account says, that when he attempted to speak, his memory failed him and he could not utter a word. Amidst these conflicting accounts, it is safest to judge by the result. Abelard started on his way to Rome to support the appeal which he had made ; it was by no means a desperate case, for he had, as has been noticed above, a party in the Sacred College. But by the time that he had got as far as Cluny, his heart had failed him ; there appears in many passages of his writings a hesitation, as though if he could but have reconciled Aristotle and the Church, he would have been orthodox ; his conscience was not at rest, and the sight of St. Bernard at the council had awakened it anew. His had been a long and weary life, made up of headstrong passions and signal misfortunes ; and his troubled spirit longed for rest. When therefore the Abbot of Citeaux came to Cluny, and offered to make his peace with St. Bernard, Abelard was prepared to make a confession of faith which was equivalent to a retractation of his errors ; and when the Pope's letter arrived condemning his opinions, it found him already prepared to submit. Abelard, broken in health and spirit, lived for three years in the peaceful cloister of Cluny, and died a sincere penitent in 1142.

Thus most effectually did Cistercian teaching fulfil its task. Abelard left no school behind him. His work in the schools had been simply one of destruction. His teaching had nothing positive ; and when once he had hidden himself in the cloister of Cluny, nothing more is heard of him.

It was easy therefore to confute Abelard so far ;[1] but St. Bernard had another task to perform. How were the sons of the Church to recover a healthy tone after being spoiled by this baneful teaching?[2]

---

[1] St. Bernard went straight to the point when he attacked Abelard as holding opinions contrary to reason, as well as to faith. Quid enim, he says, magis contra rationem, quam ratione rationem conari transcendere.

[2] The Abbé Ratisbonne, in his beautiful Life of St. Bernard, compares Abelard's doctrines to Kant's Antinomies of pure reason. This is paying Abelard's philosophical powers a great compliment. He is much more like Locke on the Reasonableness of Christianity.

For this purpose it was not enough to refute, or even to substitute truth for error, they must also learn to love the truth. And to effect this was the object of all Cistercian teaching. A moral discipline was required to heal the diseased will. With a philosophy, in reality far deeper than that of Abelard, though it did not profess to be philosophy at all, St. Bernard made the acceptance of religious truth to depend upon the will. Faith he defined to be a willing and certain foretaste of a truth not yet made manifest. Truth is offered for acceptance, not to the intellect, but to the conscience. The Church does for us the office of the intellect; it puts the faith for us into an intelligible form. And so the creed, the intellectual object, as it may be called, of our faith, comes to us from without. It is a certain, definite, and substantive thing, embodied in words by the Church, and coming to us in a clear, unbroken sound, for the Church speaks but one language. Just as words are to us the interpretation of what we feel, by giving us a classification for our sensations, so do the words of the Holy Church interpret for us what we know of God. But St. Bernard went deeper than this; the real and heavenly object of our faith comes to us through the Sacraments, and so God Himself is the real cause of our knowledge of Him; and it is love, by which we are united to Him, which fills up, as it were, the outline of the Church, and gives a meaning to our imperfect words beyond what they have of their own nature. Love, therefore, is the proper antidote to Rationalism; and St. Bernard did much more towards healing the wounds of the

Church, when he preached his Sermons on the
Canticles, than when he refuted Abelard, in his
letter to Pope Innocent. Why, indeed, should he
seek by premiss and conclusion for Him whom he
has found already by love? " To those who thus
seek him," says St. Bernard,[1] "the Lord cries out,
Noli me tangere, Touch me not ; that is, Quit this
erring sense ; lean on the Word, learn to go by
faith : faith, which cannot err ; which seizes on
what is invisible, feels not the need of sense, passes
the bounds of human reason, the use of nature, the
bonds of experience. Why ask the eye for what
it cannot see? Why stretch forth the hand to
grope for what is above it? Let faith pronounce
of me what is not unworthy of my majesty. Learn
to hold for certain, to follow in safety, what it
teaches thee. Touch me not ; for I have not yet
ascended to my Father. As if when He has once
ascended, He would either be willing to be loved,
or we capable of touching him. Yea, but thou
shalt be capable, by love, not by the touch ; by
desire, not by the eye ; by faith, not by sense.
Faith in the depth of its mystic bosom comprehends
what is the length and breadth, and depth and
height. Thou shalt touch Him with the hand of
faith, the finger of desire, the embrace of devotion ;
thou shalt touch Him with the eye of the heart.
And will He then be black?[2] Nay, the beloved
is white and red. Beautiful exceedingly is He who
is surrounded with the red flowers of the rose and
the white lily of the valleys, that is, the choirs of
martyrs and of virgins ; and who, sitting in the

[1] In Cant. 28.   [2] Song of Solomon, i. 5.

midst of them, is himself both a virgin and a martyr. Ten thousand times ten thousand are around Him, but needest thou fear lest thou shouldst mistake some other for Him, when thou seekest Him whom thou lovest? Nay, thou wilt not hesitate whom to select out of them all. Easily wilt thou recognise Him out of the thousands more beautiful than all; and thou wilt say, This is He that is glorious in His apparel, travelling in the multitude of His strength."

Before such teaching as this, no wonder that Rationalism fled away; cold and dead as it is, it cannot hold before warmth and life. But Cistercian teaching had a great influence on the Church after it. Its opposition to the scholastic method was most salutary; it gave a breathing time to the Church, and prepared it to receive the teaching of the great schoolmen of the thirteenth century. The church was not yet ready for the schools, or rather the schools were not ready for the church; men must learn to love the truth before they can safely philosophise upon it. St. Bernard and St. Aelred were not mere negative opponents of Rationalism; there is a great deal of positive theology in their works, dressed in the commanding eloquence of St. Bernard and the sweet language of St. Aelred. No one can read the masterly refutation of the Errors of Gilbert de la Porée without wondering at the acuteness as well as the deep knowledge of theology possessed by St. Bernard, the more wonderful because Gilbert's errors belong rather to the Pantheism of the thirteenth than to the Rationalism of the twelfth century. The ques-

tions so beautifully treated of in the Sermons on
the Canticles are precisely the same as those which
appear in the Summa of St. Thomas, how the
nature of God is very oneness, and there is nothing accidental in Him, how angels see all things
in the Word, how the soul of man is naturally
eternal, how grace differs from the substance of
the soul. In St. Aelred the same thing is observ-
able; none can help being struck with his clear
and orthodox language on the subject of the Incarnation, while he rejects what he calls scholastic
subtleties. The influence of St. Anselm is very
easily to be traced in his writings, so that in some
parts of his Mirror of Charity he is much more
of a schoolman than St. Bernard. Still it is true
that the office of the Cistercians was to oppose
the scholastic philosophy, which the age could not
as yet bear. Citeaux purified the schools by keeping
aloof from them; it was reserved for another order
to make an inroad into the schools themselves, and
to purify them by establishing Christ's banner in
the midst of them, and marking them with His cross.
Thus God ever in His goodness provides for the
wants of the Church. First came St. Anselm, the
saintly philosopher, to stir up the intellect of the
Church; and then St. Bernard and St. Aelred to
check the pride of intellect, and then last of all
the great Saint, who could safely doubt of all, for
he knew beforehand how to solve all doubts at the
foot of the crucifix, St. Thomas Aquinas.

LIFE OF

ST. NINIAN

BISHOP OF CANDIDA CASA
AND APOSTLE OF THE SOUTHERN PICTS
CIRC. A.D. 360–432

ADVERTISEMENT

Our knowledge of St. Ninian is chiefly owing to the Life of him by St. Aelred, which has been principally followed in these pages. Its genuineness was, indeed, questioned by the Bollandists, but apparently without any reason. It has been uniformly referred to as St. Aelred's by a long chain of English writers, nor is there any other known as such. The copy in the Bodleian Library is part of a MS. (Laud 668) containing works undoubtedly his, which was written within twenty years after his death; and one in the British Museum (MSS. Cotton. Tib. D. 3), of the close of the twelfth or beginning of the thirteenth century, distinctly attributes the authorship to him. The chief reason assigned by the Bollandists for doubting its genuineness is, that the opening words of their copy, which they do not quote, are not the same as those given by Pitseus as St. Aelred's. His words are "Multorum bonorum virorum." Those at the beginning of the Prologus in our MSS. are "Multis virorum sapientium." The difference is so slight that it would seem most probable, and from other considerations it is almost certain, that the person who made the copy for the Bollandists, overlooked, as he might easily do, the Prologus, and began with the Life, of which the first words are, "Gloriosissimam beati Niniani"; since in other respects their MS. appears to have been the same as ours.

The Service of St. Ninian's Day, from the Aberdeen Breviary, was not seen until this Life had nearly passed through the press. The historical references coincide almost entirely with what had been written, being derived for the most part from St. Aelred's Life. The only points which call for notice are, that the words "patriæ pater genuit patronum," which occur in a Responsary, look as if the Saint was considered to be a native of Galloway; and that the "brother," mentioned as the companion of his journeying, is called "collega," as if he had been a brother of his monastery, not a relation.

LIFE OF
ST. NINIAN

CHAPTER I

INTRODUCTION

How many of us have never heard of St. Ninian!
How many, on hearing of him, would carelessly put
aside the thought of his history, as a matter of no
concern, as a tale of former days, of what once was,
and is no longer, in any way which connects him
with us, or us with him. But this is a thoughtless
way of viewing any subject. All things may be
connected one with another; the works of former
times may have exercised an influence which still
lives. Still more is this the case with Saints. The
world passes away, and the works of the world, and
men, so far as they are of the world, and unite
themselves with the world, pass with it; but they
who are gifted with divine life, and united to Christ,
abide for ever; now more truly living than when
the world saw them.

If there be one whom the Church has recognised
as a Saint, there is a work of Divine Grace at which

we should pause, and turn aside, and view with
reverend awe; there is a child of Adam renewed
in the Divine image; one in whom a work has
been wrought, which is begun in many and per-
fected in few. His history, could we see it as it is
— his inward history—how eventful would it be;
how many a crisis would it involve! What motions
of Divine grace—what watchful Providences—what
a correspondence on his own part to the calls of
Heaven! What a precious tale of deeds and sufferings, of watchfulness and self-restraint, of prayers
and heavenly aspirations! How intense is the interest excited by examining some work of human
skill, and tracing its beauty, or contrivance, or
finished art! How full are the natural works of
God of all that is calculated to engage our attention,
to awaken surprise, delight, and admiration. With
how much more of deep feeling then should we
view the spiritual creation, and trace out there the
workings of providence and the effects of grace.
Beautiful as is the natural world, the fair budding
of spring, and the grass and trees, and the clear
shining after rain, they are but faint images indeed
of holy men, and of their varied graces, whose
sweetness Scripture shadows out by the choicest
objects of sense. And as we gratefully commemorate
the glory and goodness of God, as shown in these
passing works, still more should the manifold and
abiding graces of His Elect call forth our thankfulness and praise.

But, it may be said, little is known of St. Ninian.
It is true. Yet this might almost enhance our interest
in him, and our wish to know that little. How many

are there in every rank of life who pass from this world unrecognised, save by a few, yet high in the Divine favour and of great attainments in sanctity. That Saints should be distinguished in any marked way, seems to be owing to (what we may call) the accident of their being brought by circumstances into positions which have elicited their hidden graces, and manifested them to the world. But as their holiness is independent of its visible effects, so those effects are no measure of it. By the world, men are estimated for their influence on its fortunes; and in proportion as they have influenced it, is the degree of honour assigned them. But sanctity is independent of such outward manifestations or visible fruits. Though, in St. Ninian's case, if we believe those who in olden time so greatly venerated this holy man, there were not wanting abundant sensible tokens of his power and prevailing intercession. Even Protestant writers [1] allow that he had the gift of miracles, and the numerous worshippers at his shrine, three or four hundred years ago, believed, and would allege facts in proof, that they received blessings, even miraculous ones, through his prayers availing with God.

Among ourselves, there has been a long suspension of that everlasting remembrance in which the righteous ought to be held, that affectionate interest with which we ought to cherish those who in their day have laboured for the Church, and been marked by special gifts of grace. But it is not many centuries since the name of St. Ninian was one of the most honoured in the Calendar,

[1] The Magdeburg Centuriators, tom. 4, 1429.

and people flocked from every part of the island to visit his shrine. His memory has, indeed, had singular reverses. From the fifth to the twelfth century, it was scarcely known beyond the limits of the wild district where he had laboured and died. The only records of him were in the memory of his people, or written in a barbarous and unknown language. The succession of his See was interrupted. Successive tribes of uncivilised Celts occupied his country, and seemed to have obliterated almost every vestige of his earthly labours. But seven centuries passed, and his memory rose from its obscurity; his power was recognised, his shrine was frequented, and his intercessions sought. Amid the wild wars of Scotland and the Border, a safe conduct was provided for pilgrims who were visiting his church, and kings sought his prayers. Their piety was mixed, doubtless, according to the character of individuals, with even the grossest superstition; still it implied a general recognition of his sanctity; and the reason they would themselves have given of this devotion was, that they had experienced blessings through it; and that such was, in some instances, at least, the case, is the most natural and obvious account of the matter.

That little should have been known of his history need not surprise us. He lived in a dark period of British history, and laboured among a rude people. In the centuries following his death, Galloway was the scene of frequent wars, and changed its masters and its inhabitants. The Southern Picts whom he had converted were in time merged among the other races who inhabited the east of Scotland, and it was, as to the world's history, as if he had never lived. But this is not different from what we might expect. Of how many other distinguished Saints have few traces been left in history! Of how many of the holy Apostles is it merely recorded that they preached the gospel in certain remote districts, and were martyred! Of the fruits of their preaching, of the Churches they founded, no certain vestiges remain. Yet their names are written in heaven; their works are recorded there; and the souls who, through their means, though of distant ages and of barbarous languages, were brought into that Communion, where all learn one language, and are formed after one model, and are brethren and fellow-countrymen in Christ, are blessing and praising God for the mercy he showed in their conversion. It may be to the increase of their blessedness to be thus humbled; to have their works hidden from the world; that having no reward of human praise here, they may enjoy a more ample recompense in heaven.

Do not think slightingly then of St. Ninian because he is little known; but rather let us trace out with reverential love what may be learnt of him. We know more of him, and on better authority, than we do of many more exalted Saints; and if in searching out what may be known of him, we seem to be led into dry and antiquarian matter, let it not be an ungrateful labour. It may be repaid by the contemplation of his graces.

And there are circumstances which give a peculiar interest to St. Ninian. Besides his being one of our

own Saints, and the earliest Missionary, and first
Bishop in Scotland of whom we have any authentic
record, he lived at a time when there was a change
taking place in the mode in which conversions to
the faith were made. The barbarous nations were
now pouring in upon the Christians, and threaten-
ing the destruction of the empire of the Church, as
though it were not Christ's. St. Ninian was one of
the first of those who turned back the arms of the
invaders, and reduced them by meekness and truth,
under the gentle and happy sway of the gospel.
Again, conversions had hitherto been of individuals,
now they became national; that of the Picts was
one of the first. And the system on which missions were conducted in the countries of Europe
found one of their earliest types in him.

It may, indeed, very naturally be asked, what
do we really know of this ancient Saint, and, considering his age, country, and circumstances, what
authentic records can there be of the events of his
life?

Of the history of Britain at that time (the close
of the fourth and early part of the fifth century),
the notices, whether civil or ecclesiastical, are very
few, scanty, and unsatisfactory. It was St. Ninian's
lot to live at that critical period, when the Roman
power was breaking, and the empire was giving
way under internal divisions, and the inroads of
the Northern tribes. And Britain, which had been
raised from a wild and savage condition to considerable civilisation, was again to be thrown back
into a more miserable barbarism by the inunda-
tions of the Caledonians, and the occupation of the

Saxons. They were too much engaged in fighting to write narratives of what they did; and any memorials they had were lost in the troubles which followed. Of its ecclesiastical history we are still more ignorant. The age of St. Ninian may be looked on as one of which almost nothing is recorded in the annals of the British Church; so that we must form our ideas of this particular period by what we know of the times preceding and following it. It would come in to fill the blank between the third and fourth chapters of the account of the British Church, which is prefixed to the life of St. Augustine.[1]

Of one, then, who lived in such an age, what records can we have? May not the history be given up as entirely uncertain? I conceive not; and for these reasons. Personal history is preserved when public events are unrecorded and forgotten. Nay, in all history it is often through the narratives of the lives of individuals alone that many circumstances of public importance have been preserved to us; it is round the individual that interest centres, and his doings which are remembered. We know how children are impressed by the words and deeds of individual worthies, when of the general course of the history they have no clear ideas, so that the best histories for them consist of a series of personal tales. And it is so with men generally, and particularly in a simple state of society. Among Christians this is still more the case; since with them the affectionate remembrance of those who are gone is heightened

[1] No. iii. of this Series, [and Vol. III. pp. 190, 198 in this edition].

by religious reverence, and sanctioned and sustained
by the commemoration of the departed. It is to
the individual Saint that Christians look, rather
than to the events of general history; for they view
him as the work of Divine grace; whilst the course
of the world, though in its progress and issue the
effect of His providence, is in detail but the manifestation of man's wilfulness and misery.

We cannot suppose but that the Picts, among
whom St. Ninian had introduced the Gospel, would
retain the memory of one to whom they were indebted for all they held dear. And in Galloway
he had left a standing memorial in the church of
stone, which was looked on with no little interest
by the admiring Britons, and was thought to give
a name to the place where it stood. He left a
monastery, too, and that would be the means of
preserving some records of him. That such records
were preserved we know, on the authority of the
earliest witnesses we could have—the most learned
and accomplished scholars, and the most holy men
of their age—Bede and Alcuin.

In Bede's time the Southern Picts were still
existing as a separate race, and testified to having
derived their Christianity from St. Ninian; and
Whithern, with his church and tomb, was a visible
memorial. A Saxon succession of Bishops and a
Saxon monastery had been established here, on the
conquest of Galloway by that people. So that in
Bede we have the testimony of one who had full
means of informing himself on the subject, as to
the main incidents of St. Ninian's life; as also
had Alcuin, of whom there is a letter still extant,

written to the Brethren of the Saxon Monastery of Whithern, recognising the miracles and holiness of the Saint. And after this we find incidental mention of St. Ninian in different writers, all treating the chief facts of his life as matter of authentic history.

These are, however, only portions of information incidentally given, indications of a larger store existing among the people whom he had converted, and where his Church and monastery were. Among them we might expect that records would exist (as among the other Celtic tribes in Wales and Ireland), written in their own language, and from that very circumstance little known to the rest of the world. Galloway had been overrun by different tribes, but (with the exception of the brief occupation by the Saxons) they were all of the Celtic race, and their languages, though different dialects, were mutually intelligible. And we know that in the twelfth century lives of the Saint were extant in their language.

This we learn from the testimony of St. Aelred of Rievaux, who was requested by the brethren of the convent of Whithern to compose a life of their Patron Saint in Latin. In an Introduction addressed to them, he speaks of the disadvantage arising from the life of the Saint only existing in a barbarous language (or being written in a barbarous style), which obscured his history, and interfered with the pleasure and edification of the readers. It seems to be implied that more than one life was extant in Celtic, and perhaps in Latin, but that very rude and barbarous, and that St. Aelred selected as the groundwork of his life the one which seemed to him the most authentic. And it is possible that a life referred to by Archbishop Usher, as existing among the Irish, may be the representative of some of the others.

We regard this life, then, as representing what St. Aelred considered the most authentic account then existing of St. Ninian, an account not improbably, in tradition at least, almost contemporaneous with the Saint, and supplying the information which Bede and Alcuin possessed respecting him.

Of the authority of St. Aelred as a biographer, little need be said. He, whom even Bede calls a second St. Bernard, was endued with that kindred sanctity which fitted him to be the biographer of a Saint; and his education in the Scottish court and long friendship with the king, and in particular his connection with Fergus, the lord of Galloway, and his labours for the restoration of religion in that country, as it led him to tread in the footsteps of St. Ninian, would enable him to ascertain all that could be learnt of authority respecting him.

The work was written towards the close of his own life, between 1153 and 1166. It agrees in style with his other works, and is every way worthy of him. Being intended for spiritual reading and edification, it contains much that is inserted for that end, and throws the sentiments which might be supposed to influence the Saint into the dramatic form of a soliloquy or speech. Perhaps in one or two points it is liable to the charge of anachronism, from the writer's imagining the existence of the customs of his own time, in the days of which he is writing. It is a singular gift in a writer to be able to strip himself of the habits of thought to which he has ever been familiarised, or even constantly to keep in mind that practices existing in his own day are of recent origin. It ought to be added, that St. Aelred's Life bears internal marks of truth, from its correspondence with other history in minute points of chronology, with the circumstances and habits of the age, and with the distinctions of the tribes who occupied the country, as the researches of the latest writers have determined them. Indeed, from St. Aelred to the present century, almost all who have written about St. Ninian have fallen into some error or other from which he seems to be free. This life soon became a popular work in our monasteries, if we may argue from the numerous copies which seem to have been made.

It was abridged by John of Tinmouth, and from him was inserted by Capgrave in his collection. It has received the highest sanction from the Scottish Church, as selections from it were read as Lessons for St. Ninian's day, in the Aberdeen Breviary. There are copies made within a few years after St. Aelred's death, in the Bodleian and the British Museum; and it has been printed, though without the Introduction, by Pinkerton, in a collection of old Lives of Scottish Saints.

Later writers mention further circumstances respecting St. Ninian, but we have little evidence of their truth. They may in some cases be regarded as traditional stories, and have credit given to them as not being intrinsically improbable; in others the silence of St. Aelred respecting them may be taken as a fair proof that he did not know, or did not believe them. The Irish life referred to by Archbishop Usher does not appear entitled to much consideration.

CHAPTER II

ST. NINIAN'S EARLY DAYS

THE date of St. Ninian's birth must be placed about the middle of the fourth century. Alford has given 360. We may rather conceive it to have been a few years earlier, as in 357, so as to make him forty years of age at his consecration as a Bishop, in 397.

His name has been variously written and pronounced. We now uniformly call him Ninian, as he has usually been called in England, and so his name is given in the Roman Martyrology and by St. Aelred. In Bede, however, the name is Nynias, in William of Malmesbury Ninas, in other writers Ninus. In Scotland he is popularly called Ringan, the word being pronounced Rin'nan, or Rinnian, or (as in the Shetland Isles) Ronyan. In Ireland, both Ringan and Ninian. How the difference in the first letter arose (for the rest is much the same in pronunciation) we have no means of conjecturing.

The father of the Saint, as his biographer explicitly states, was a British Prince. To appreciate, however, the condition of such a person in the age of St. Ninian, we must forget the associations which we usually connect with the Ancient Britons. This was no longer a country occupied by wild savages, with half-naked and painted bodies, who lived in assemblages of miserable huts, buried in woods and protected by morasses. This state of things might exist in those parts of the Island which were unsubdued or unoccupied by the Romans; but those in which they had now for three centuries been predominant, had, like their other provinces, become assimilated to the habits of the conquerors.

Under this transforming system, a complete change had been made in the appearance of the country and the habits of the people. Forests had been cleared, marshes drained, bridges thrown over the rivers, and roads formed, intersecting the whole island, and affording speedy and secure communication. Towns sprung up, which imitated the cities of the continent. They had their temples, basilicas, and theatres adorned with painting and sculpture; their shows and exhibitions. So that in a period of three hundred years, Britain advanced in wealth and prosperity, and her artisans rivalled in activity and skill those of the continent; "every production of art and nature, every object of convenience or luxury, was accumulated in this rich and fruitful province." The remains which are still left among us, bespeak the advance of luxury and civilisation. The tesselated pavement, the marble bath, the elegant vase, tell what Roman taste had produced in England; while we still use, after a lapse of sixteen hundred years, the roads which her labour formed.

With these changes there rose up a corresponding alteration in the native population. They became Romans; filled the ranks of the legions; acquired the rights of citizens, and naturally imitated, as the model of refinement and civilisation, the dress

language, and manners of the Italian. The British
language still continued as the mother tongue of the
great body of the people, but even that was in a
measure Latinised, and among the higher classes,
Latin was generally spoken. The pleadings of the
courts were conducted in it, and the British youth
were taught to speak it by their grammarians and
rhetoricians, whose instructions formed the chief part
of Roman education. Even in the days of Agricola
Latin was cultivated, and the natives excelled in
eloquence; the sons of the British chieftains received
a Roman education, and began to adopt the Roman
dress; and in the fourth century, these beginnings
had issued in the complete assimilation of the Provincial to the Roman habits; and the son of a British
prince may be conceived not to have differed much,
in point of manners and civilisation, from the inhabitants of any other part of the empire.

Alford, indeed, smiles at the flattery of his biographer, in exalting the Saint to the worldly distinction of the son of a king. St. Aelred, however,
or his Galwegian authority, was quite aware of the
meaning of this title when applied to a British chief.
He says, in speaking of Tuduval, a petty prince in
Galloway, "That the whole island was divided into
portions subject to different kings." Like the other
Celtic nations, the Britons consisted of distinct tribes,
with various subdivisions of septs and clans, each
under its own chieftain, and these subordinated to
a superior one. Thus the four Kings, whom Cæsar
speaks of in the one kingdom of Kent. These
national subordinations, living on under, and through,
the Roman period, and naturally prevailing most on

the outskirts of the empire, are supposed to have been the origin of the clans of the Scottish border. St. Aelred would identify the position of the father of our Saint, with the kings who governed the whole of the Cumbrian Britons till within the memory of his own time; though this is giving him a wider extent of authority than he probably possessed.

To suppose St. Ninian the son of one of the minor chieftains under the Roman sway, is not assigning him a very high or improbable distinction. These kings, indeed, from their lands, or the contributions of their tribes, often acquired considerable wealth, and this coincides with what is said by his biographer of the sacrifice he made in relinquishing his father's house and his prospects in Britain, as well as with all we hear of his education, and his acquaintance with the full extent of theological teaching, which his own country could supply.

St. Ninian's father then was a petty chieftain of a British tribe, and, as we should infer from St. Aelred's description, on the north - west coast of Cumberland. It is true that the claim of Cumberland to this her one only native Saint may be disputed, and the right we have to introduce St. Ninian into a series of English Saints. For two other parts of the island have been generally assigned. On the one hand, though without any alleged ground so far as we can ascertain, North Wales is stated to have been his birthplace by Leland, Bale, and others; while he has most commonly been regarded as a native of Scotland, and it has not unnaturally been supposed that he was born near Whithern, the seat of his future Bishopric; not unnaturally, because it was to labour for the restoration of religion among his own countrymen, primarily, that he was sent from Rome. The inhabitants of Galloway, however, were of one and the same race with the Britons of Cumberland, and so were really his countrymen, even if he were born in Cumberland ; and as we go on it will appear that his mission at first was not directed to Whithern, but that after landing and preaching in his native country, he chose that as his permanent abode. St. Aelred is certainly an unprejudiced witness. His authority was a Galwegian life, and he was writing his narrative for the Church of Galloway, and he had strong affections for that country. Still he states, as the received opinion of his day, that the coast of Cumberland by the Solway was the birthplace of the Saint. His words are, "in that district, as it is thought, which lying in the western parts of the island (where the sea, stretching out, as it were, an arm, and forming two angles on each side, separates what are now the kingdoms of the Scotch and English), is proved, not only by the authority of histories, but also by the memory of some persons, to have had kings of its own, even to the latest times of the Saxons." [1] This arm of the sea is evidently the Solway, which on the cession of Cumberland to Henry II., 1153, became the boundary of the two kingdoms ; and it was on the western shore of the Island, and in a district which had kings of its own,

[1] "In ea, ut putatur, regione, quæ in occiduis ipsius insulæ partibus (ubi Oceanus quasi brachium porrigens, et ex utraque parte duos angulos faciens, Scotorum nunc et Anglorum regna dividit) constituta, usque ad novissima Anglorum tempora proprium habuisse regem, non solum historiarum fide, sed quorundam quoque memoriâ comprobatur."

" usque ad novissima Anglorum tempora " ; that is, till the end of the Saxon times. The Cumbrian Britons had kings of their own till the year 946, when the last of their princes, Dunmail, fell in defence of their narrow territories, and Edmund gave the conquered country to the Scottish kings. The British inhabitants continued as a separate race in the time of St. Aelred, and took a conspicuous part in the Battle of the Standard.

It is quite clear that Galloway was not the country intended, for it had lords of its own, who were in power in Aelred's day, and some time after ; and as he was on terms of intimate friendship with Fergus, the then lord, he would certainly not speak of them as matter either of history or tradition.

Pinkerton indeed in a note on St. Aelred's life, supposes as others had done, that Strathclydd, the Scottish portion of the great northern settlement of Britons, is the district referred to. But there are these objections to the view. Strathclydd, which lies on the opposite side of the Solway, and stretches to the Clyde, would scarcely have been described as in the western parts, in connection with the mention of that sea, as it is its south-eastern coast only which abuts upon the Solway. Again, though the Strathclydd race of kings had continued till 975, or perhaps 1018, when there is the last mention of the inhabitants of Strathclydd as having a king ; yet it does not appear why they should be mentioned in connection with the Angli—the Saxons—who had not occupied that district for some centuries previously, and then only for a short time and very partially. Indeed the " usque ad novissima Anglorum tempora "

would not seem to have any meaning as regarded
any part of Scotland, where, in St. Aelred's days, the
Angli still continued in as much power as at any
previous time.[1]

And there is a remarkable confirmation of our
view in Leland s account ; for though he represents
North Wales as Ninian's birthplace, and throughout
his history differs materially from St. Aelred, yet he
says that the country the Saint first visited as a
missionary, was the coast of Cumberland, " between
St. Bees Head and Carlisle," and Galloway. This is
what we conceive him to have done, supposing that
part of Cumberland to have been his birthplace, and
so far it coincides with St. Aelred's account, that he
first went to his native place ; except that Leland,
quite erroneously it would seem, places that missionary visit before, instead of after, his residence at
Rome.

It is allowed that St. Aelred's description is obscure, but to suppose it to describe the Cumbrian
coast seems the most natural interpretation. Let us
then assume that St. Ninian is an English and a
Cumbrian Saint. In that case he would be one of
the great tribe of Brigantes, who occupied the whole
of the northern counties of England. The district
where he was born was in those days one of considerable importance. It lay close to the wall of Severus,

---

[1] The name Cumbria was given to the whole district occupied by
the Cwmry, in Scotland and the north of England, sometimes includ-
ing even Galloway. The Scottish part was called Strathclydd ; the
English, to which the name of Cumberland was afterwards appropriated, Reged. We must not, therefore, claim the authority of
writers who call St. Ninian a native of Cumbria, as they may have
meant, of the Scottish portion.

which there came to its western limit, and for the defence of this line a very large proportion of the Roman forces was stationed in the neighbourhood ; and it was near the point where the great line of road through York to Carlisle terminated. These circumstances made the district a busy and excited one, and gave many opportunities of intercourse with the Romans, and the rest of the world. Still it was the busy scene of camps and warfare, for the country was intersected by roads, and filled by garrisons ; and its position on the Scottish border must even then have made it a restless and unsettled dwelling-place.

In a religious point of view, it is possible that this free intercourse may have brought a knowledge of the Gospel earlier amongst the natives of this district, than of others which were in actual distance less remote. We know so little of the religious history of Britain at this time, that we must judge much by probabilities, and the parallels of other countries. There had long been a Bishop at York, and probably the small size of the island would have promoted a more general conversion of the people than in France, where, at the same period, a large portion of the country were still unconverted. In the towns, Christian Churches would be established ; but in country districts, the people might still be to a great extent pagan. Indeed, it was to complete the conversion of the inhabitants of the western side of the island, as well as to root out the errors which prevailed among those who were Christians, that St. Ninian was many years after sent back from Rome. That the father of

St. Ninian was a Christian, is mentioned as a distinction.

We might probably infer, from the prince of the district having accepted the gospel, that it would be promoted among his countrymen, that Churches were built, and clergy fixed among them. St. Ninian's reverence for Churches is mentioned by his biographer, as a mark of his youthful piety. Now, not far from the sea-coast, in the very part of Cumberland where we conceive St. Ninian to have been born, and of which his father was the chieftain, there is a church, the architecture of which has been supposed to indicate its being built during the Roman occupation of Britain — that of Newton Arloch, in the parish of Holme Cultram. It is, then, not an improbable conjecture, that this church, which, unlike the rest of the British churches, was built of stone, may have been connected with the family of our Saint. Shall we imagine its erection the work of the British prince, and his son baptised, and praying there? Or the fruit of the return of the Saint from Rome, when, as his Cathedral at Whithern was built of stone, a corresponding work of piety was performed, in the rebuilding the Church of his native district. Anyhow, if such, as is by no means improbable, be the age of the Church, and this the birthplace of St. Ninian, we cannot but connect them with each other.

The very circumstance that Christians were living surrounded by a heathen population, assisted them to realise that they were a distinct people, enjoying peculiar privileges, and under especial obligations, separated from the world, as in profession, so in

duties and in destinies. It was a state which gave
a vivid force to the language of the New Testament,
and a manifest visibility to the Church ; and their
faith may well be supposed to have been united
to personal earnestness and conviction, to actual
renunciation of the world, and a life corresponding
to their calling. Such the father of Ninian is said
to have been ; " one of such faith and merit, as to
be thought worthy of a son through whom the
deficiencies in the faith of his own people might
be supplied, and a distinct tribe (the Southern Picts)
brought to a participation in the mysteries of our
Holy religion."

His mother has been supposed to be one of a
family of Saints. The notion is not unnatural. In
those days, when the few names we know are those
of Saints, we should wish to imagine that they, at
least, knew, and were connected with, each other.
And the instances in sacred history, the selection of
families for privileges, the rewarding the children
for the piety of their parents, and the obvious effects
of association, common education, and mutual intercession, would lead us to think it likely. All this
would suggest the notion, till it passed into a probability, and guesses became reports, and their very
likelihood made men believe them. Thus one would
account for the tradition, that the mothers of St.
Ninian and St. Patrick, whose name is said to have
been Conch, or Conchessa, were sisters of St. Martin
of Tours ; thus uniting, by the ties of blood, these
holy men. This statement, as regards the mother
of St. Ninian, is found in a MS. Catalogue of Saints,
at Louvain, and in Hector Boethius, and other later

writers, of little authority. But to say nothing of the improbability that the daughters of a Roman officer, in Pannonia or Italy, should have married two Britons, the life of St. Aelred would be decisive against it. It is not to be supposed that he should not have known it, had it in his day been matter of probable tradition. Yet he not only omits it, but implies that St. Ninian's knowledge of St. Martin arose from the Life of the Saint, by Sulpicius.

A brother is mentioned by St. Aelred, in the later part of St. Ninian's life, as his companion in his episcopal travels in Galloway. His name was Plebeius; and he is spoken of as his equal in sanctity. He, probably, was one who stayed in his father's house, and on the return of Ninian from Rome, became his fellow-labourer in the conversion of their countrymen, and his helper, by example and admonition, in personal holiness.

Born of such parents, our Saint "was in infancy regenerated in the sacred waters of Baptism." So his biographer begins his history — with the first element of spiritual life, the source of all his graces; and very beautifully does he describe the preservation of the purity then imparted. We might, indeed, wish to know the circumstances by which the youthful Saint was surrounded; the events which befel him, and the temptations he surmounted; but it seems as if we were to view him as Angels might love to do, in his true spiritual condition, looking only to the Divine work in him, not to those temporary and earthly accidents by which it was carried out; for of them no record is left us. It is this inward life only which St. Aelred records, and the graces in which it developed itself. We must imagine the outward circumstances of his condition as best we may.

"The wedding garment," he says, "which he then put on," that pure bright clothing of the soul by the gifts of grace, which the white robes of the new-baptised figured, "he preserved unsullied." Such was his special blessedness; as one of those virgin souls which follow the Lamb whithersoever he goeth. "Victorious over his faults"—those tendencies to evil which remain in the soul, like the Canaanites in Israel, to exercise the Christian warrior in watchfulness and obedience—"he presented it, spotless as it was, in the presence of Christ. And coming thus pure for the gift of Confirmation, he deserved, by the sanctity of his character, to have, as the enlightener of his holy heart, that Holy Spirit whom at first he had received to purify it."

"Under this Divine Guide, whilst still a child, yet with no childish mind, he shrunk from everything contrary to religion, from all that was opposed to chastity, to right conduct, or the laws of truth; and ceased not to cultivate with the understanding of a man all that was of the law, of grace, of good report, whatever was of service to his neighbour and acceptable to God."

The circumstances of this holy childhood we must imagine — the examples of religious parents, the blessedness of a house where no sentiment unfavourable to piety was ever heard, the training of a saintly mother, his first lisping prayers, his reverend introduction to the Church. His first lessons in sacred reading, his little playmates, his youthful trials, his first schooling; of these we only know that their influence issued in his sanctification and growth in grace. One means of this, St. Aelred specially intimates—the study of Holy Scripture, that meditative study which is the only way to let its truths take a deep and sure root in the heart.

"Blessed," his Life proceeds, "was he whose delight was in the Law of the Lord; in His Law did he meditate day and night. He was like a tree planted by the water side, which brought forth his fruit in due season."

This fruit was abundantly produced in the after-life of St. Ninian. Let us observe the preparation for it; the early practice of meditating on Holy Scripture, by withdrawing the thoughts from dissipating objects, and calmly and silently turning them to God; dwelling upon His word, and extracting from it all its sweetness. This is that studying, exercising one's self in, meditating, thinking on it, which we hear so much of in the Psalms. It is very important to accustom children to this practice, that they may not merely read over certain portions of Scripture, but, taking, a few verses, dwell on them in silence, endeavouring to enter into their meaning, to realise what they contain, and apply it to themselves. "To read little and think much," is a rule of Bishop Taylor's.

But in subordination to this sacred reading and meditation, we cannot doubt that Ninian had all those advantages of secular learning which Britain afforded; and these were not inconsiderable. At the neighbouring town of Lugubalia, our Carlisle, he would have the means of acquiring the preparatory learning of the encyclical course,[1] as no doubt the military establishments in the neighbourhood would induce even a higher class of teachers than ordinary to resort thither.

At York, which was in turns with London the seat of government, still greater opportunities would be afforded for completing his secular studies; and the zeal and earnestness with which he would avail himself of them, his after-history will abundantly testify.

Of his character in this part of his life St. Aelred writes, describing it as the fruit which in its season was brought forth from his continual meditation on the divine law, and the purifying and enlightening influence of the Holy Spirit. "He brought forth his fruit in due season," he says, "fulfilling in riper years what he had with the utmost devotion learnt in youth. His devout reverence for Churches was wonderful; wonderful his affection for his companions. He was temperate in food, sparing in words, assiduous in reading. His manners were engaging, he abstained from jesting, and ever subjected the flesh to the spirit."

---

[1] See Life of St. German, No. IX. of this series, pp. 14, 15. [In this edition, Vol. II. pp. 153, 154.]

CHAPTER III

ST. NINIAN'S RIPER YEARS

PROCEEDING (we may well suppose) from this spiritual mind, and the fruit of it, was that mental energy and resolution which soon distinguished him. Indeed it could not fail to be so. It is matter of common observation, how remarkably the understanding of a poor and uneducated man is developed by religious earnestness. Such a one is awakened from sluggish indifference. The end of his being is set before him, and he feels that he has duties to discharge. The value of Christian knowledge begins to be appreciated, meditation on divine truths expands the faculties, and leads him to see the connection of religious ideas; and love of the Object of Whom something is known, creates a holy eagerness to know more.

The young and noble Briton, with few advantages indeed, yet earnestly desirous to use those few, had more given. He began in careful self-government, unfeigned reverence for Holy things, in sweetness of temper and purity of heart. The Holy Spirit, whose firstfruits were love, joy, peace, longsuffering, gentleness, goodness, faith, meekness, self-control, imparted in due season and fuller measure his sevenfold gifts. Such is the true course of attaining divine wisdom. Holy Scripture, in enumerating these gifts, mentions first that which is the highest, and therefore the last attained; in the actual order they are inverted, and become the steps of wisdom; first is *fear*, the beginning of wisdom, fear of offending God and losing our souls; then *reverence* for every manifestation of the Divine will and His truth; hence *knowledge* imparted to the docile heart; then *counsel* guiding us to choose our course each day aright; then resoluteness and *strength* to adhere to it; *understanding* readily to discern the Divine will and to enter into the meaning of His words; and lastly, as the crowning point, *wisdom* in the contemplation and perception of the highest truth.

Far different in its origin is that unpractical temper which would treat the truths of our most Holy Faith as matters of mere intellectual knowledge, and seek to know what is and what may be said about them, in a curious and disputatious spirit, tampering with most sacred things. Such a temper can only end in darkness, ignorance, and error, even if it retains the outward expression of the truth; for it is quite compatible with the neglect of relative duties, self-indulgence, angry passions, and gross habitual violations of the divine law. Nay, from its offensiveness to Almighty God, and profane familiarity in His most Holy Presence, and the hardening of a heart which has been accustomed to close the affections and the will against the most influential truths, it is most likely to lead to falling away from grace and final departure from God.

But far different was the case of St. Ninian; humility, purity, and love were the elements of his

Q

character. In him holiness of heart was the principle which led to an earnest desire after divine knowledge. There was One Supreme Object of his affections, and on that same Object his thoughts would ever be fixed : where the heart is kept in the love of God, the mind will turn to the knowledge of Him. And it was the working of this simple principle which determined the course of his life. He had been taught the principles of the faith, and he sought to realise more and more what is revealed respecting the Heavenly Father, and the Eternal Son and the Holy Ghost. He was constant in drinking in at the fountain of Eternal Life in the Scriptures, and tracing there the manifestations of the truth ; and the result was a yearning after a more exact knowledge of Religious Truth, after that Truth which would be consistent with itself, and harmonise with the statements of Holy Writ.

"Before the mind," it has been said, "has been roused to reflection and inquisitiveness about its own acts and impressions, it acquiesces, if religiously trained, in that practical devotion to the Blessed Trinity, and implicit acknowledgment of the Divinity of Son and Spirit, which Holy Scripture at once teaches and exemplifies." "But as the intellect is cultivated and expanded, it cannot refrain from the attempt to analyse the vision which influences the heart, and the Object in which it centres. Nor does it stop here, till it has, in some sort, succeeded in expressing in words, what has all along been a principle both of the affections and of practical obedience."

Such seems to have been the state of St. Ninian's

mind; and a most critical period it was in his spiritual history. For whereas the Divine arrangement is, to provide, by the gradual teaching of the Church, that knowledge which the religious mind desires, the circumstances of the British Church at that time failed to supply it. His heart would have responded to the notes of truth, but they were not truly and clearly heard.

It is not a pleasing task to depreciate the estimate which may have been formed of the religious condition of Britons at any period; but a writer of St. Ninian's life cannot avoid the subject; it stands full in his way, for the whole of our history turns upon the fact that the teaching of the British Church at that time was very imperfect and erroneous. His biographer is explicit on this point, and the evidence from other sources inclines the same way. Bede's statement as to the prevalence of Arianism, does not imply merely that when the British bishops consented to the suppression of the true doctrine at Ariminum, our church, like the rest of Christendom, wondered to find itself Arian. On the contrary, he speaks of a peculiar prevalence of error here; an infection of Arianism first, and that followed by every form of heresy; and the cause he assigns for it in the fickleness of the national character, would lead us to expect what he intimates, the inconsiderate reception of errors, and the want of any sound or stable teaching of the truth; "novi semper aliquid audire gaudenti, et nihil certi firmiter obtinenti."

Nor is it at all inconsistent with this, to believe that the Bishops adhered to the Nicene formulary, and that such was the profession of the British

Church generally. In 353, they had unwillingly yielded at Ariminum, but in 363, St. Athanasius, in his letter to Jovian, enumerates them among a long list of nations who acknowledged the Creed of Nice. Persons might agree to the form in which the Catholic doctrine was expressed, and feel shocked at the idea of separating themselves from the faith and communion of the whole Church, and yet not have any deep hold on the truth itself, or, when they came to explain what they meant, any accurate knowledge of it. We may well imagine more active minds openly Arianising; more religious and less intellectual ones obscure and inconsistent in their statements, and quite unfit to teach dogmatically; and this would coincide with the fact of the Bishops submitting under their trials to an Arianising formula.

St. Jerome and St. Chrysostom have repeatedly, indeed, been referred to, as witnessing to the orthodoxy of the British Church, but the passages really bear very slightly on the subject, and rather suggest a different view; for in each case the mention of Britain is introduced to establish the universal prevalence of the practice they are speaking of; it existed even in Britain; and Britons were regarded as very exiles from the rest of the world. "The Gospel has prevailed over heathenism," argues St. Chrysostom;[1] "besides the Scythians, Moors, and Indians, even the British Isles have felt its power, and churches and altars are established there." "That it is not lawful to have a brother's wife,

[1] St. Chrys. tom. 10. 638, tom. 1. 575, tom. 3. 71, Ed. Ben. are the references made by Stillingfleet.

resounded even in Britain," besides other remote
and barbarous countries. Again, in a passage more
to the point, of which the beauty itself will be an
excuse for quoting it at length, speaking of the
study of the Holy Scriptures, he compares them to
a "Paradise of Delight, not like that of Eden confined to one place, but filling the whole earth, and
extending to the utmost bounds of the habitable
world. 'Their sound is gone out into all lands, and
their words into the ends of the world.' Go to the
Indians," he says, "on whom the rising sun first
looks; to the Ocean, to those British Isles (so does
he speak of us); sail to the Euxine; go to far
southern climes; everywhere will you hear all professing the philosophy of the Scriptures; with
different voice, but no different faith; the tongues
discordant, but the minds in unison."

But beautiful as the passage is, and comforting as
the sentiment it contains, yet it is much too general
and rhetorical in its style, to found any accurate
view upon. The passage quoted from St. Jerome [1]
is from a letter from SS. Paula and Eustochia to
St. Marcella, wishing her to come to visit the holy
places in Palestine. Their spiritual guide, St. Jerome,
was supposed to have composed it, and so it had
passed under his name, but the Benedictine editors
are of opinion that it was not written by him.
"Christians," they say, "from all the world visit
those sacred places. The Briton separated from
our world, if he has made any progress in religion,

---

[1] Ep. ad. Marc. tom. 4. p. 2. 441, Ed. Ben. There are several
other passages in Jerome to the same effect.

leaving the setting sun, seeks a place known to him only by report and the mention of it in Scripture."

There does not seem in these passages anything to oppose the distinct statement of Bede, as to the prevalence of error. Their tone would rather lead us to think that the British Church was not very highly esteemed by the rest of Christendom. And quite consistent with this was their condition, when the Bishops in vain endeavoured to resist the progress of Pelagianism. The life of St. Ninian certainly represents the state of the Church to have been such that he could find no complete teaching of the truth, and that it was on account of the errors which prevailed that he returned as a missionary among them.

As respects schools for theological teaching, there does not seem to be evidence of any previous to the visit of St. Germanus, except perhaps the monastery of Benchor; and it is doubtful whether this existed at the time of which we are speaking. That there were such schools, however, is not questioned. Indeed, there were among the contemporaries of Ninian, some whose character for learning was acknowledged throughout the Church. Pelagius and Cælestius, sad as is the remembrance attached to their names, were men of distinguished talents and learning. The former, born 354, it has been said, was educated at Benchor, and became superior of it in 404.[1] His abilities and accomplishments were recognised by the best and greatest Doctors; he was on terms of familiar intercourse and correspondence with SS. Jerome, Augustine, and Paulinus,

[1] Usher de Prim. B. E. p. 207.

and highly esteemed and loved by them.   The writings of Cælestius, a native of Scotland or Ireland, before he became heretical, were universally admired for their orthodoxy, learning, and virtuous tendency. Somewhat later, St. Patrick flourished, and Fastidius and Faustus later still.

But even if there were schools of theological learning where such men were trained, of what use could they be, if they did not hold that faith which it was their duty to teach?   There may be existing in a country an ample establishment of places of education for every age and every rank, yet what are they worth if the truth has departed?   It is the body when the spirit has fled; the salt without its savour; the lamp unsupplied with oil.   It is worse. Not teaching the truth must be training the mind in error.   And it is not wonderful, though Britain about this time did send out men of distinguished talents, that those who did not humbly seek instruction elsewhere were more or less heretical Pelagius and Cælestius were almost contemporary with Ninian and Patrick.   How remarkable is the different issue of the histories of these fellow-countrymen.   Ninian (and as some say, Patrick too), with little name for learning, and in their lifetime probably little known in this world, pursue the course of humility and obedience, seek the City for no earthly object, but for the inestimable pearl, the knowledge of Christ—cultivating a saintly character, and prepared at the bidding of their superiors to leave the privileges, and happiness there enjoyed, for the arduous office of converting their heathen and barbarous countrymen.   Pelagius and Cælestius,

passing from, it may be, the more civilised parts of
the island, looked up to, even in Rome, as distinguished men, enjoy the society and esteem of
the learned and the saintly—attain name and distinction in the Church—follow their own ways, and
leave their memories branded with the awful note of
heresy. Of Pelagius's numerous works scarcely a
fragment remains. " I went by and lo! he was gone;
I sought him but his place could nowhere be found."
" They are like the chaff which the wind scattereth
away from the face of the earth." But "the righteous
ive for evermore, and his memory is blessed."

But to pursue the course of St. Ninian's history.
The time we are speaking of is probably prior to
the year 380, and so before the Council of Constantinople, A.D. 381, had finally destroyed the Arian
party. Then it was that the earnest desire of
learning the true faith took entire possession of St.
Ninian's mind. He sought instruction from the
best teachers his own Church afforded, but could
not obtain it. He felt their teaching was imperfect.
It did not harmonise with what he knew was true,
nor accord with those Scriptures which he had ever
studied. He had a teacher within—that inward and
divinely kindled Light which illumines the mind of
many an unlettered peasant, and gives him a real
perception and understanding of the truths of the
Creed, and of the sense of Holy Scripture. He had
learned the elementary truths of the Gospel, and a
religious life had impressed them on his mind as
living realities. Thus much light was thrown on
the meaning of those Holy Scriptures on the
thought of which he had lived when a child. For

the knowledge of the Rule of Faith, as St. Aelred, with the primitive fathers, calls the system of Christian Doctrine, was an entering into the very mind of the Spirit, which is the true key to the understanding of His most holy Words. That mind is expressed in various forms, pervading every part of Psalm and Prophecy, History and Epistle; and we shall best understand them, not by critical investigations into the meaning of words, but by learning more of the mind of the Author; just as one who knows but in a very slight degree the views of a writer, will apprehend his meaning with readiness and certainty, while one who weighs the words and criticises their force with the utmost jealousy, will find them full of ambiguity and un-certainty, and at last arrive at a doubtful and probably erroneous conclusion. The Scriptures had been the subject of his constant study and medita-tion from early youth—of a practical, devout study, that they might be the guide of his life and the model he aimed to imitate, and now the hidden things they contained were being revealed to him, and continually more light thrown upon them, as they were made more practical, and connected with the truths of the Creed.

With this inward perception of Divine Truth, St. Ninian could perceive the inconsistencies of the teaching of the British Ecclesiastics, and its dis-crepancy from the Scriptures. In him were the words made good, "I have more understanding than my teachers, for Thy testimonies are my study. I am wiser than the aged, because I keep Thy commandments."

Disappointed of help where he most naturally and dutifully looked for it, what was he to do? It was not perhaps to be expected that he should be led into a perfect knowledge of the truth by the light within, independently of external teaching. In the case, indeed, of an accomplished and highly illuminated teacher, or one precluded from the means of instruction, or as a gift of special grace, one would not presume to limit its possible range. In such cases the development of truth by holy and loving meditation, and devout study of Holy Scripture, may surpass conception. But to St. Ninian the means of further instruction were open, though at a great and trying sacrifice, that of forsaking his home and all that was dear to him on earth.

Before, however, this step was taken, whilst he sought for further teaching, we may conceive his trials to have been very great. There was the temptation to indifference, to seek no more of that which he already had in a larger measure than most around him, and to turn the thirstings of his ardent mind to those objects (such as they were) which occupied the thoughts and aims of most of the young nobles of his time; and the checks and difficulties he met with would suggest themselves as reasons for such a course. But he was not disposed to feed on the husks of swine after having tasted of that which was sweeter than honey and the honeycomb, more to be desired than gold and all manner of riches—the knowledge of Him who passeth knowledge.

On the other hand, there was the temptation to rest in what he knew, in intellectual self-satisfaction, to feel pride in superior attainments, to point out the errors of others, and argue on the illogicalness of their conclusions—to show that they could not prove what they maintained, and to make a display. But surely no earnest mind could do this. It was the truth which he desired to know; to be thought to know it was matter of indifference to him. To prove others wrong could but be an occasion of sorrow, unless it aided himself and them in attaining truth.

A more subtle temptation remained; to throw himself on the resources of his own mind, to trust to the deductions of his own intellect, either from the text of Holy Scriptures or the doctrines he had already been taught. For this he was too humble. The immensity and awfulness of the subject, and the consciousness of his own imperfections, both of will and understanding, might well make him draw back from so perilous and uncertain a work. Reverence would shrink from touching with a young and uninformed mind subjects which it only regarded as objects of veneration. Moses was bidden to put his shoes from off his feet before he approached the Holy One. The cherubim cover their heads against the dazzling brightness of the earthly manifestations of Divine glory. It is only where the mind has been trained into the knowledge of the faith, and is influenced by great sanctity and humility, that it can safely use the reason in matters of faith. Others must be content, and, if they have the elements of holiness, will be desirous, only to be taught by those of higher attainments than themselves.

What then was he to do? St. Aelred thus describes his state. "He intently applied his mind to the study of Holy Scripture; and when he had, in their way, learnt the Rule of Faith from all the most learned of his own nation, being possessed of a discerning mind, he perceived, according to the understanding he had himself by Divine inspirations gained from Scripture, that they fell far short of perfection. Hence his mind was thrown into uncertainty; and unable to rest in incomplete knowledge, his heart swelled within him; he sighed; his heart grew hot within him, and while he was thus musing the fire kindled. What, he said, shall I do? I have sought in my own country for Him whom my soul loveth, and have not found Him. I will arise! I will compass sea and land! I will seek that truth which my soul loveth!"

In this state of mind Rome naturally presented itself as the place to which he should have recourse. She, who for centuries had been the queen of nations, was now attaining a greater glory, as the chief Church of Christendom, the centre of the Christian world—the home of faith and devotion—the point to which all that was great and good drew as to a safe refuge. High as was her bearing in the eye of the world, yet greater still was the interest which attached to her in the eyes of a Christian. Man saw her noble edifices, her wealth, her power; yet that outward kingdom and glory was but a shell to guard an inner principle of life, and was now breaking in pieces to allow of its development. Here was a Church which the chief of the Apostles had founded and taught, and for which they had shed

their blood ; a Church which had carefully preserved
the faith as it had received it, by the Holy Ghost
dwelling in it. To her, as a guide, the chief writers
of the western Church had directed those who sought
to know the truth; and during the long Arian
struggle, she had been the main support of the
faith ; and the purity of her belief, and the completeness of her teaching were known and acknowledged
by all.

"To this Church," St. Irenæus had said long ago,
"on account of its higher original, all Churches
must have recourse." And Tertullian, "Go to the
Apostolic Churches to learn the faith. If thou art
near to Italy, thou hast Rome, where we also have
an authority close at hand. Blessed Church! on
which the Apostles poured their doctrine with their
blood. Let us see what she hath learned, what she
hath taught." This was the Church, which the
Council of Antioch shortly before had called "the
School of the Apostles and the Metropolis of
Religion"; and Theodosius in an edict, published
just at this time, A.D. 380, respecting faith in the
ever blessed Trinity, commanded that all the nations
under his rule "should steadfastly adhere to the
religion which was taught by St. Peter to the
Romans, which faithful tradition had preserved,
which was now professed by Pope Damasus, and
by Peter, Bishop of Alexandria."

These are the sentiments St. Aelred attributes to
St. Ninian, in a soliloquy which embodies the views
that might naturally be supposed to influence him.
"I have in my own country sought Him whom my
soul loveth, and have not found Him. I will arise,

I will compass sea and land to seek the truth which my soul longs for. But is there need of so much toil? Was it not said to Peter, Thou art Peter, and upon this rock will I build my Church, and the gates of Hell shall not prevail against it? In the faith of Peter then there is nothing defective, obscure, imperfect; nothing against which evil doctrine or perverted sentiments, the gates as it were of Hell, could prevail. And where is the Faith of Peter but in the See of Peter? Thither certainly I must go, that leaving my country and my relations, and my father's house, I may be thought worthy to behold with inward eye the fair beauty of the Lord, and to be guarded by His Temple." And of the temptation which would draw him back. " The deceitful prosperity of life smiles on me—the vanity of the world is attractive— the love of my relations wiles me to stay—difficulties and personal sufferings deter. But he who loveth father and mother, saith the Lord, more than Me, is not worthy of Me, and he that taketh not up his cross and followeth after Me, is not worthy of Me. I have learnt too that they who despise Kings' palaces, attain to heavenly kingdoms."

Such were his feelings. And should it seem strange to speak of a young Briton as making any great sacrifice in leaving a distinction almost nominal in a remote country, regarded as scarcely belonging to the Roman world, for the metropolis of the empire, the seat of refinement and luxury, of taste, literature, and intellect, of all which was calculated to engage the interest and sympathy of a Christian— should it be thought that the change was one to be gladly caught at—let it be considered that it was not the leaving Britain for Rome merely, which indicated the devotion of St. Ninian. This might have been done from the lowest motives, ambition, curiosity, pleasure, and might not have implied the tearing asunder of any ties; as many have made pilgrimages from the mere love of wandering. The circumstances and the end determine the character of the action. The sacrifice of worldly interest might have been small; but it was a sacrifice of all he had, and that without any earthly recompense, and He who rewarded those who left their father, and all that they had, though but an interest in a fisherman's poor stock, would have accepted him.

Relatively speaking, however, the sacrifice was considerable. If the eldest son, he would hold the rank of Tanist, as the destined successor to the reigning king; and his country was no longer, as we have seen, that in which the captive Prince had wondered the Romans could envy his poor cottage. Many of its Princes possessed considerable wealth; in their days of independence they had coined gold and silver, and in all probability still continued to possess hereditary revenues. And Roman manners had introduced even into Britain objects which that wealth might purchase. Their elegant and costly works, their notoriously extravagant luxuries, show that Ninian could have found ways of expending his inheritance which the children of this world would have envied; baths, and costly marbles, inlaid pavements, and all the elegancies of art. For objects of ambition he might have aimed, at least, to be the chief among his countrymen; or by engaging in the service of Rome have risen, as other provincials had done, to high distinction. Even the imperial purple was not beyond the grasp of an ambitious spirit. The British legions about this very time made Maximus Emperor, and the great Constantine has been said to be a native Briton.

But these things were seen in their true colours by Ninian. He had renounced them in his Baptism, and his heart had never returned to them. The world, with its charms of pleasure, its prospects of wealth or ambition, had no hold on him. His real trial was from a deeper attachment—affection to his friends, a sacrifice made more painful in proportion as Christian piety increased his love to them. Almighty God seems ever, as it were, to retain a hold upon us, so as to be able to inflict sharp pain for our correction, or give us the opportunity of overcoming it from love to Him ; and this especially through our affections. Men hardened by ambition, covetousness, and indifference to religion, yet retain deep and tender love for wife or child ; and the loss of them, or the sorrows which befall them, are continually means of awakening them to a sense of religion. So in those who for Christ's sake have weaned their affections from all other earthly objects, their very progress in goodness, while it gives them strength to forsake even what they best love for Him, and keeps them from setting their affections on them, yet makes their love more tender and deep, and the pain of separation in itself greater, entirely though it be compensated for by the overflowings of Divine consolations.

Such seems to have been St. Ninian's chief

struggle; but the remembrance of his Lord's calls, and the greatness of His promises, prevailed, and he went out where Christ seemed to call him.

It has been reported that his father had at first wished him to keep in the way of life which his birth and circumstances naturally pointed out, and that it was with great unwillingness that he yielded to his son's desire to give up the world for a life devoted to religion. This, however, must have been earlier, when St. Ninian gave himself up in his own country to the pursuit of religious truth. Still there is a peculiar pang when a final step is taken, which breaks off entirely hope which may against hope have been secretly cherished; still more when that step took from their home him whose distinguishing sweetness and affectionateness must have made him beloved, whilst he was reverenced. But all these considerations sank before the great object he had in view, and he left his home, and as his biographers say, "like Abraham, he went out from his country and his father's house."

Two other reasons have been assigned for his visiting Rome. The first is a conjecture of Alford's, that he went to take advantage of the schools, the original of our universities, which had been established on so large a scale, and with so systematic a discipline by Valentinian. They had been instituted in 370, and with a special view to the education of provincials. It is plain, however, that this view is quite inconsistent with the picture given us by St. Aelred. It was for no advantages of secular learning that the humble and affectionate Ninian left his parents and his home. It was the need of religious teaching, of that knowledge which is life eternal, which caused and justified his sacrifice. Besides, the students were not allowed to continue after they were twenty years of age, which would make Ninian so young on his going there, as to give an entirely different character to his visit. He would in that case appear to have been sent, as it were, to the university by his parents. It is enough to say that this is purely a conjecture, and not only without foundation, but inconsistent with the earlier histories of the Saint. Camerarius again represents his visit as occasioned by the rules of the Culdees, to whom he supposed him to belong, who required those who were to be consecrated Bishops among them, to have previously visited the Limina Apostolorum. But this is apparently an anachronism, as the Culdees do not appear in history till above a century after St. Ninian's time.

Leland, too, places the visit to Rome after he had been engaged in missionary labours in Britain; but he gives no authorities, and mentions the subject so incidentally, and without noticing the different account given in the received Lives, that we should rather suspect him of a mistake in memory as to the Saint's history, than of so slightingly opposing the best authorities for the history.

CHAPTER IV

ST. NINIAN'S JOURNEY TO ROME

THE date of this journey we cannot accurately determine. It was certainly before the year 385; for the Pope by whom St. Ninian was consecrated and sent as a missionary to Britain was not the one in whose Pontificate he arrived in Rome. St. Siricius was his consecrator, and he was elected Pope on the death of St. Damasus in 385. Prior then to this date, and during the Popedom of St. Damasus, was the time of St. Ninian's arrival; and we should conjecture that it was prior to the year 383, as there is not in his Life any reference to the convulsion occasioned by the revolt of Maximus, which introduced great changes into Britain and Gaul, by the emigration of a considerable portion of the British nation to Brittany. Perhaps 381 may be conjectured, when he was twenty-one years of age or upwards.

By the assistance of the Itineraries we may trace the route by which Ninian would travel from his northern home, near Carlisle, to the great city. The road began either on the south of the Solway, or in Annandale, and ran through Carlisle by Old Penrith, where a noble military way may still be traced, thence by the vale of the Eden to Brough,

and over the dreary hills of Stainmoor. Here
Ninian would have the last glimpse of those mountains within sight of which he had spent his youth,
and the remembrance of which, with all the associations of friends and kindred, is so deeply engraven
on the heart. He would cross the moorlands and
travel along a road which runs by Bowes and
Catterick, and which we still enjoy as an inheritance from our Roman conquerors, and so to York.

This was, as we have said, the second city of
Britain, the residence of the governors, and the
See of an Archbishop, and here most probably the
young prince would receive commendatory letters
to other Catholic Bishops, and particularly to Rome.
Hence he would proceed by the great line of Watling
Street to London, and Sandwich. This was the
port from which they sailed for Boulogne. Passing
through Rheims, then an episcopal city, he would
come to Lyons, that first cradle of the Church of
Gaul, consecrated by the memory of her martyrs,
and her sainted Bishop, St. Irenæus. It was now
a great city, but more interesting to St. Ninian, as
it was now probably presided over by one who,
during the period of Arian trials, had been the
firm maintainer of the Catholic faith—St. Justus.
He was the friend of St. Ambrose, and Bishop
from 370 to 381, when he resigned his office and
retired to Egypt, to embrace a monastic life, and
end his days in devotion and peace.

The direct road from Lyons to Milan over the
Great St. Bernard, was steep, narrow, and impassable
for carriages ; another from Vienne by the Little
St. Bernard, was more circuitous but easier ; they

united at Aosta. His biographer especially mentions that he crossed the Gallic Alps, to impress us, as it would seem, with the arduousness of a journey, terrible from its natural difficulties, and dangerous from the robbers who infested it; for not many years before St. Martin had been attacked here, and saved from murder only by a miracle.

He now entered Italy, and came among cities and Churches associated with the names and lives of Saints distinguished in the history of religion; and these would be the objects on which his thoughts would fix. Nature indeed spread before him her most sublime and then her loveliest scenery. The world presented riches and splendour. He might encounter on the road the magnificent equipages and retinue of the wealthy Roman, coaches of solid silver, mules with trappings embossed with gold, horsemen preceding to clear the way, and a train of baggage and attendants, cooks, slaves, eunuchs, marshalled like an army. But he was proof against these seductive imaginations; the *nil admirari* is not so effectually produced by any philosophy as by the calm recollection of the Christian, whose guarded eye does not allow him to forget the shadowy nature of what is seen, and the reality of those things which are not seen; and he would esteem above all the beauties of nature or of art, the Church in each place he came to, and the pious Christians whom he might meet with.

And there was one of these places which was connected in an interesting way with his own future history — Vercelli, through which the road from

Lyons to Milan passed. Its late Bishop, St. Eusebius, had introduced here, for the first time in the western Church, the union of the clerical and monastic life, which was afterwards adopted by St. Ninian. St. Eusebius had died ten years before, but the system was still kept up; and it may not be out of place here to give St. Ambrose's description of it, as it will by anticipation describe the episcopal life of St. Ninian.

The Bishop and Clergy lived together in one house, shut out from the world, and adopting the way of life of the Egyptian monks, having all things in common, and devoting their days and nights to continued prayer and praise, labour and study. "Can any thing," says the Saint, speaking of their society, "can any thing be more admirable than their way of life, in which there is nothing to fear, and every thing worthy of imitation; where the austerity of fasting is compensated by tranquillity and peace of mind, supported by example, made sweet by habit, and cheered by virtuous occupations. A life not disturbed by temporal cares, nor distracted by the tumults of the world, nor interrupted by idle visits, nor relaxed by intercourse with the world." Thus, under the eye of the Bishop himself, Clergy were trained up, of whom he personally knew the blamelessness, piety, and zeal; while their characters were so esteemed, that other Churches sought their Bishops from him, and many distinguished Prelates were sent out from his school.

In after days, St. Ninian, on the coast of Galloway, might recall to his mind the time when he had seen Vercelli, and the first model of a system which, with some modifications, was soon generally embraced, both by missionaries and in settled churches, and is the original of the chapters of our cathedrals.

The road brought him from Lyons to Milan, which from the year 303 had been the chief residence of the Emperors of the west, and soon assumed the splendour of an imperial city. In the number and beauty of the houses, the gay and polished manners of the people, and the magnificence of the public buildings, it seemed to rival, and not suffer in comparison from the proximity of, Rome. In this place St. Ambrose was Bishop, and even to the eyes of the world that great man would appear the most important object in Milan. The popular voice had taken him from a high civil position to be their Bishop, and he was such an one that Theodosius recognised in him a realising of all a Bishop ought to be. His people were devoted to him, and his influence could withstand and control the highest earthly sovereigns. And yet so simple was his life that Ninian might have seen or conversed with him. He gave himself wholly to the work of the ministry. Constant in prayer, by day and night, he slept little and fasted daily. Yet he was accessible to all. St. Augustine generally found him surrounded by crowds of persons and full of business. His time which was not thus occupied, and it was but little, was given to refreshment or reading, and he read where any one might come to him ; no one was hindered, nor was it usual for them to be announced, so that Augustine would come and stay in the room, and leave again, unwilling to interrupt him. He preached every

Sunday, and Ninian may have listened to that eloquence which melted the stubborn heart of him who afterwards was St. Augustine, and which we may read with so much admiration.

But Rome was his object, and he hastened forward. The Via Flaminia brought him to the shore of the Adriatic, to the fatal Ariminum, connected with recollections most distressing to every Christian, and to a Briton still more so, as the scene where the Bishops of his Church had fallen into an allowance of heresy. But better days were coming to the Church; for, whilst the Eastern Bishops had met at Constantinople, and republished the Nicene Faith, in the year 381, perhaps the very one in which St. Ninian was travelling through Italy, councils were held at Aquileia and Milan, where St. Ambrose was most distinguished for his zeal for the maintenance of the true Faith. Keeping along the coast to the Metaurus, the road there turned inland, and crossing the passes of the Apennines, led on to Rome.

And what a scene must Rome have presented to St. Ninian as he beheld it on his approach, and saw the wide gilded roof of the Capitol, or the gorgeous splendour of the Palatium rising above the innumerable buildings which surrounded them. Or as he passed through the Forums, or under the Temples or Basilicas which overhung its streets, how vast must it have appeared in the multitudes of its people, and the grandeur of its edifices. Above a million, some say many millions of inhabitants, were enclosed within a circuit of twenty miles. The luxurious villas and gardens which were spread around it, hemmed in the portion occupied by dwellings, so that the houses rose to a tremendous and dangerous height, far exceeding the limit of 70 feet,¹ which law had imposed; yet these were broken by wide places around on which stood the most magnificent specimens of ancient architecture; and porticoes, arches, columns, and statues, were seen on every side. The palaces of the nobles, now numbered at nearly 2000, from their enormous establishments of slaves, were little towns of splendid architecture, with marble columns and gilded statues, each comprising within itself "every thing which could be subservient to use or luxury, forums, temples, fountains, baths, porticoes, with shady groves and artificial aviaries." An overgrown population of poor and idle citizens occupied at an enormous rent the different floors and rooms of the crowded houses, intent only on the daily doles of food and the public entertainments of the Circus.

The pomp of heathen worship still remained, though its privileges and revenues were diminished. Half the senate at least still adhered to the ancient superstitions, and garlands, processions, and victims might be seen, while the smoke and odour of sacrifices and incense still rose on every side. The rich, unoccupied by political or mercantile pursuits, spent their days in idle and frivolous pleasures, and a continual round of dissipation. There might be seen the rich senator, in elegant and costly dress, making his way through the streets, attended by some fifty slaves; or sailing in his barge, screened by silken awnings and listening to luxurious music. Their wealth was enormous, and it was seen in their display of gold and silver plate, the magnificence of their establishments, the number of their slaves, and the lavish expenditure of their exhibitions and public entertainments. Luxury and refinement seemed to have reached their utmost limit, and the great metropolis of the world to be sinking down, worn out by its own effeminacy.

There were, indeed, schools of learning, supported and regulated by the state, and a great university, to which students from every part of the empire resorted, to obtain the advantage of a Roman education; and the philosophical professor might be known by his peculiar dress. The teachers were for the most part men opposed to the Christian faith, who, by a revived and modified Platonism, explained away the grosser features of Polytheism, and put forward views of philosophy and morals, which, with the utmost zeal and talents, they opposed to the doctrines of the Gospel. Here Ammianus publicly read his admired history, the eloquent and virtuous Symmachus pleaded almost with fanaticism for the toleration of the religion of their fathers; and the philosophers (as Eunapius and Libanius) published explanations of the popular religion, and attributed miracles to the distinguished leaders of their schools, which had not long before received a temporary patronage under the apostate Julian.

Such were the varied and strange objects which, so far as it was not Christian, Rome presented to the view of the British stranger who now made his way along its streets. Nor indeed would the Christian community seem exempt from the corruption of the atmosphere in which it lived. Besides the Catholics, we must remember, there were numerous bodies of heretics, especially Manichees, assuming the name of Christians, and sometimes concealing themselves among them, who endeavoured, by their subtle disputations, and professions of austerity, to gain over converts from the true faith. These were most numerous at Rome, and lived in a miserable way, dispersed through all the quarters of the city, and though professing a severe life, really given up to self-indulgence, and bringing reproach upon their name by their immoralities and crimes. Here might be seen parties of Sarabaites, vagabond and pretended monks, who lived two or three together, under no rule or government, exhibiting pretended sanctity, as a cloak for indulgence, fasting for display, and when a feast came, giving way to excess. Superstition, too, doubtless existed among the people, and vices inconsistent with the religion they professed. For the good, it has been said, are as grains among the chaff; here one and there one, from the accident of their position, stand prominently out, and are discerned almost buried in the surrounding mass, which gives its own complexion to the whole. These things would strike the eye of the casual observer, and it might, perhaps, too, surprise one who had not considered that the Church was a net inclosing bad and good, and that the irreligion and superstition of the mass of men would abuse and discredit the holiest system.

If St. Ninian had not thought of this, there would doubtless be much among the Roman Christians to shock and to distress him. That Church he had looked to, as the model of excellence and the guide to truth; to be taught by her he had relinquished home and friends, and now he saw, even in her bosom, and under the very eye of the Saintly Bishop, gross and evident sin. "I know," says St. Augustine, "that there are many who adore sepulchres and pictures"; and so by superficial or evil-disposed persons, among heretical or pagan contemporaries, the Church was accused of introducing a new idolatry of martyrs and relics, and substituting as objects of divine worship those whose tombs were consecrated by the veneration of the people.[1] "I know," proceeds the Saint, "that there are many who drink to excess on occasion of burials, and make great feasts, under pretence of religion."[2] Among their testimonies to their generally consistent and virtuous lives, the very heathens we find charging Christians with immorality, with the more earnestness because of its contradicting the rules they professed. Violence, party spirit, ambition, found a place among them. The election of the present Bishop—for at Rome the whole body of Christians had a voice in the choice of their Bishop—had been attended with violence and bloodshed. The clergy were often secular in their habits, endeavouring to gain favour with the rich, and using their influence to obtain

[1] As by Eunapius and Faustus the Manichee, quoted by Gibbon, c. 28, notes 60 and 88.
[2] St. Aug. de Moribus Eccl. Christ. I. c. 34.

legacies; so that the civil power interfered by law to check the evil. The wealthy were infected by the luxury of the age and yielded to the pleasures and dissipation common to their class. It might fall to St. Ninian's lot to witness the sad abuses which were practised on the vigil of some martyr, corrupting the holiest services to evil; abuses such that the celebrations themselves were suppressed by St. Ambrose, and the abuses provided against, by the influence of St. Augustine.

But indeed, how could it be otherwise, when the world was flocking into the Church. "In speaking against such men," is St. Augustine's answer, "you do but condemn those whom the Church herself condemns, and daily labours to correct, as wicked children. It is one thing that we are commanded to teach, another we are commanded to correct, and forced to tolerate till we can amend it." For the last seventy years the emperors had been, with few exceptions, professed Christians; they had encouraged the same profession in others, and men influenced by the consideration of worldly interest, and with no serious sense of religion, would outwardly embrace it. And let us not forget that by doing so, faulty as the motive might be, they yet brought themselves and those dependent on them, under a holy discipline, and to the enjoyment of privileges, and inward influences, which might prevail in their children's case if not in their own, and lead them to eternal life. Still this prevalence of an external profession could not but have the effect of lowering the apparent

standard of Christian holiness. It needed a coun-
teracting influence, that the Church might still be
the light of the world and the salt of the earth;
and it found it in the visible separation from the
world, and eminent sanctity of those who followed
out their baptismal vows by the relinquishment of
all earthly ties, and the professed adoption of a
religious life. The Holy virgins and monks it was
who now kept alive the flame of piety, and were,
so to say, the soul of the Church. And their
holiness testified perpetually against the unworthy
lives of others. This is ever to be kept in mind
when we read (as in St. Jerome or St. Sulpicius)
of the evil and worldly lives of the clergy of their
time. They had before them high living standards
of the devotion and sanctity suited to the Christian
calling, and saw more vividly any departure from it.
It was the disciple and biographer of St. Martin,
and the monk of Palestine, the admirers and
advocates of perfect self-denial, and the ascetic
life, who chiefly speak of the evils prevalent among
Christians. That they discerned these evils implied
that the principle of right, the conscience of the
Church, was sensitive and whole. There are ages
where Christians so lose the true standard, that
they are unconscious of their loss.

This may guard us against misjudging the Church
which St. Ninian now visited, whilst in endeavouring
to portray its real condition, we repeat what contemporaries have said of the evils which existed
in it.

Externally indeed the Church of Rome had now
attained to great splendour and magnificence. The

time had come when the wealth of the nations poured in to her, and "she decked herself with jewels as a bride doth." The very Christians who had endured the last and most trying persecution of Dioclesian, raised up more splendid churches than he had destroyed. Long before, during her earlier persecutions, the sacred vessels were of gold and silver. Martyrs suffered because they refused to give up the holy trust, and we know the details of them from the very inventories made by the spoilers.[1] If, then, confessorship be an argument for sanctity, and sanctity for a perception of the truth, we have this authority for decking with magnificent adornings the Christian Churches, as the Jewish Temple was by Divine command. In Rome, the Basilicas had been given to the Church, noble oblong buildings, with rows of columns running lengthwise, and forming, as it were, a nave and aisles. Other Churches were erected over the tombs of Martyrs, where the awful service of the Christian Sacrifice was performed, according to the majestic and simple Liturgy which the Church had received from St. Peter. The taste and magnificence of the present Pope had contributed much to adorning the sacred edifices, and enhancing the grandeur of the services. For the continuous praise of the ever blessed Trinity he had provided for the chaunting of the Psalter night and day, with the Doxology as we now use it. He had built two Basilicas, and given costly offerings of gold and silver vessels to others. Around the altars, lamps of gold, and wax lights in massive candlesticks, burnt by day and

[1] Bingham, 8. 6. 21.

night, dispelling the natural light. The perfumed cloud of incense rose up in the solemn service of the Mass. Gold and silver vessels, and precious stones furnished and adorned the Churches, and garlands and flowers hung around; nay, the devotion of the people made them hang up, on cords of gold, memorials in precious metals of the blessings they had received in answer to their prayers, or through the intercession of the Martyr, over whose grave the Church was raised.[1]

Such were the Churches and Services of Rome, and so deeply was St. Ninian influenced by them, that his first work, on returning as a Missionary into Britain, was to build a Church after the Roman fashion, and there, with the faith of the Roman Church, to introduce her custom in the celebration of Divine offices.

There was one object of surpassing interest, to which first he made his way—the Churches where the martyred remains of St. Peter and St. Paul were laid. The body of St. Paul had been buried a little distance from Rome, on the Ostian road, where his Church now stands; that of St. Peter, on the Vatican, probably by the Jewish Christians who lived in that quarter. Afterwards part of each was laid beside that of the other, in vaults in their respective Churches, that as they were lovely in their lives they might not be divided in death. These were recognised as their burial-places at the end of the second century, and at this time, St. Jerome says, "the Bishops of Rome offered the Holy Sacrifice to God over the revered bones of departed human

[1] Bingham, 8. 8. 2.

beings, and considered their tombs as Altars of Christ." The Vatican, where the more splendid vault and Church were placed, was known as the Confession of St. Peter and the Limina Apostolorum. Hither sentiments of devotion drew Christians, at this time, from all parts of the world, emperors, consuls, and generals, says St. Chrysostom, devoutly visited the sepulchres of those who in their lives had been lowly in the world, but were now exalted.

To seem to be, were it only in imagination, brought near to those chiefest of the Apostles, and most blessed Martyrs, must have been esteemed by St. Ninian a singular privilege. It is a natural sentiment which men of all ages are affected by. "We move," said the philosophic heathen, "in those places where there are, as it were, the very footmarks of those we admire and love. For my own part Athens itself does not so much delight me by exquisite and magnificent works of art, as by calling to mind those greatest of men; where each was wont to live, to sit, and to discourse; and their burial-places I look on with the intensest interest." How much more to a Christian to trace in Rome the places which had been consecrated by the footsteps, the blood, the very remains, of the Apostles. To recall the image of St. Paul, the aged prisoner, his deep knowledge of Christian Truth, his zeal, his constraining eloquence, his patience, his charity;—or of St. Peter, full of love for his Lord, of humility, of readiness to die and to prefer a death of pain for His sake. It was the belief that their spirit and doctrine were preserved here which brought St. Ninian from his distant home. Rome had killed

them—Rome for which they had laboured and inter-
ceded; and the blood of Martyrs, like that of their
Lord, cries for mercy on their persecutors, and brings
blessings on the Church for which they had shed
their blood. So they became the life of Rome.
Persons taking a mere external view saw this.
Rome went to decay, and "like Thebes, Babylon,
or Carthage," says the historian of her fall, "its name
might have been erased from the earth, if the city
had not been animated by a vital principle which
again restored her to honour and dominion. Two
Jewish teachers" (so he speaks), "a tentmaker and
a fisherman, had been executed in the circus of Nero,
and five hundred years after their relics were adored
as the Palladium of Christian Rome": and a glory
and a kingdom were given to it before which the
ancient empire sank into inferiority.

To these shrines St. Ninian came, with a heart
full of devout sentiments; with gratitude that he
should have been brought to this great object of
his desire; that he, a Briton, from almost another
world, might approach the very remains of the
Apostles; and with earnest prayers for the further-
ance of his designs. "He shed tears," as the simple
narrative proceeds, "before the holy relics of the
Apostles, as pledges of his devotion, and with many
prayers commended his desire to their patronage."

CHAPTER V

ST. NINIAN'S LIFE AT ROME

AFTER having thus performed his devotions at the tombs of the Apostles, St. Ninian sought the Pope, and laid before him the object of his journey. It had long been usual for Christians, in travelling from one part of the Church to another, to take with them commendatory letters from the Bishop of their own Church, which should be an evidence of their being in the Catholic Communion, and a recommendation to the Churches which they might visit. Such we suppose St. Ninian to have brought and to have presented to St. Damasus, who had now for nearly twenty years occupied the holy See, having been elected at sixty years of age, in 366. By this aged Saint he was most kindly received, and the object of his leaving his home and seeking the Church of Rome heartily entered into and approved. St. Damasus, himself, was a man of taste and learning. Some of his sacred poems and official letters have come down to us. He was also a great encourager of learned men, and prompted them to undertake works for the service of religion; one especially, the Translation and Commentaries on the Scriptures by St. Jerome, was the fruit of his suggestions, for which alone he deserves our gratitude. This Saint was probably with him about the time St. Ninian came : he resided at Rome for two years, at the wish of the Pope ; and assisted him in these last years of his life in writing those important letters, on many nice and important points of doctrine and ecclesiastical rules, which the See of Rome, consulted and appealed to from every part of Christendom, had continually to send out. And it may throw light on the real character of St. Damasus, who is said to have wrought miracles in life and after death, to consider him as supporting under strong unpopularity the austere and simple-mannered Jerome, and selecting him as his confidential adviser ; and as entering, with the kindness and interest of a father (for he embraced him, it is said, as his own son), into the views of the devout Ninian, who, from a simple desire after the knowledge of Christian Truth, had given up all the world had to offer him. For, outwardly, St. Damasus lived in a splendour which emperors might envy, and had a mind which delighted in great and magnificent works. Whilst Christian Bishops in general lived with simplicity, external humility, and often in poverty, the Bishops of Rome were surrounded by pomp and grandeur. But under this external splendour how often in every age has there been concealed a true poverty of spirit and a self-denying life. St. Jerome, who knew well the character of the Pope, and whose sincerity and severe standard of Christian holiness renders his testimony most valuable, designates him as "of holy memory."

St. Ninian was received by him with the utmost kindness, with, as has been said, the affection of a father. He laid open the object for which he had come to Rome ; and how highly does it speak for the deeply devout character of the Pope, now nearly eighty years of age, that he should enter into and approve a course which had about it so much which in other matters we should call romantic. How rarely do we find the aged capable of entering into the feelings of the young, in cases especially, where worldly interests are concerned, and the usual course of action is departed from. The mere natural disposition of old men leads them to look on the self-forgetfulness of the young as a kind of folly, which experience and sobriety of spirit will wean them from. Such is the temper to which intercourse with the world, and the downward and hardening tendencies of our evil nature, incline us, even towards what is right, and good, and noble, in the temperament of the young. But not such is the aged Christian. He has learnt by experience the true value of that Pearl of great price, and the worthlessness of the world's best treasures. In him love has been warmed and deepened ; and self-sacrifice become a practical and habitual principle. So that, whilst he has the discriminating eye which sees the true path of duty, and distinguishes between a course suggested by mere emotion or self-will, and that to which the guidance of the Holy Spirit leads the youthful scholar in the saintly life, he yet is not wanting in the fullest sympathy with all that is noble and disinterested in his spirit. The Christian mind is one in all, and produces a mutual sympathy in those in whom it exists. Diversities of race and climate, of station, age, employment, which swallow

up the whole character in others, are but an outside
clothing to Christians, and fade away before the
unity of that in which the moral being really consists. And age and youth love to dwell together
in sympathy and peace.

Ninian was placed by St. Damasus under the
care of teachers, who instructed him systematically
in the doctrines of the Faith. He was, as Bede
expresses it, *regulariter doctus*. We do not, indeed,
know what provision was made for the teaching
of Christian doctrine to individuals. It would seem
as if, as yet, it had not assumed any very systematic shape. From the first, the teachers (Doctors)
formed one class of the Christian ministry. They
whose gifts, extraordinary or ordinary, qualified
them more especially for the office of instructing
others in the Faith, would be employed in preparing converts and catechumens for baptism; and
it seems most probable that they would themselves
advance in the study of Holy Scripture, and the
Christian writers, and in the further training up
of others. And this was one use of the Minor
Orders of the clergy, in which, according to the
rule of the apostle, they served a sort of probation
for the diaconate; and under the eye of the bishop,
and the teaching of the Doctors, prepared themselves for the higher offices. At Alexandria the
Church taught all learning, human and divine. In
other Churches, secular and preparatory knowledge
of the arts and sciences, was learnt from the established heathen institutions; and Christian knowledge from their own Clergy.

Under the care of his present teachers St. Ninian

had every reason to rejoice in the step he had taken. " The youth, full of the spirit of God, perceived that he had not run or laboured in vain, as he now understood that from their unskilful teachers, he and his countrymen had believed many things opposed to sound docrine." He met with that satisfaction which the mind feels in the consistency of the truths put before it ; and still more the peace resulting from the confidence which such harmony inspires, that it is indeed the truth itself respecting the Supreme Object of his desire, love, and reverence ; and not a shadow which it grasps instead. And the Holy Scriptures, now explained in their true sense, harmonised with the doctrines inculcated.

The advantages he enjoyed, in this respect, were very great. The Roman church was indeed the school of the true faith, and in its atmosphere heretical teaching was at once discovered. The controversies of the day had caused the truth on the most essential Doctrines to be elicited and defined ; and for the interpretation of Scripture, the learning, and deep and clear understanding of the Sacred writers, possessed by St. Jerome, if not directly engaged in teaching St. Ninian, must yet, without doubt, have had their influence on those to whom St. Damasus committed him for instruction. It was the time, too, when the spiritual understanding of Scripture was being brought out so much by St. Ambrose. And all the teaching he then obtained, whether from the lips of his instructors or the writings of the great teachers of the Church, was eagerly learnt and carefully stored up by St. Ninian for his present comfort, and to be brought out in future years for the instruction of others. In St. Aelred's words. "Applying himself with entire eagerness to the Word of God, he drew from the views of different teachers, as the laden bee from various flowers, the rich honey with which he filled the cells of wisdom, and stored them in the hive of his heart, to be kept there, to be meditated on, and afterwards brought out for the refreshment and support of his inner man, and the consolation of many others."

It was indeed a worthy recompense, that he, who for the love of the truth had thought lightly of home, country, wealth, and pleasures, should, so to say, be led into the innermost shrine of truth, and admitted to the very treasures of wisdom and knowledge; should receive for carnal, spiritual; for earthly, heavenly; for temporal, eternal goods. He was happy. For he had now found a home; for what is a home but a place where we meet with abiding sympathy—where we feel we can repose on those who love us, and whom we love. He had left a home which was dear to him; one which he might well and holily love; but he had found another, where he had what his own home could not give, the knowledge of his Saviour. He had a new father in the holy Damasus, and guides and directors in his wise teachers, and doubtless many brethren, for not in vain would he pray, " Let such as fear Thee, and have known Thy testimonies, be turned unto me." And Rome was full of objects for a Christian to admire and love.

It so happens that, chiefly from St. Jerome's letters, we know much of the spiritual history of the Roman Church, and of what occurred there about this time ; and, as St. Ninian must have been influenced by what was going on, and our estimate of what he was must be to a greater degree formed by knowing the characters held in esteem at that day, some longer reference to them may be excused.

For the first two or three years of his stay St. Jerome was residing there, beloved and esteemed by the good for the holiness of his life, his humility, and learning. Intimately associated as he was with St. Damasus, particularly in his theological studies, it is not unnatural to suppose that the young inquirer after truth had opportunities of drinking in the lessons of wisdom from his lips. For the Saint suffered, it is said, from sore eyes, and so was led to spend more time in oral teaching and conversation. One of his chief employments was to answer the inquiries of those who consulted him on the interpretation of Holy Scripture, and he was ever ready to afford the benefits of his instruction to those who sought it. There can be little doubt that St. Ninian would earnestly desire to hear him, or that opportunities would be given him.

Not long after his arrival another event occurred which must have been most interesting to him, and have made him feel as in the very metropolis of the Church. In the year 382, a council was held in Rome, at which Bishops were assembled, whose names have ever been honoured, and whom St.

Ninian through life might remember.   St. Ascholius, Bishop of Thessalonica, was here, the intimate friend of St. Athanasius, one who had laboured in the conversion of the Goths, a work like that to which the latter part of St. Ninian's own life was to be devoted.   St. Epiphanius, too, the aged Bishop of Salamis, and Paulinus of Antioch, had come with St. Jerome, and spent the winter of 382-3 in Rome, lodging in the house of the holy widow, St. Paula. Epiphanius, now above seventy years of age, had lived through the troubled times of Arianism.   He was the scholar and the dear friend of the sainted hermit, Hilarion, and his own life had for many years been spent in religious solitude, whence he had derived a severe and unbending character, and was now highly honoured in the Church.   St. Ambrose was here, and lodged in the house of his sister, St. Marcellina, to whom he was indebted for the blessings of a religious education, and for a bright example of sincere piety.   She had thirty years before put on the religious habit, and devoted herself to a life of singular holiness in retirement, silence, and prayer,—the secret cause, it may be, in some degree of that glory which shone forth in her brother.

It was a time when many Roman ladies of high rank and wealth retired from the world, and devoted themselves in their own homes, and with their near relations, to the exercises of religion and works of charity.   Each house was a little monastery, where prayer and praise, and fasting and watching, dwelt with love and abundant almsgiving, and works of mercy for the souls and bodies of others—widowed mothers, with their daughters, giving up the enjoyment of wealth and station, and withdrawing to be nearer God. Such was the natural way in which, before the systematic introduction of monastic rules, pious Christians adopted a mode of life which enabled them to serve God without distraction, in prayer and the practice of charity.

Such was St. Marcella, whom St. Jerome calls the glory of the Roman ladies. She had, after losing her husband, early endeavoured to imitate the ascetics of the East, of whom she had heard from St. Athanasius. She refused to marry again, and employed herself in works of devotion and charity. Her example was followed by many noble maidens, who placed themselves under her care, and many religious societies were formed in consequence.

One of the most distinguished of her spiritual children was St. Paula, whom she had comforted on the death of her husband, and induced to forsake the world. St. Paula was descended from one of the noblest Roman families, and had given up great riches and a high place in society, to seek consolation in God. She had now adopted a life of retirement and poverty in the possession of wealth, inquiring out the poor and relieving them with her own hand. "She could make," she said, "no better provision for her children than by drawing on them by her alms, the blessings of heaven." Her time was chiefly spent in religious reading and prayer. She avoided the distractions of society, seeking only the edifying conversation of religious people. At her house, as was said, St. Epiphanius and Paulinus were lodged, and St. Jerome was her spiritual guide during his stay in Rome. There were many others, some of whom, in the society of their own families, formed religious retreats; others united together, under the guidance of a holy and experienced matron. It is most interesting to see the way in which these associations sprung up. The spontaneous growth, as it were, of a deep sense of the truths of religion, and of love to God and man. The example of the solitaries of Egypt had but to be set before them, and they whose hearts were prepared followed it. A few were influenced at first, and from them it spread to greater numbers. They were possessed with the desire of leading a heavenly life on earth, and embraced it under such forms as naturally suggested themselves. We call their houses monasteries, but they are so different from what we usually associate with the name that it is apt to mislead us. They were simple and natural associations of religious persons, living in ordinary dwellings, and devoting themselves to a strict life of silence, abstinence, and prayer, to labour and works of love; and they might rise up spontaneously in any Church where there was the spirit which at first gave them birth.

The monasteries of Rome, as being religious communities formed in the very heart of the city, are highly commended by St. Augustine. "The religious lived together, under the care of a virtuous and learned priest, maintaining themselves by their own labour, ordinarily having but one meal each day, and that towards night; some fasting for longer periods, even for three or more days, but no one being forced to undergo austerities he could not bear." It was most natural for St. Ninian to join some such body; for he was separated from his country, without any ties in the world, or any home but what the Church offered, and so to unite himself to a body of like-minded brethren, in a society of religious men, living together under some rule, was the obvious course by which to seek for support, sympathy, and improvement. Here he was free from the wretchedness and the sights of evil which a life in the city would bring. He might live in silent study, or laborious occupation, enjoying the blessing of undistracted attention to Divine things, without the chill of solitude, the presence of his brethren assisting him to realise that of those unseen Beings who are ever around us. The examples of holy men, seen in their daily round of employments, their humility, recollection, patience, industry, and self-denial, how great a privilege to one who was endeavouring himself to grow in grace, and to learn to copy what was good and profitable in others. And that he adopted this course, which was what the most religious people of his time would do, is confirmed by the circumstance, that St. Siricius, who chose him to be a Bishop, particularly favoured the practice of selecting the Clergy from such monastic bodies.

Thus St. Ninian lived for the next fifteen years, fifteen years of what is called the best part of a man's life, gradually advancing in that holiness which was afterwards manifested in his works on earth, and his availing power with heaven; growing in gentleness, self-devotion, and recollection, and meanwhile making progress in the depth and ac-

curacy of his views of Divine truth, and in the
understanding of Holy Scripture. It was, according to men's present views, a long time to spend
in comparative inactivity, where the missionary
life was that for which he was destined. It was,
as they say, shutting up in a cloister, power, and
energy, and goodness, which might have been more
usefully engaged in doing good to others. But
very different from the hurried eagerness of men
for immediate visible results, is the calm majestic
march of the Divine dispensations, and the course
of those of His servants in whom they are imitated.
He waited four thousand years before He undertook His work. He would have His servants well
matured in knowledge and love before they take
in hand the offices they are designed for, and is
willing that there should be a long and seemingly
unprofitable toil, in preparing deep and strong
foundations for the structure He would raise. One
well prepared and sanctified character exercises far
more influence for good, than many ordinary ones.
Such an one is a true standard of what we should
aim to be, and as such attracts the hearts of those
who are prepared to receive the truth. He is fit
to guide, and by his deep practical wisdom, and
weight of character, has a constraining power over
even unwilling minds. St. Ninian might have
engaged early in missionary labours, and have
been as others are. He waited, growing more and
more in holiness; and he went forth to work
miracles, and to convert the nations.

Nor should it surprise us, that so long a time
should be spent in the study of Divine truth.

Nearly as long a time given exclusively to that highest object of the human mind, was not of old thought too much for preparing one who was to teach others. It is our low standard of theological attainments, which makes a few months seem enough to prepare for expounding the mysteries of the Gospel; and it is our diversion into matters only accidentally connected with Theology proper, which leads us to conceive the knowledge of the divine unnecessary, if not prejudicial to his practical usefulness in influencing the hearts of men. Criticism and Antiquities, Church History and Evidences, viewed externally, and by themselves, are thought, and rightly so, to be of little use to one who has the care of souls. But such is not the case with Theology, properly so called, that is the knowledge of what we are to believe, and what we are to do; the more exact knowledge of Him, Whom truly to know is everlasting life; the true vision of Whom keeps the soul and its affections in their right position, whilst errors and false views distort and deprave them; this is real Theology. It is Dogmatic Theology which contemplates, defines, and gives exactness to our views of that truth by which we are sanctified; Controversial Theology, which enables us to guard the truth from corruption, and to watch against the first inroads of error. Surely, to a holy mind, such contemplations are alike the highest employment of the understanding, and tend most to his own sanctification, and his power of teaching others. St. Thomas, the most profound of schoolmen, was the most devout of Saints, and the most powerful preacher. His prayers are among the choicest treasures of the Church. His sermons awakened and converted the most ignorant and hardened sinners.

And as regards Moral Theology, with its hand-maids, Casuistical and Ascetic, contemplating what we ought to be, and to do, in principle and detail, and how we may attain to a saintly temper ; what time and thought can be too much for attaining to exactness of knowledge here, by one who is really to be a guide to others? How many nice points are to be determined ! How many difficult questions in the treatment of the souls of men in their varied spiritual conditions ! What grave con-sideration of duties and principles ! It betokens indeed that men have fallen into a low religious condition, when they cannot even estimate the value of deep and long continued study on such subjects. If it be kept in mind that Theology, rightly so called, is the knowledge of God, and how we may please Him, it will be evident, that as the one great requisite for the study of it is a holy life, so it is the first business of the Clergy to attain proficiency in it, and that no extent of real attainment can be too much—they ought to draw all their care and study this way. This will be the guide of their course of study, and will arrange in due subordination the various other branches of know-ledge, and enable them to derive from each what it can minister to their highest end. It will secure the knowledge of those truths which are essential, will determine the extent and the end for which we should pursue the rest. No subject of human knowledge will then be without its use and due position.

Of the course of study St. Ninian would go through, we may form probably a very fair notion from a Treatise of St. Augustine, written not long after, designed to direct the studies of those who were to be teachers of others.

The main object to which he directed the student was the right understanding and explanation of the Holy Scriptures. This seems to be viewed as the chief business of the Christian teacher, and it is to this end that all other studies are made subordinate. But first, he was to know those principles to which all interpretations must be conformed — the principles of Christian Faith, Hope, and Charity. Of Faith, in the full knowledge and understanding of the Creed; of Hope, and of the sum of evangelical morality in the love of God above all things, and of our brethren in Him, and for His sake; and any interpretation which is inconsistent with these principles, whether as sanctioning immorality, or erroneous doctrine, must be wrong. Next, presupposing that the student has, by personal religion, entered on the steps of wisdom, beginning with the fear of the Lord, he is to learn the rules and principles of literal and spiritual interpretation, the latter being the chief study of the expositor. In connection with this, he is to acquire a knowledge of Scripture criticism, of the right text, and translation; of history, natural science, logic, and all other subjects which may be useful to him as subsidiary learning. Lastly, he is to study how to express to others what he himself has learnt, by acquiring the art of Christian eloquence. The first and second of these subjects

T

we may conceive would form the principal part of St. Ninian's studies, the doctrines of the faith and Christian love, and the spiritual interpretation of Scripture, for both of which he would find so great assistance in the works of contemporary writers, or of those who had gone before; as well as by the oral teaching of the doctors, of the Roman Church.

So much of apology, if it be needed, for St. Ninian's living for fifteen years, in what the world would call a comparatively narrow sphere at Rome, but really, in a life of labour, thought, and constant endeavour after improvement.

Every thing here combined for his advancement in fitness for his great destiny. Rome was the centre of the Christian world. Errors and disputes were heard of, examined, and determined there; each improvement in the rules of holy living, each practical advancement in Church discipline and conduct, was brought into this great resort and emporium of the Christian world, while the steady orthodoxy of the Church enabled it to look with discrimination on the opinions and practices which rose up around it.

The details of St. Ninian's life here are quite unknown, but general history relates many events, which must have exercised an important influence upon him.

Within three or four years after his arrival, St. Ninian sustained a heavy loss in the death of his kind patron, St. Damasus, who died the tenth of December, in the year 384; being then nearly eighty years of age. He was succeeded by St.

Siricius, who, twelve years after, was to consecrate and send out St. Ninian. For some time he was unacquainted with him, as was natural in so large a Church, and when St. Ninian did not occupy a prominent place. St. Ninian, therefore, deprived of the friendship and countenance of St. Damasus, was left to go on in the ordinary course.

About this time he was, most probably, admitted to the minor orders as a Reader. For we have the rules which St. Siricius sent to the Church of Spain, immediately on his election, February 385, in which he determines the regular gradation of offices. One who from infancy was devoted to the service of the Church, was to be baptised before he was fourteen, and placed in the rank of Readers. If his life was approved till he was thirty, he was made an Acolyte and Sub-deacon, and if judged worthy, a Deacon, after having previously made a promise of continence. Then, after five years' service, he might be admitted to the Priesthood, and, after ten more, to the Episcopate. Such was the long probation and service for the sacred ministry in those days. And though, very probably, in St. Ninian's case, as in others, peculiar circumstances might be a ground for departing from it in some points, we may suppose it observed on the whole : and that he went through the regular course of clerical offices in Rome.

Meanwhile important events were occurring around him ; events in which the whole Church has since been interested. The conversion of St. Augustine and his baptism at Milan, occurred at Easter, 387 ; and the latter part of that year, after the death of his mother, and whole of the following one, he spent at Rome. It is not unnatural to suppose that he and St. Ninian might meet; the more humble talents of the Briton, being in the eyes of St. Augustine far more than compensated by that spotless purity of heart which enjoyed the blessedness of seeing God. The one baptised in infancy had by habitual obedience, kept his robes unstained. The other, washed from a load of actual sins, was now at the eleventh hour labouring more than any, and by his zeal and earnestness making way beyond them.

About this time, too, the Emperor Theodosius visited Italy, and great exertions were in vain used to prevail on him to favour the depressed cause of paganism; it was his resolution which led to the entire fall of the ancient superstition. His visit to Rome in 389 gave the last blow to idolatry. He entered the city with Valentinian, and then it was that the most distinguished families embraced Christianity, the Anicii, Probi, Pauli, Gracchi. The people ran in crowds to the Vatican, to venerate the tombs of the Apostles, or to the Lateran to be baptised; but few adhered to the ancient superstitions. The temples were filled with cobwebs and soon fell to ruin; and the idols were left alone under their roofs with the owls and the bats.

The time was now approaching when he was to be called to that work for which the providence of God had long been training him. Year after year had passed, and, to himself, it might seem as if he was doing but little service, and was an unprofitable servant: but a preparation was going on in the practice of humble obedience, and in His own good time

God called on him to take his great work in hand. The duties of the offices he had been placed in afforded an opportunity for his good qualities to be seen and generally recognised. Purity, wisdom, and circumspectness, are the points specially mentioned ; and those of them which may be considered as intellectual gifts, are just of the kind which would be formed and developed by religious principles ; the absence of hurry and excitement, calm considerateness, a fair estimate of others, are the natural fruits of that confidence in God which trusts that all will be controlled for good, which sets their true value on the things of the world and the events of time, and so is without anxiety ; of charity, which despises no one, but sympathises with their difficulties, puts itself in the place of others, and enters into their views ; and of honesty and simplicity of aim, which has no bye ends to entangle, or duplicity to involve it. It is from these qualities that wisdom in counsel springs. And to be gradually entrusted with offices of responsibility, in subordination to higher authority, the learning practically to rule and to be ruled, in the successive steps of the lower clerical offices, was the very means to form the mind of the future saint to this prudence in judging and circumspection in acting. And his excellences by degrees became generally matter of remark, and brought him under the notice and, ultimately, into esteem and familiar association with St. Siricius.

"While he was spoken of by all as chaste in body, wise in understanding, provident in counsel, circumspect in every word and deed, he rose to the favour and friendship of the Pope himself."

The advantages to be derived from this position
were, we need not say, very great, in fitting him for
the work in which he was to engage ; and the knowledge of it gives us peculiar means of ascertaining the
views which St. Ninian entertained on many important subjects, and which he brought into our own
country. For we know those of St. Siricius ; and, considering that after this intimate acquaintance with
him the Pope fixed on him as the fittest person to
correct the errors which prevailed among the British
Christians, we cannot doubt that Ninian's views coin-
cided with his own ; the more so as his professed
intention was to teach in Britain the doctrines of the
Roman Church.

The decretals of St. Siricius sent to the Church of
Spain in 385 have already been referred to ; they
recognise, it need scarcely be said, a monastic system,
as an established custom, approved and encouraged
by the Church. A strict penitential discipline and
the celibacy of the Clergy are presupposed as right,
regulated and enforced. A formal expression of the
same views was elicited by the heresy of Jovinian,
who, amongst other errors, maintained "that virgins
have no more merit than widows or married women,
and that there is no difference between abstaining
from meats and using them with thanksgiving."
With these easy doctrines it is no wonder he had
many followers at Rome ; persons who had long lived
in continence and mortification, married and returned
to a soft and unrestrained life. It did not, however,
number any Bishop among those who embraced it,
and in the year 390 an assembly of the Roman
Clergy was held, and the doctrines declared to be

contrary to the Christian truth ; and by the unanimous advice of the Priests and Deacons who were present, and we can scarcely doubt St. Ninian was among them, Jovinian and his followers were excommunicated.

CHAPTER VI

ST. NINIAN'S RETURN TO BRITAIN

AND now we may pass to the time when the Saint
was called to the high duties of a Bishop and a
Missionary. The activity and vigilance of St. Siricius
prompted him to act upon those feelings of sym-
pathising interest which give to every Church which
is a healthy member of the great Catholic body, a
deep concern in the welfare of every other part. If
one member suffer, all the members suffer with it.
Still more should he feel it who occupied the chief
See of Christendom ; on whom, in an especial manner,
it seemed incumbent to watch and provide for all, to
support the weak, to correct the erring, and to convert
the unbelieving ; and Siricius seems particularly to
have felt this interest in our remote and despised
country. It was compassion for half taught and mis-
guided Christians, for heathens and barbarians, for
whom the Son of God had shed His precious blood—
for immortal beings, who, unrescued, might perish for
ever, but by the power of the Gospel, would be
exalted to everlasting bliss, and swell the ranks of
the angelic choirs. It was compassion, such as two
centuries afterwards moved his successor, the saintly
Gregory, to yearn over the wretchedness of our Saxon
ancestors. These feelings in their case would go

beyond the ordinary compassion which Christians generally would have; they would feel with the blessed Apostle that they had the care of all the Churches, and that the weak and the scandalised were the special objects of their sympathy.

And in the case of St. Siricius there was happily one at hand peculiarly suited for the work before him. St. Ninian had waited long for this call to the office for which Divine Providence had all along designed, and been preparing him. Perhaps he would have no thought of undertaking so great a work, or if ever a desire had crossed his mind to impart to his countrymen the unspeakable blessings he had himself obtained, it might be repressed as not to be thought of, till some guiding of Providence, or obedience to authority should determine it to be his duty, and sanction his undertaking it. For it is not to be imagined that Ninian had forgotten Britain. How should he? Means of communication were regular and speedy; events of moment were frequently occurring; his countrymen, who, as we have heard, made religious visits to the Holy Land, would often draw to the city, to offer their devotions at the tombs of the Apostles; others would resort among the provincials for the advantages of the schools; others again, like himself, for religious improvement. Of one such we know, St. Piran, the Cornish Saint, whose Church in the Sand was recently brought to light. He was a native of Ireland, and born about 352. When about thirty years of age, and so nearly at the same time as St. Ninian, having received some imperfect information about the Christian Faith, he travelled to Rome for more complete instruction.

He is supposed by the Irish writers to have been consecrated at Rome, and returned home, accompanied by four Clerics, who were all afterwards Bishops. With them St. Ninian would hold converse, and hear the language, which, harsh as it may seem to us, would sound sweet in his ears, as the language of his home. By these means his information and interest in Britain would be kept alive. And when the holy Father, whose authority and wish would be a command, called him to this work, we may imagine that with his deep humility, and shrinking from an office to which he would seem quite unequal, there would be some warm feeling kindled, in the hope that he might be a blessing to those he loved so well.

In St. Aelred's words, "The Roman Pontiff had heard that there were in the western part of Britain some who had not yet embraced the faith of our Saviour,[1] some also who had heard the word of the Gospel, but from heretical or ignorant teachers; and by the impulse of the Divine Spirit, he, with his own hands, consecrated this man of God to the

---

[1] It is most probable that attention was drawn to the condition of the British of this district by the publication of St. Jerome's work against Jovinian, which occurred in the year 393 or 394. It was written at the request of some Christians at Rome, and excited great interest there. In the second book he mentions that he had himself, when a youth in Gaul, seen some of the Attacotti, a British tribe, who ate human flesh; and adds still more revolting details as to the habits of their people. This tribe occupied the country between Loch Lomond and Loch Fine. Such a statement could not fail to excite inquiry, and lead the Pope to ascertain the real state of the unconverted people, who, being of the same race, were within the limits of the empire. The mission of St. Ninian was the natural result.

office of a Bishop, and sent him with the Apostolic Benediction to this people."

This event most probably occurred in the spring of the year 397. The date is determined by a circumstance which is on other accounts interesting, and intimately connected with the history and future character of St. Ninian. It is, that on his way to Britain, he visited St. Martin of Tours, whose name had recently been made known through the whole Church by Sulpicius's life of him. Now St. Martin, according to the best authorities, died in November 397. The life in question was a narrative, written by Sulpicius, for his friend St. Paulinus of Nola, without any view to its becoming public. It was, however, communicated by Paulinus to others, and so spread with unprecedented rapidity. This occurred within a year before the death of the Saint, for it was after the death of St. Clare in the previous November. And the sensation it produced in Rome and throughout the Christian world was incredible. The booksellers having at command only the slow process of the human hand could not have it copied so fast as to meet the demand, and could sell it at almost any price; it was considered the most gainful work they had ever had. No book was so much read, or so eagerly sought after; it was in every one's hands, and everywhere the subject of conversation. For it related of a living Bishop so near them as in France, sanctity almost unequalled, and miraculous powers, such as were not then possessed by any one; and these recorded in graceful language, with the Latinity of the purest ages, and the unaffected simplicity of a friend writing to a friend of what he had himself seen and known; and with the deep and affectionate reverence of a disciple, for one who had guided him by example and instruction into the ways of holiness and peace.

From this work, St. Ninian, as St. Aelred relates, ardently desired to see and converse with the holy man whose ways were depicted there, and accordingly, on his way to Britain, diverged to Tours to visit its Bishop.

We, too, have the beautiful picture which Sulpicius has drawn, and for St. Ninian's sake, that we may know the sort of person whom he looked on as a model; and for our own, that we may in this way see the Saint ourselves, we will go along with him to the Hermit Bishop, whom our northern Churches venerate so highly.

St. Martin had long lived as a recluse, and when the people of Tours would have him, in spite of his poor clothes and mean appearance, to be their Bishop, he kept up his holy solitude as much as he could, in a cell adjoining his Church. This, however, proved more liable to interruption than he wished, so he went into a lonely spot a mile or two from the town, where a sweep of the river left a level grassy plain, which was shut out from the country on its landward side by a line of precipitous rocks, and accessible only by difficult paths. Here he fixed his abode, and to him gathered others who desired to be under his guidance, and, forsaking the world, to imitate his humble and mortified life. They were about sixty in number; some lived in cells built by themselves, many in caves in the rocks, and that in solitude, except when they met for prayers, or at their meals, and labouring, many by copying books, for their own support. Above all, the Saint himself drew the hearts of holy men to him by his humility, meekness, and deep knowledge of religious truth. He was quite an illiterate man, yet readily solved the difficulties of Scripture. But his real life was hid with Christ, and he was in continual communion with Him, unceasingly praying, either by direct supplication, or the inward lifting up of his soul to God. His humility was remarkable; he judged no one, he condemned no one; he was never irritated, never depressed by sorrow, or excited by mirth, but ever bearing in his looks a kind of heavenly joyfulness. Christ only was on his lips, and in his heart compassion, piety, and peace. Besides all this, there was an awfulness thrown around him by the visible tokens of the Divine presence in the miracles he had wrought, miracles which have a degree of evidence rarely to be met with.

To visit this saint, then, so marked by traits of personal holiness, and the awful manifestations of Divine authority accompanying his deeds, was the object of St. Ninian on his way to Britain. "He diverged to Tours," says St. Aelred, "filled with the Holy Ghost, and touched by an eager desire of seeing him."

Meanwhile St. Martin had been prepared for his coming. "By the grace of prophetic illumination, the virtues of the new Bishop were not unknown to him. He was taught that he was sanctified by the Holy Ghost, and would be the instrument of the salvation of many; and, in consequence, with what joy, devotion, and affection did he receive him." Their time was spent in holy converse and aspirations of divine love, Ninian, doubtless, being eager to learn from so great a saint, and profiting by his readiness to solve the difficulties of Scripture, and to speak of Christ and the rules of holy living. He also gained another advantage. His wish was to introduce religion into his country in its completeness, to present it before his people, not only in the statement of doctrines and rules of practice, but as visibly embodied in the Church and manifested in her sacred services; it was his intention to imitate, "as the faith, so the customs of the Roman Church in building Churches and arranging the services"; and he requested St. Martin to furnish him with masons for the work. " In the tabernacle of the Lord two columns are joined together, and two cherubim stretching out their wings touch each other; now borne up on the wings of virtue they withdraw to be with God; now standing and letting them fall they condescend to their neighbours. So these saints returned from heavenly objects to the things of this world." At last they parted. " They had feasted on their mutual conversations as on heavenly banquets, and separated with embraces, kisses, and tears shed in common. St. Martin remained in his See. Ninian hastened to the work for which he had been sent forth by the Holy Ghost."

Such is the sympathy of holy men; such their love, seeming not to need the usual preparations of human friendship; but as they each have ad-

ST. NINIAN'S RETURN TO BRITAIN 303

vanced towards the one model, the image of Christ
enabling them to understand each other at once.

On his way through France and Belgium, as Camerarius reports, St. Ninian was anxious to labour for
the conversion of the people, and great numbers
were the fruit of his preaching. The authority however is very recent, and though he may be regarded,
like other later writers, as preserving and perpetuating a tradition of a much earlier date, the evidence
is so slight, that we must leave the matter simply to
recommend itself by its internal probability.

And now, after an absence of many years, St.
Ninian is again in sight of the shores of Britain,
and gazes on its white cliffs as he nears his native
land. But greatly is he changed. He had gone
forth, young, uninformed, seeking to be taught the
truth. He returns in mature age, with solid judgment, deep knowledge, confirmed faith, commissioned
to instruct others, and to impart to them those true
views of doctrine, and those many lessons of holy
living which he had been storing up. But with
how great a responsibility did he come, and with
how little earthly help. In Rome he had been
surrounded by those who sympathised with him,
and were engaged in the sacred pursuits he had
been devoted to ; counsel, consolation, and aid were
ever at hand. Now was he to stand alone, with a
half barbarous people around him, whom he had
to labour to convert, or to correct, scarcely knowing
how they would receive him, or how he should find
access to their minds.

On the part of his countrymen however the greatest
interest was felt in him. We know how strongly

the inhabitants of remote districts are interested in
those who have left the seclusion in which they
live, to make their way in the world. There is
among such people a strong feeling of community,
which makes each one a relation as it were to all
the rest ; and if one goes out from his native village
to make his way in a larger sphere, deep interest
is felt in his success, and a desire to hear of him.
The old remember him as a child, and his father
and father's father. The young were the companions of his boyish days. If he becomes distinguished and honoured, all seem to have a share in
it. And Ninian had been a youth whose goodness
and engaging manners would especially gain their
affections. He was a Briton, the son too of one
of their own princes, to whom it was natural they
should cling with peculiar attachment as associated
with the remembrance of what their tribes had been ;
for amid the improvements of Roman civilisation,
many ardent spirits would look back on the wild
glories of their uncivilised days, and cherish the
recollection of the renown and independence of their
race. We may imagine the interest with which they
would hear of the esteem in which their young
countryman was held, the position which he occupied
even in the chief city of the world ; and the joy
with which they would receive the news, that he
was to be restored to them as their Bishop. He was
the son of their king, but he had humbled himself
by relinquishing secular dignity, and now was exalted
by a far higher spiritual office. The children of this
world, the more they valued its gifts of wealth and
power, the more they would conceive that he had

made a sacrifice; and they who had the opportunity of seeing any thing of the peace and joy he had in Christ, would see that he had not been wrong in making it. Here was a living instance of giving up the world for Christ. What it was to be a Prince they saw, and they would think much of it. The Bishop might have had these goods of wealth and honour, but he preferred to be a servant of Christ, and of the people of Christ, to struggle with poverty, to submit to hardships, to overcome ill-will, unkindness, and obstinacy, by meek endurance. The sacrifice they could appreciate; and when they heard him speak of leaving all to follow Christ, and of taking up the cross, his words would come home to them, for what he said was real; it had an interpretation in his own doings.

This will in a measure account for the great success which attended the first opening of his work amongst them. It is described as an outbreak of enthusiasm, which ran through the people, and enabled him at once to do the work of years.

If he preached at all as did the great models of his day, we cannot wonder at it. They preached as men who realised what is unseen, for the great truths of eternity were the groundwork of all they said; and they came forth from deep and earnest meditation on these truths, to speak of them to others, with earnestness and affection, their own minds being filled with the ideas and affections which corresponded to them. As one who had really seen some land of bliss, or awful suffering, or impending danger, they spoke of them in a natural and real way, and by their very sincerity, and the

vivid impression of their own conviction of all they
said, they carried others along with them. They
could trust to the spontaneous flow of their minds,
for they had been schooled by severe lives and
serious thought, to deep awe and reverence, and
been trained in the full and exact knowledge of
Christian truth ; and as Bishops almost exclusively
were preachers, they had long time for thought,
experience, and sobriety, before they undertook so
high an office. They could speak freely, for they
spoke of what they really knew by personal experience, and long acquaintance with the ways of holy
living ; and this without erroneous and vague statements, or the risk of irreverence, familiarity, or
excitement.

It was the age of Ambrose, Chrysostom, and
Augustine ; and Ninian came into Britain, as it
were, from their school, with all the fulness of view
and varied thoughts which an acquaintance with
Christians and Christian Theology, in its highest
form, would give. And this was expressed to the
Britons in their own language ; that language which,
unlike most of the other subjects of the empire, they
still retained and cherished, and which would be
more likely to be preserved and usually spoken in
remote and mountainous districts, as Cumbria and
Galloway. And we know how it gladdens the
hearts of the Celts of these days, in Wales and
Ireland, to hear their own language, and how they
think no harm can come in it ; and can imagine
what the Britons would feel at hearing it from St.
Ninian.

It may be they were of the same imaginative and

susceptible temper which we find in those remains of their race, for the effect of the Saint's preaching was immediate and very great. " Crowds of people collected together and came to meet him ; there was unbounded delight among them all, and wonderful devotion. Every where did the praises of Christ resound, for they all held him as a prophet. At once, the active labourer, entering his master's field, began to pull up what was ill-planted ; what was ill brought together, to disperse ; to pull down what was built amiss." This was his first beginning. " Afterwards, having cleared the minds of the faithful from all their errors, he began to lay in them the foundation of the holy faith ; to build the gold of wisdom, the silver of knowledge, and the stones of good works. These all he taught by word, exhibited by example, and confirmed by numerous miracles."

CHAPTER VII

ST. NINIAN IN GALLOWAY

THE province which was assigned to St. Ninian seems to have been the western portion of our northern counties, and the Scottish Lowlands, south of the Wall of Antoninus. In the direction of the heathen, it was, of course, unlimited; the field was open for him to convert all he could. In Scotland there were, probably, very few Christians; in the English portion they were but partially converted and very ignorant. What arrangement was made between the new Bishop and the Bishop of York, or of any unknown See, in whose diocese this country was lying before, we cannot tell. The British Bishops might gladly receive amongst them a missionary Bishop, as they afterwards did St. Germanus, to assist in eradicating evil and promoting the good of their people; or there may have been some definite district assigned to him; and of this it may be that a trace remained in the limits of St. Kentigern's diocese of Glasgow, which seems to have taken the place of St. Ninian's, and extended to the Cross on Stainmoor.

This district was occupied by different tribes of Britons, having the same language and character, except that those in England were more influenced by Roman civilisation. Those to the north consisted of five tribes, whose country had been formed into a new province, by Theodosius, A.D. 367, under the name of Valentia. They lay between the two walls, and were in an intermediate state of civilisation, between the inhabitants of the ancient provinces, who had for centuries been under Roman influence, and the wild unsubdued inhabitants of the Highlands. Their country was but partially occupied by the Romans, who used it chiefly for military occupation and defence against the Caledonians; and though the inhabitants were Roman citizens, those who lived in the more remote portions of the district probably differed little from the barbarous state in which Cæsar had found our whole island.

It was among the English portion of his people that St. Ninian first laboured. His history implies that, as was natural, he first went among his own people and the friends of his early years, to impart to them the inestimable benefits he was commissioned to diffuse; and in accordance with this, Leland distinctly speaks of his first mission as being to the coast of Cumberland, between St. Bees Head and Carlisle.

The circumstances of the country were not, however, such as were in any way suited for his long continuance or permanent establishment there. Cumberland lying just within the southern wall and being filled by military establishments,[1] was now the scene of warlike preparation, and the fearful anticipations,

---

[1] There were stations at Moresby, Ellenborough, Burgh by the Sands, besides Carlisle and Penrith, and those at Stanwix, Bowness, and along the line of the Wall.

and miserable realities of a bloody and exterminating warfare. It was a time of bitter distress to the Provincial Britons; and sad, indeed, was the sight presented to St. Ninian. The peace and tranquillity he had left in his native land was at an end. It was just the time at which the wild hordes of Picts, who had been restrained whilst the vigorous hand of Theodosius held the reigns of empire, were again, a year or two after his death, coming like a flood over the fair fields and rich and civilised abodes of the Provincials. In the following year, 398, it was necessary to send two additional legions into Britain to save the province from utter ruin; and it was now but thirteen years before it was finally abandoned by the Romans.

St. Gildas has depicted in strong colours the savage invaders, and the wretchedness of the helpless Provincials. It needs, however, no exaggeration to represent the greatness of their sufferings. They had long been shielded by the power of the empire. Four legions evidence alike the danger from the barbarians and the security of the inhabitants. They had, from the first, been taught to forget their warlike habits in the luxuries of ease, and to delight in a slavery which presented itself in the form of comfort and refinement. The works of long continued peace—the improvements of civilisation—the beauty of their cities — their costly and elegant houses, now fell before the destroyers, whose cupidity they had excited. Hardy and warlike Picts poured from the fastnesses of the Highlands; poor, uncivilised, unclothed, what the Britons themselves had been 300 years before. Their ill-will was in-

creased by the very circumstance that their countrymen had identified themselves with the invaders,
whose yoke they had themselves with difficulty
avoided. Rapine, bloodshed, and cruelty followed
in their course, and the Provincials, unable to cope
with them, were driven from their peaceful homes,
and witnessed the destruction of their cherished
possessions, and the death of their dearest friends.
Such were the miseries which met St. Ninian on
returning to the home of his childhood, and led to
his retiring to a more peaceful district to establish
his Church. It is not improbable that he was
accompanied by some of his family, who might
seek a refuge on the retired shore of Galloway, from
the rapine and harassing inroads to which their
old homes were exposed. We find, at least, that
his brother was his companion in after years, and,
as one ancient Life reports, his mother and relations
were settled near him. His father may have died
before he saw, on earth, the face of his son, or
witnessed the blessings which he brought to his
countrymen. He was removed from the joy of
seeing the fruits of Ninian's preaching ; from the
distress of beholding the calamities of his country.

The plan which St. Ninian proposed to adopt for
carrying on the work of a missionary Bishop, required a place where he might erect a Church, where
he might himself permanently live, and form a
religious society. For this it was most important to
select a position which would be retired, and secure
alike from the interruptions of a rude soldiery or the
outrage of barbarian tribes. And the place which
he chose was singularly adapted for his purpose.

The country between the walls was the very
ground on which the battles of the contending armies
would continually be fought; like the suburbs of a
besieged town, which neither party spared, but made
the arena of their mutual combats. To the south-
west, however, the extensive promontory of Galloway
stretched beyond the scene of war, and being guarded
by the sea on either side, had on the whole remained
almost undisturbed by the changes which had gone
on around it. It was removed from the ordinary
course of the invading Highlanders, and had not
itself any objects to attract their rapacity. It had
scarcely been affected even by the Roman power.
Agricola, in the year 83, had contemplated an expedition to Ireland, and with this view, had overrun
the country; roads had been made, and encamp-
ments formed, but, afterwards, as he seems not to
have had any object in pursuing the natives into
their fastnesses, its remote situation made it little
frequented by the Romans. It appears to have
continued without giving much occasion for military
establishments, for few Roman remains are found
in it.

What is now a bare and uninteresting district,
where the slow progress of plantations endeavours
to compensate for the want of natural wood, was
then covered by thick forests, and occupied by
Britons, living in all their uncivilised simplicity.
The tribe was called the Novantes; and Ptolemy
mentions their two towns as Rerigonium and
Leucopibia. The latter was the one which St.
Ninian fixed on as the site for his Church. It was
conforming, so far as he could, to the ancient rule,

to fix the seat of a Bishop in a city, that the shepherd may be where his flock principally are found; and in this place the greatest number of Christians would be gathered. Of its identity with Whithern there can be no doubt, and the very probable and generally received conjecture is, that the Leucopibia of our present copies of Ptolemy should be Leucoikidia—Whitehouses; so identifying its three names, Leucoikidia, Candida Casa, and Whithern, which is derived from the Saxon ærn, house. Baxter suggests that it is so called from the practice of the Celts (he says Picts, but there were no Picts in Galloway till long after this time) to whitewash their houses. It seems most probable that the name was prior to St. Ninian's arrival, and not derived, as commonly said, from the Church he built; for whatever be made of the latter part of the word, Leuco speaks for itself, and Casa like ærn, seems rather to indicate an ordinary dwelling than a Church. There had been a castra stativa close adjoining the town which is the only Roman position traceable in Galloway; and a road which Agricola had formed along the coast, had been continued to Leucopibia. But in their present pressing circumstances, the encampment doubtless would be abandoned. The town itself lies but two or three miles from the extremity of the promontory, which branches off from the main one of Galloway, and running far into the sea, forms almost the most southern point of Scotland. It is thus without access by land except on the north; and being naturally difficult of access, and out of the direct line towards Ireland, is now one of the most retired places in Scotland. Few had any inducement to visit it from the north; and its southern and western sides are guarded by lofty and precipitous rocks, and only here and there afford access for vessels.

Here, then, St. Ninian might securely fix his See, removed from the troubles and dangers which occupied the rest of Britain; and hence go forth to traverse the wild woodlands for the purpose of evangelising the people. At the same time, the town was probably, as we may judge from the encampment and the road, one of the most important which the natives had; while the promontory, called Burrow Head, which rises near it, is seen from and commands a view of the extensive diocese in which his lot was cast.

One looks with interest at the position of the Minsters of York or Lincoln, which are conspicuous through the whole surrounding districts—ever present remembrances of Divine Truth, and marks of him who sits there the spiritual father of the flock. Such was the position of St. Ninian's See. As you stand on the fine headland, with sea on every side, you almost look down on the mountains of the Isle of Man, which rise out of the sea, before you. To the right stretch the successive promontories of Galloway almost to Port Patrick; the Hills of Wigtonshire, Kirkcudbrightshire, and Dumfriesshire, rise in successive and lofty ridges, from the shores of the Solway, to the north; while, due east, you may trace the coast of Cumberland, to St. Bees Head, or even to Blackcomb, backed by its fair blue hills, so picturesque in outline; and as the light and shade alternate on the view, you may make out each bay and headland, and even the white houses by the shore. Surely this was a place where the Saint might stand and survey the field in which he had to work. He had given evidence enough that he was no idle dreamer or slave of weak affection. Still we may well suppose that when he looked down from this central point, and had before him headlands and mountain tops which marked out the wide district committed to him, he would regard with especial tenderness, the distinctly marked shore where he had been baptised and spent his youthful years;—those hills which he had looked up to from his home. They would recall the remembrance of those who were gone, and awake more fervent prayers for his country, now in the scene of distraction and warfare.

We have said that the manners of the people had been but little affected by the influence of the Romans. It is probable that their way of life was very much what that of the Britons had been before they were refined by Roman colonisation, or as those of their neighbours the Mœatæ, who at the beginning of the third century inhabited barren mountains and marshy plains, had no manured or cultivated lands, but fed on the milk and flesh of their flocks, or what they got by hunting, or some wild fruits; fish they never ate, though they had great plenty of them, and when in the woods they fed on roots and herbs.

There still remain in Galloway, circles, and Cromlechs, and Cistvaens, traces of what St. Ninian might see lingering as a broken, but still living system. The Druid religion was proscribed by the Romans.

It was a strong, too strong a bond to be allowed to remain among the Britons; but the superstition was still deeply rooted in the minds of the people, and a reverence long after hung around the enclosures which had been consecrated by Druid rites. At present, therefore, they must have been in a wretched religious condition; the public exercise and ministers of their own religion, were proscribed, and the truth had made little progress amongst them. There were indeed Christians, but in an ignorant and ill-informed state; and to revive religion amongst these persons, and to correct their errors, was one great part of his work.

St. Ninian's plan was not merely to disperse Clergy in separate districts through the country, but to concentrate his strength in one point, and there to have a Church in some degree worthy of the design for which it was intended. The Churches of the Britons were generally of wood. In the cities no doubt, when the Romans had introduced their arts, and wealth abounded, the Churches, like the other public buildings, would be of stone; but in remote and poorer places where wood was plentiful, it was more natural to make them of that material. It was ready to their hands; stone they did not need, and could not afford, and might not have the art of working; as St. Ninian had contemplated in taking his masons from Tours. Bede speaks of the Church as built of stone in a way unusual among the Britons. His words probably apply to the form as well as the material of the building, as he afterwards contrasts the Churches of the Picts with the Roman fashion. These Pictish

Churches, and those of the Britons of Bede's days, and of the Irish, were of wood; such they now are in Norway, where neither skill nor labour are spared in the beauty of the workmanship with which they are adorned.

St. Ninian however desired to use materials for his Church, which, by their strength and permanence, might image forth the perpetuity of that Kingdom to which it belonged; and in which the services might be performed with becoming dignity. He had Rome in his mind; and as he had there doubtless planned what he would raise on the wooded shores of Britain, he might often now in thought return to the majesty and splendour of the Ritual and Churches of the Apostolic See; so that whatever simplicity and poverty there might of necessity be elsewhere, the Cathedral at least would afford a model of what was aimed at, and which might be copied in their measure by the other Churches. Such doubtless was the practice, that the Mother Church of the diocese should be the place in which the due order of Divine Service might be kept as a guide to the rest.

Natural piety would move St. Ninian to this work, as indeed it had all along been near his heart. But it must also have been very important in its effects on the people, as a perpetual witness to the truths he taught. That we should give of our best to God, and that what is spent on places specially dedicated to His service is in some more immediate way given to Him, is a natural sentiment. This sentiment is implanted in the human heart, in common with those others which seem to have produced every where, among people who had any sense of religion, an external form and expression of it. Places appropriated for sacred services, where God was believed to be especially present; an order of men set apart to serve Him, offerings of our best and costliest possessions, and grace and beauty in the ornaments of His House, and the conduct of its services,— these are the spontaneous dictates of the heart, and carry with them the evidence of their being a part of natural religion, as well as what we commonly call such. Surely it is with this view that we should look on the fair forms of ancient art, their temples, their graceful processions, their choric poetry, as the offering of natural piety to the Supreme Being. Corrupted and polluted it is true they were, but so were the fundamental doctrines of essential religion ; and as we are used there to sever the over-laying errors from the elementary truths, and think it no prejudice to the Divine original of the true portions, that corruption should have attached to them, so let us regard the ceremonies of the heathen, and the taste and wealth they lavished on them, as the yearnings of the human soul after Him, to Whom it desires to do all homage.

And the consideration was very important in reference to the conversion of the heathen, as well as to the maintenance of religion among Christians ; for instead of falling in with their true and right notions as to what a religious system ought to be, we may by a neglect of external Religion directly clash with what they conceive we ought to do, which they will the more deeply believe, the more they are prepared by natural piety for embracing the Gospel.

Instead of Churches, by their very forms and ornaments, and services, being silent and ever present
preachers of the truth, embodying practical devotion,
as being its fruits, they may give the lie to our
professions, and hinder the reception of religion.
We have power, we have generally wealth. Ninian
had not much of either, yet he made no delay, but
made it his first work to build the house of God on
a scale which excited the admiration of the people,
and suited the high purposes for which it was set apart.

It was during the time the Church was building,
that is, in November 397, that St. Ninian was divinely
warned of the death of St. Martin, and so deep was
the veneration he entertained for that holy man, that
he dedicated the Church under his name ; a name
it afterwards retained ; though, when the Saint by
whom it was built, and whose remains were laid
there, became more known, it was commonly called
St. Ninian's, and is spoken of as dedicated to him.

In Rome they built the Churches over the tombs
of the Martyrs, and so dedicated them to their
memory, and in other places it was usual to deposit
some of the remains of a martyr under the altar of
the Church, which was to be consecrated, a practice
observed by the great Saints of the age. At
Whithern however there was no martyr, and St.
Ninian had not brought any relics, so it seemed as
it were providential that St. Martin, one of the
greatest Saints of the age, though not a martyr,
should yet be honoured thus, and he to whom
St. Ninian owed so much be regarded as the patron
of his Church, and the model to be perpetually kept
in view by his people.

I pass by the story which the present tradition of the country reports, that St. Ninian first settled in the Isle of Whithern, three or four miles from the present Church and town, and afterwards removed to that which was his ultimate position. It seems incompatible with the history, which speaks but of one place, and that the one where he at first engaged in building his Church ; for it was in progress at the time St. Martin died, that is within a year after his arrival in Britain. There is an old dismantled Chapel, as it were a landmark, on the top of one of the hills in the Isle, which the people connect with St. Ninian, and consider the oldest Church in the kingdom, as if it were his Church. It is however much more recent than even the ruined Church of Whithern; it is a plain oblong Chapel, with very thick walls, and one narrow pointed window in each of the sides, with niches, and the other recesses usual about the east end : a lone deserted place without roof, which from its thick walls and simple form, suggests the notion of great antiquity ; but certainly is not connected with St. Ninian.

At Whithern then he gave a visibility and local habitation to the Church. The service of God would here be daily celebrated with the simple dignity which befits the image of heavenly things, and the unseen presence of Saints and Angels. The rites which the Roman Church had derived from her founders, or introduced in after times, as the spontaneous expression of the spiritual mind, the language, if we may say it, the very bearing, and graceful movements of the Spouse of Christ, would there be embodied, and form after the like model the minds of those who came to worship, or abode continually in her courts. With the building there was a society of religious persons formed, living with their Bishop, consisting of Clergy to maintain the unceasing services of the Church, to prepare for the higher offices, or to teach the people, and of laymen, who sought here to lead a devout life under the shadow, and within the very walls of the sanctuary.

That St. Ninian should form such a society was antecedently probable. The monastic life had been introduced and sanctioned in the western Church by the most revered men; and the association of Bishops with their Clergy or other religious people, had been recently adopted by those whose judgment St. Ninian would be most guided by. St. Siricius, it has been said, preferred to choose Clergy from monks; what then was more natural than that the Bishop should himself form, and rule such a society? He had himself too probably lived in one at Rome, and would love its religious calm for the sake of his own improvement.

For the account of this indeed and the remaining events of St. Ninian's life, and the institutions and system which he adopted, we are chiefly indebted to the accounts of his miracles, which form the rest of St. Aelred's life. But this, for obvious reasons, will not appear a valid reason for questioning their truth, considered as common facts. A long time, certainly, had elapsed between St. Ninian and St. Aelred; and though we must put at a much higher date the composition of the life, from which St. Aelred derived his history, still some considerable time may have intervened, during which we must trust to the traditions of his Church. It may then be said we have little evidence for these facts; we have, however, all which the circumstances of the case admitted. And we have this in particular, that they were believed by men who had much more means of judging than we possess. They were believed, I mean on the whole, for it is very possible that Alcuin, St. Aelred, and the Scottish Church generally, received them as they were handed down, not attempting to distinguish—to receive part or to reject part, where they had little or no grounds for making such distinction. To us, however, they convey much real information as to the way of life of the Saint. I do not mean by mentioning circumstances which might have been inserted by the narrator; but by the facts which form the very groundwork of the story, so that if the miracle was believed, which it must have been in very early times, it must have been the case that these facts were also generally believed. And a general and early belief in common facts would be admitted as evidence by many who would hesitate to receive it for uncommon ones, particularly if these common facts were what might otherwise be expected. Nay, we may go further; they who consider that St. Ninian was a friend of St. Martin's, engaged in the work of converting a barbarous people, and who are familiar with the authentic history of the saints of that age, will look on miracles as things to be expected, as what under the circumstances were natural; and so they will, in the same way, give an assent to the miraculous narration, as what may very possibly, at least, be true; though from the nature of the evidence they would not positively affirm it in each particular case; and in the same spirit they may praise God for His glories thus manifested, as they may for those of His natural works, though they are in doubt or error as to the physical facts. Hymns are not the less religious because they are philosophically untrue; nor is the piety unacceptable which saw traces of the deluge in the shells upon the mountain top, though recent investigations have taught us to doubt of their connection.

To return, then, to our history; it appears that one of St. Ninian's earliest works was the formation of a religious community, where he and his Clergy might live together, having all things in common. It is, of course, most probable, that he adopted the plan from those of St. Eusebius of Vercelli, St. Augustine, and especially St. Martin, and that his society, as theirs did, would consist of laymen as well as clergy.

The evident advantages of such an institution led to its general adoption in the missions of the following age. It was a home where sympathy, support, and counsel, might be had from men like minded, and engaged in labouring for the same great ends. Hither men were gathered, who desired to serve God more entirely than they could do in the world, to lead a heavenly life, in contemplation, prayer, and praise. It became a very school of sanctity, where men earnestly desiring virtue associated round one of known sanctity, to be guided by him in their way to heaven, to copy the traits of holiness in him and in their brethren. Thus was a body formed which gave light to others, so that men were drawn out of the contaminating and lowering influence of the world, and brought together under a strict rule and with a professed aim after holiness.

And this must have been of singular importance at a time when Christianity was now becoming the religion of the many, and whole nations were being converted. It presented a difficult problem to the heathen philosopher, how the mass of society could be renewed, when the few in whom the principle of goodness was implanted were scattered, unseen, and lost among the numbers who surrounded them, and by whose way of life, as they possessed no higher visible standard, they were lowered and corrupted. The Gospel undertakes to effect it by gathering out these scattered instances of goodness, and uniting them in one visible society, by the tie of a professed standard of practice; to be a city set on a hill, a light put upon a candlestick; providing, moreover, for training up, and forming the characters of others, by instruction in the truth, and a life regulated by holy discipline. Such was the Church itself, in its first ages, when the few Christians were closely bound together, and broadly distinguished from the unbelievers who surrounded them. At the time, however, when this was no longer possible, when the world came into the Church, and all were members of that society, it pleased God gradually to introduce into the Church itself minor combinations of its holiest members, who, without the danger of individual profession, and bound by obligations which humbled them in the thought of their shortcomings, might continue as memorials of what had existed in a former age, and schools and models of practical

religion. We have schools for all other arts, for all
those acquirements which need rules and practice,
and, above all, imitation, seeing how others do what
we wish to learn. In secular matters we recognise
the advantage of an experienced teacher and cor-
rector, of being united with others engaged in the
same pursuits, and of the improvement derived from
observing how they attain to excellence, or how they
fail in the minute details of their daily work; surely
it is only reasonable to have some similar institutions for learning the most important and the most
difficult of all acquirements, that of a holy life, and
the practice of the varied graces of the Christian
character. How many a practical difficulty might
thus be solved! How many a soul which had en-
tangled its course, and rendered its perceptions of
duty obscure and uncertain, might here be relieved!
The chief part of Christians have duties in the
world, and they have, amongst the Saints, patterns
and guides for leading a devout life in the discharge of those duties; but some are ever called
to a life where they may serve God more directly,
and these are especial means of keeping up the
general tone of religion, and supply helps and en-
couragements, as well as a true standard, for those
who are in the world.

Such may the Saints of Whithern have been, pre-
senting by their purity, meekness, heavenly minded-
ness, and peace, a specimen of what the fruit of
Gospel righteousness is; a contrast to the pride,
and worldliness, and violence, which reigned among
the heathen; and a special means of attracting to
the Church, all in whom the elements of purity and

goodness had life and activity. Devotion was the end of their association and their rules—to imitate on earth an angelic life ; to this all was subordinate ; for this they rose betimes, they fasted, they watched, they kept a constant guard on their senses and their thoughts. Thus to please God they cultivated all Christian graces, humility, obedience, and love ; they were silent to converse with God, turning their eyes from the objects of earth, that the mind might see those of heaven, and seeking in this life to be cheerful, resigned, and happy. The system of the monks would necessarily have its modifications when adopted by clergy, whose office called them to be accessible to their people, to go out on journeys and to preach and to administer the Sacraments to a scattered people. But even then they carried with them in silence, recollection, and prayer, and the devout saying of their Psalter, the spirit and the practices of their holy home, and by their gentleness and humility would win over the poor and simple people among whom they laboured.

They probably supported themselves by their own labour, and such voluntary offerings as might be made to the Church. The former belonged to their life as monks, the latter as clergy. Their chief food was vegetables ; leeks are especially mentioned ; these were the produce of a garden of their own, which was under the care of one of the brethren, whose business it was thence to provide the supply necessary for their daily repasts. It was a simple life deriving support from the grateful earth ; a condition which maintained in them a continual dependence on Him who feeds the young ravens, and enabled them to sympathise with the poor; as being themselves without provision from day to day, and having really made themselves poor for the sake of Christ. Nor should it surprise us that at times they were almost in want of the necessaries of life; since, for some time, St. Ninian had to struggle against much opposition, and his labours seemed to produce scarcely any fruit.

It was in such a time of need that the traditions of Galloway represent the Saint as receiving a supply of food by miracle. And before we allow ourselves to judge lightly of the simple tale, let us recall the numerous instances in Holy Writ in which miracles were wrought for supplying bodily wants; perhaps there is no class of which the cases are so many. The Bishop and his brethren went one day into the Refectory, but their usual meal of leeks and other herbs did not appear. The brother who should have provided them was called. He had only the disappointing tale to tell, that they had no provisions left, all the leeks had been put into the ground for seed, and none remained for them to eat. Perhaps it had been a bad season and their garden crops had failed. The Saint bade him go to the garden and bring what he found. He was astonished at the command, knowing there was nothing there, but habitual obedience and the thought that the Bishop could not command any thing without good reason prevailed. He went, and behold, the process of nature was anticipated, and the herbs were found not grown up only but in seed. There is a very useful lesson at least taught here, to obey though it seems useless; difficulties vanish from the path of the determined.

And by this simple way of life, and the exercise of useful arts, as the Egyptian monks made mats or baskets, and the cultivation of their garden, and afterwards by keeping flocks and herds, they would suggest many a useful lesson to the uncivilised people around them, and introduce among them improvements which were otherwise unknown. This has ever been a part of the work of missionaries in barbarous nations, tending to the real improvement of the people, winning a way to their good-will, and teaching them to look up, in things spiritual, to those who were so willing and able to help them in earthly concerns.

But there was one other object to which St. Ninian made his monastery especially subservient. His own religious history, the wants he had felt, and the privileges he had enjoyed, and the very design for which he had returned to Britain, would lead him to regard sound theological training as of the utmost importance for his clergy. He had himself sought in vain for those who could teach him the truth ; he had seen the evils which resulted from the want of a steady holding to the right faith, in the unsettledness and spiritual deadness which prevailed. He had come to remedy those evils. Where could it be better effected than in his college? This was healing the fountain, it was providing that those who, each in his own sphere, was to teach others, should himself be in doctrine as well as life a model for them to imitate. The advantages he had enjoyed at Rome he came to impart to Britain; and the monastery at Whithern was the place where the system of theological teaching he has known there would be adopted for his own clergy.

He would himself first, as they were able to bear it, lead them into a full and exact knowledge of the truths of religion, by such a course of oral and catechetical instruction, as would transfuse into their minds the great ideas with which his own was impressed. He would accustom them by rule and instance to an accurate literal exposition of Scripture, and still more to that wonderful system of mystical interpretation, which the spiritual mind spontaneously suggests, and, when duly instructed in it, carries through the whole of Scripture. And in both he would aid them by the study of the works of the earlier fathers, and of the living lights of the Church, the great masters of dogmatical and interpretative Theology, St. Augustine and St. Jerome. Nay, it will appear that he perpetuated his teaching by composing works, probably for their benefit. In consequence Whithern became a school from which the teachers of the northern Church were sent out.

Another very important part of his institution was a school for the young, rising up, as in some of our Sees, under the shadow of the Cathedral, as in olden times it formed an essential part of the Capitular establishment. It was most important to rescue, as far as might be, the children of heathen or evil-minded parents from the contaminating influence of their homes, and both with them and others to keep the young mind from losing the innocency of its regeneration, and to train it in habits of virtue, and the knowledge of the truth. It was indeed sowing seeds, which might for a long time seem buried, but would at last grow up to noble trees. And from among the brethren, as in after times, there would be found those who teach the little ones, and themselves be both refreshed and improved by it. Refreshed by the sweetness and simplicity of their innocent minds, naturally thinking no evil, without anxiety, ambition, or guile; which is to the harassed mind what a garden of flowers is to the weary, where they may repose amid fair objects, and where all is peace. Improved, because their own ideas would be cleared, and made more real by having to impart their knowledge to the unsophisticated minds of children. Nor was the Bishop without his own share in the work. He taught the children himself, not unmindful of the precept to feed the lambs, just as Gerson, the great Chancellor of Paris, is said through life to have maintained the practice of weekly catechising little children. It was a mark of the sweetness of St. Ninian's character that he was loved and reverenced by his little ones; and this circumstance was so prominent among his works that the characteristic which one historian gives him is, that he was a distinguished trainer of children.

Connected with this, there was a story for which people could, in St. Aelred's time, point to what were held to be living evidences, which brings out the Bishop as the father of these little ones. But it is best to adopt or paraphrase the words of St. Aelred. "Many, both of the more noble and the middle rank, placed their children under the care of the Saint, to be taught the knowledge of religion. These he instructed with learning, and formed to habits of virtue, restraining by wholesome discipline the faults to which their age is liable, and implanting virtues by which they might live in sobriety,

justice, and piety." It happened on a time that
one of the boys offended, and preparations were
made to punish him. The boy, in alarm, ran away ;
but knowing the power and goodness of the Saint,
and thinking he should find a solace in his flight
if he did but take with him anything belonging to
the good Bishop, he took off the staff on which
St. Ninian used to support himself. In his eagerness
to escape he looked out for a boat which might carry
him away. The boats of the country St. Aelred
then describes. They were of wicker work, large
enough to hold three men ; over this wicker work
a hide was stretched, and the boat would float and
be impervious to the waves. They are the same
boats which Pliny and Cæsar describe, and in
which the Britons would cross the sea to France or
Ireland, or even go voyages of many days. They
are called currachs or coracles ; they were long in
use in the Western Isles, and still are among the
fishermen on the Wye.

There happened just then to be many large ones
making ready on the shore. The wicker work was
finished, but the hides not put on. He very in-
cautiously got in, and the light boat at first kept
on the top of the waves, the water not at once
making its way through ; soon however it did so,
and there seemed no prospect but that it must fill
and go down. He knew not whether to run the
risk of leaping out or staying and sinking. In the
moment of his distress, however, he thought of the
holiness and power of St. Ninian ; contrite for his
fault, as though weeping at his feet, he confesses
his guilt, entreats pardon, and by the most holy

merit of the Saint begs the aid of Heaven. Trusting, with childlike simplicity, that the staff was not without its virtue, as belonging to the Saint, he fixed it in one of the openings. The water retreated, and, as if in fear, presumed not to pour in. "These," says the saintly Aelred, "these are the works of Christ, Who did say to His disciples, he that believeth in Me the works that I do, shall he do also, and greater things than these shall he do."

A gentle wind arose and forced on the little boat, the staff supplied the place of sail, and rudder, and anchor to stay his course. The people crowding on the shore saw the little ship, like some bird swimming along the waves, without either oar or sail. The boy comes to shore, and to spread more widely the fame of the holy Bishop, he in strong faith, fixed the staff in the ground, and prayed that as a testimony to the miracle, it might take root, send forth branches, flowers, and fruit. Presently the dry wood shot out roots, was clothed with fresh bark, produced leaves and branches, and grew into a considerable tree. Nay, to add miracle to miracle, at the root of a tree a spring of the clearest water burst forth, and poured out a glassy stream, which wound its way with gentle murmurs, grateful to the eye, and, from the merits of the Saint, useful and health-giving to the sick.

With what interest would this tale be told to the pilgrim strangers, and the tree and fountain shown as the evidences of its truth in those days of simple faith! And with hearts lifted up to God, and trusting in the aid of St. Ninian's prayers, many a poor sick man would drink of the clear stream.

Men of this day may smile at their simplicity; but better surely is the mind which receives as no incredible thing, the unusual interposition of Him who worketh all things according to the counsel of His own will; better the spirit which views the properties of a salubrious spring as the gift of God, granted to a faithful and holy servant, than that which would habitually exclude the thought of the Great Doer of all, by resting on the Laws of Nature as something independent of Him, not, as they are, the way in which He usually works; or thanklessly, and as a matter of course, receive the benefit of some mineral waters.

However, we were speaking of St. Ninian's school, and we have seen the aged Bishop, for the event is related near the close of his life, leaning on his staff, and ordering the boys to be punished; and we see too what kind of scholars he had, and how deep was their veneration for him, even when they were doing wrong; how simple their faith in the presence and power of the Almighty.

Another narrative brings more before us the personal habits and religious life of St. Ninian, and this we should much wish to know. We have followed him through his holy childhood, and his pure and humble youth, have seen in opening manhood his deep and reverend love of Divine knowledge —his relinquishing the world—his progress in piety and perception of the Truth. And one characteristic which had been formed and strengthened by his obedient love of Him, who is unseen, was now brought out, the fixedness of his thoughts amid the distractions of the world, and his attention to Divine things. This indeed is the state in which reason shows us we ought to be ; for it is to have our thoughts dwelling on what is true, permanent, and most concerning, instead of what is transient and unreal. And to him its effects were most blessed, enabling him to sustain a calm and tranquil mind amid the hurry and trials of his toilsome work ; leading an angel's life, diligent and laborious, and doing all things perfectly, as the angels unceasingly minister for us ; but without excitement and hurry, even as they, by retaining the contemplation of the Divine glory, and a simple union with the Divine will, are undisturbed. It had doubtless ever been his practice from the time that as a child he turned his thoughts and loving affections towards his Heavenly Father, and afterwards dwelt in pious meditation on the truths he laboured so earnestly to learn. And he sustained it by keeping a constant guard against wandering, dissipated thoughts ; by occupying his mind in holy things, that the house which had been swept and garnished, might yet never be found empty ; by not seeking to know anything which did not concern him. He was assisted by a practice which we often read of in the lives of Saints, that of reading or saying the Psalms, or earnest meditation, at times when circumstances would most tend to dissipate the thoughts ; which probably every one feels to be the case in those seemingly unoccupied times, when one has to walk or travel alone. Then it is for most people, perhaps, impossible to keep the thoughts fixed without some external help, the very moving and changes that occur distract and unsettle them. To guard against this and another evil, that of idle and vain conversation, St. Ninian, on his journeys, always carried his Psalter and some book for religious reading; and, besides saying the Psalms, when he stopped to rest, or to refresh his horse (for he used to ride on his long travels through the rough woods and hills of his diocese), he would take out his book and read with careful attention.

And to secure himself from any unnecessary occasions of distraction, he seems to have observed the rules which our good Bishop Wilson gave himself, and so has most forcibly given us. " Never be curious to know what is passing in the world, any further than duty obliges you; it will only distract the mind when it should be better employed." " The best way to prevent wandering in prayer is not to let the mind wander too much at other times, but to have God always in our minds in the whole course of our lives."

We may here quote the beautiful language of St. Aelred. It was intended as a lesson for lay people, living at home, as well as for professedly religious men. It was to be read in the long winter evenings in the hall, as well as in the refectory. It has been read in many a house and many a monastery, in the olden times of merry England; it may have awakened then a sense of the importance of guarded thoughts, and the danger of curiosity. It may do so for some one now.

" When I think," says the good Abbot, " of the very religious habits of this most holy man, I am filled with shame at the slothfulness of this our miserable generation. Which of us, I ask, even at home among the members of his own family, does not in social intercourse and conversation, introduce more frequently jocose than serious subjects, idle rather than useful, carnal than spiritual ones. Those lips which Divine grace has consecrated to praise the Lord, or to celebrate the holy mysteries, are daily polluted by detraction and worldly talk, and whilst they feel a distaste for the Psalms, the Gospels, and the Prophets, they run the live-long day through the vain and shameful works of men. And when they travel, is not the mind like the body, in continual wandering, the tongue in idleness to any good? Reports of the characters of ungodly men are continually brought forward; the gravity suited to a religious man is destroyed by laughing and stories; the affairs of Kings, the duties of Bishops, the ministrations of the Clergy, the contentions of the powerful, above all, the life and character of every one is the subject of discussion. We judge every thing except our own judgment; and what is more to be grieved at, we bite and devour one another, so that we are consumed one of another. Not so the blessed Ninian; crowds hindered not his tranquillity, nor did travelling interfere with his meditations, nor his devotions become lukewarm through lassitude. Wherever he was journeying he raised his mind to heavenly objects in prayer or contemplation, and when he turned aside on his journey, to rest himself or his horse, he delighted to take out a little book, which he always carried for the purpose, and read, or said

Psalms, for he felt what the Prophet David says, 'How sweet are Thy words unto my throat, yea, sweeter than honey unto my mouth.'"

Nay, it was said, so highly favoured was his practice, that by special grace the very rain was turned aside from falling on him, forming as it were a vault above and around him. And once it happened, to give the substance of St. Aelred's narrative, that he and his brother, called Plebeia, a man of equal holiness, were on a journey, and as was their wont, solaced themselves with the Songs of David. When they had travelled some distance they turned from the public road to rest themselves awhile, opened their Psalters, and were refreshing their souls with religious reading. Presently, the bright clear sky was clouded over, and the rain fell heavily; the thin air, however, like an arched vault, formed over the servants of God, and continued as an impenetrable wall against the falling waters. Whilst, however, they were saying their Psalms, St. Ninian turned his eyes from the book, an unlawful thought, nay, an unrestrained desire, affected his mind. The supernatural protection was withdrawn, and the rain fell on him. No useless lesson this—that the unseen guardianship which is over us in prayer, which screens us from evil, that the grace which is then around us, is for the time withdrawn, if wilful distractions are admitted. His brother observed the change, and understood the cause; he gently reminded him of his fault, and the Saint, coming to himself, blushed at having been carried away by foolish thoughts, and in the same instant he threw off the imagination, and the rain was stayed.

It is to be hoped the reader will rather seize the lesson this ancient tale affords, than smile at its simplicity. Who can say how many a wandering thought has been checked by thinking of it, when the brethren of Whithern, day by day, and year after year, said their Psalter in St. Ninian's Church —checked by recalling the lesson which it teaches; of evil kept off from the soul by earnest attention, and falling unrestrained upon it when we wilfully wander.

The next miracles are connected with the trials of St. Ninian. His portion, as that of all the saints, was to follow in his Master's steps, to labour for the unthankful, to win souls by suffering, to endure reproach, to bless those that cursed him. There are intimations incidentally occurring in the latter part of his life, which show that he was often in danger from powerful men, and exposed even to the loss of life.

The chief opposer of his labours was a king of those parts, called Tuduval; the prince, perhaps, of the whole tribe of the Novantes. He was, for a Galwegian chieftain, wealthy, powerful, and influential, but withal proud, grasping, and the slave of passion and unbridled license and ambition. It may easily be conceived that he felt the opposition which existed between his own spirit and St. Ninian's, and instinctively resisted him. He felt that he belonged to a kingdom which must fall before that of which the Bishop was a minister, and strove the more earnestly because his time was short. The admonitions of the holy preacher were disregarded, his lessons of righteousness, temperance, and judgment were derided ; his teaching, nay his holy life, were assailed and detracted from ; all the influence the prince possessed was exercised to withstand him, and his doctrine was met with open and direct opposition. For a time the enemy summoned so much strength, and exercised so wide and baneful an influence, that it seems as if the conversion of the people was becoming hopeless. It was as a land on which the gentle dew and rain from heaven fell in vain ; it brought forth no fruit, but only thorns and thistles, and seemed nigh to be given up as accursed and reprobate.

But the prayers and patient sufferings of the Holy Brotherhood at Whithern, wènt up for a memorial; they wielded the weapons of the Saints, meekness, righteousness, and truth ; and their intercessions for their persecutors and defamers prevailed. When their cause seemed hopeless, the Divine arm was lifted up to help them.   He who took the lead in resisting them, the resolute persecutor and opposer of the truth, felt a hand laid on him to stay his course.   Tuduval was seized by a violent illness, which ended in the loss of sight. Laid on a bed of suffering, and precluded from the sight of the outward world, reflection brought him to himself. His conscience recalled the marked events of his soul's history, and his opposition to St. Ninian would be the most prominent.   The possibility of all proving true which he had often scoffed at ; the consciousness of his wrong-doings, even according to his own ideas of wrong ; the undefined dread of future retribution, all would combine to awaken consideration. Then the purity of the Christians' lives—their present peace—their future hopes—would suggest the thought how much better it were to be as one of them; nay, that there was something in them more than human; the miracles scoffed at before would recur to his memory, and the truth of the Saint's claims take possession of his mind. So it was; a light spread through the soul, whilst the outward organs were in darkness. Repentance and confession of his wrong-doings followed, and without delay he called for his friends, took their advice, and sent them with expressions of contrition and humiliation to St. Ninian. He besought him not to treat him as he knew he deserved, but to imitate the mercifulness of his Lord, to return good for evil, love for hatred.

We may imagine the deep joy which the holy Bishop felt at the return of one who seemed lost for ever. In his mind there was no place for glorying over a fallen enemy, no notion of personal triumph, no revengeful delay of reconciliation, but a going out to meet him whom he saw afar off. He offered up first a prayer to God, a prayer of thankfulness for this work of His grace, a prayer that his enemy might be freed from his sufferings, and at once set out with the utmost humility and devotion. At first he gently reproved him for his sin, then with healing hand touched his head, and impressed upon his eyes the sign of our salvation. At once the pain was gone and the blindness departed. Tuduval became a sincere convert, humility and purity took the place of his former vices, and he devoted himself to St. Ninian's guidance, treating him with the deepest reverence, as recognising that God was indeed with him and guided him in all his ways. The effect of this miracle of Divine grace in the conversion, even more than in the cure of the strenuous persecutor must have been very great. The power and influence which had been used to oppose, would now be devoted to aid the cause of religion, and so exercised, would indeed produce their true and proper results. To this time, probably, we may assign the general conversion of the people.

It was, perhaps, during the period of the previous persecution that the event occurred which St. Aelred next narrates. It was important as removing a scandal which might have stood greatly in the way of the progress of religion. It seems that clergy were fixed, whether before St. Ninian's arrival, or by him, in separate districts, which St. Aelred, in the language which would be most intelligible to his readers, designates as parishes. An unhappy girl who had been seduced by a powerful master, at his instigation accused the clergyman of being the father of her child. The effect was astounding. The good were distressed; the weak offended; the wicked rejoiced; and the low-minded ridiculed; the whole sacred order was blasphemed by the ungodly. St. Ninian, however, was inwardly assured of the innocence of the priest; and in full trust took the most public means of manifesting it. He proceeded to the Church, summoned the clergy and whole body of the people, preached and then confirmed. The mother appeared with her child and openly denounced the priest; the utmost excitement prevailed; shame and derision were the portion of the good; when St. Ninian called on the child just born to declare his father; a voice was given to the infant and the truth declared.

One other miracle is recorded, which, like the one of the schoolboy, was associated with a permanent record in the name of the place, and a mark in a stone, which, in St. Aelred's days, was shown in Galloway. But now we know nothing of the stone, and Pinkerton says, there is no place which he knows of the name. The miracle itself is, in some points, like one narrated by the Ecclesiastical historian, Sozomen, of St. Spiridion, a shepherd Bishop in Cyprus, who continued his simple employment in the care of flocks, after he was chosen to be a shepherd of souls. Of course there is no reason why the miracle should not have been performed by both saints. And if there be reason to think that the Almighty did exercise miraculous powers through His Saints, and that around them and in them there was a spiritual agency at work, let us be cautious how we judge these tales, let us tread carefully on what may be hallowed ground.

The story is this. St. Ninian and his brethren had many flocks and herds, which they kept for their own use; for milk and cheese would be monks' fare; and for hospitality to strangers and the use of the poor? making provision to fulfil the precept which Bishops and their chapters and all monasteries were used to keep in mind, to exercise hospitality without grudging. These cattle were kept in pasture grounds, at some distance from the monastery, and St. Ninian went to bless the herds and their keepers. The Bishop had them all brought together, lifted up his hands, and committed himself and all that was his to the guardianship of God. He then went round them, and with his staff marked the ground within the limits of which they were to stay, something like what was afterwards done as a superstitious spell. He then retired to the house of an honourable matron where he and his brethren were to lodge. After refreshing themselves with food, and their souls with the word of God, they retired to rest. Meanwhile robbers arrive, and seeing the herds unenclosed and unguarded, expect an easy prey. The cattle remain quiet, no sound is heard, no dog even is heard to bark; they enter within the limits, but do it to their cost. The bull of the herd attacks and severely gores the ringleader of the thieves, and himself, digging his hoof violently into the ground, impresses the mark of it on the rock, as if in wax. The mark remained, and the place was called in Saxon, Farres Last, that is, the Bull's footmark, Tauri Vestigium, as the Latin life explains it. Meanwhile after his regular morning prayers, St. Ninian arrives, finds the poor robber with his entrails torn out, and now lifeless, and the others running about as if insane, within the limit he had marked around the cattle. He was deeply moved with pity, and entreated that the robber might be restored to life; nor did he cease from prayers and tears till the same Power which had caused his death restored him again to life. The other robbers who seemed possessed on seeing St. Ninian, fell at his feet in fear and trembling, and begged forgiveness. He kindly reproved them, pointed out the punishment which awaited the robber, and at last, after giving them his blessing, allowed them to depart. The result was the sincere conversion of the man whose life had been restored.

Perhaps the strangeness of this narrative ought not to be any hindrance to our believing it. As the most wonderful instance of his prayers being heard, even to bringing the dead to life, its circumstances are especially dwelt on in the religious services for his day. And we are sure the people of Galloway would have been disappointed, if they had not found this story in the Life of their own Sainted Bishop; for like the tree and the spring, Farres Last must have made an early and deep impression on their minds; and often doubtless was the story told to the stranger who passed that way, and to their own little ones, and they would go to see the deep impression of the bull's foot; and the sermon which St. Ninian had preached would be afresh inculcated, and the fact appealed to as the most vivid evidence of the wrongness and the possible unexpected evil which might at any time await the cattle stealer.

We may now pass on to St. Ninian's conversion of the Southern Picts, of whom he is designated the Apostle.

CHAPTER VIII

CONVERSION OF THE PICTS

THE labours of St. Ninian extended over a wide district; and were exercised among great troubles and dangers, from the unsettled state of the country, and the continual hostilities which prevailed. The tract of country, which, so far as we know, had no Pastor but himself, stretched from sea to sea, and, besides the (now) English portion of it, from the wall of Antoninus to that of Severus. The Western part, however, was his special care. The rest was a scene of war and rapine during the chief part of his Episcopate; and after fruitless endeavours to repel the inroads of the mountaineers, the Roman forces were at length withdrawn A.D. 410, and the Provincials left to defend themselves as best they could.

The tribes of St. Ninian's diocese had retained their original divisions of clans, and though they were rendered less fit to cope with the unsubdued and uncivilised portions of the same great Celtic race, whom we know as Picts, they yet combined, and maintained themselves as a distinct people in possession of their territory. The Picts might rob, but do not seem to have displaced them. The separate princes united in the election of a common leader, and though harassed by internal broils and breaches of their federal compact, the Western tribes, with the exception of Galloway, continued for six centuries as an independent body, forming the British kingdom of Strathclydd. During all the wars which rent this unhappy district, Britons, Picts, and Scots, it is said, united in reverencing St. Ninian. He was allowed to travel, without molestation, through countries which were the seat of war. His calm presence seemed to breathe of peace and love, and to inspire awe even in the wildest barbarians. It has been so in these latter times. The Isle of Man was to be spared by the French, for the sake of Bishop Wilson, and in the wars of the Low Countries at the beginning of the last century, the Archbishop of Cambray was treated with reverence by all the contending parties, and made his Episcopal journeys unmolested in the midst of hostilities.

Who can say that it was not owing to the influence of the holy truths, and the practical goodness inculcated by St. Ninian, that the tribes of his diocese did so unite and retain a social life after the convulsions which resulted from the departure of the Romans?

And now, after many years of patient toil and assiduous teaching, having brought the people immediately committed to him, to some unity of faith and goodness of life; his ardent desire for the salvation of men prompted him to undertake the conversion of a tribe, who did not as yet know the name of Christ, and were bitterly hostile to his own countrymen. These were the Southern Picts, a division of the numerous tribes, who, secured by the mountains of the Highlands, had never submitted to the yoke of the Romans, and now in the decline of their power revenged themselves on them, and on the tribes of their own island, who had yielded and been civilised by them.

It seems that Caledonians and Picts are but different names for the same people, given originally to one tribe or other, according to the circumstances of their localities or ways of life, and then borne by all in common. As inhabitants of the forests of the Lowlands they had early had the name of Woodmen, Caledones, given them. Another portion again who occupied the plain country between the Grampians and the sea, to the north of the Frith of Forth, were called Peithi, a name which signifies inhabitants of the open country, and by the Romans, Picti (as the Welsh peithen is from the Latin pecten, and effaith is from effectus), and from them the whole race received the name. It was the coincidence between their own Celtic name, and their painted bodies, which gave a point to the well-known line of Claudian, "non falso nomine Picti," which would have had little force, if they were only called so because of their being painted. These inhabitants of the plain country are the Southern Picts. Those who remained in the fastnesses were called Northern Picts, and the distinction of these two portions of the race would become more marked, from the different habits of life, which would gradually result from their different localities. The distinction was recognised in the middle of the fourth century, when they were respectively called by the Romans, Deucaledones, and Vecturiones; of which the former, it is said, means separate or far Cale-

donians, those, that is, farther removed from the
Roman districts; and Vecturiones is another Celtic
form of Picts, P and V being interchanged, and the
rest of the word, Peithwyr, or Peithwyron, differing
from simple Picts, as Englishmen does from English.

These Vecturiones—they to whom the name of
Pict first belonged, are the tribe of which St. Ninian
was the Apostle. They had first established themselves on the Eastern coast, as has been said, north
of the Frith of Forth and of the Roman wall; and
many authors confine them to this district. Others
say that after the withdrawal of the Roman forces
they passed the wall, poured in upon the Eastern
coast of Valentia, and took up a position which
they permanently occupied, south of the Forth, in
the Lothians, and even reaching to Northumberland;
they had previously acquired more settled habits
than the mountaineers, and so were fitted to establish
themselves permanently in the countries they subdued. They existed as a separate people in the
time of Bede, who accurately distinguishes them
from those who lived within the mountain district.
It was, he says, when St. Columba went to convert
the Northern Picts, that he found the Southern ones
had been converted previously, and, as they stated,
by St. Ninian.

It seems most probable that it was after their
occupation of the country south of the Forth (supposing they did occupy it), that he went amongst
them. It was that occupation which gave them a
more distinct and permanent nationality; nor is it
to be supposed, that they should have become
Christians, and afterwards have attacked with so

much cruelty the people to whom they were indebted for the knowledge of the Gospel ; we will not think so ill of them, barbarians as they were. And the dates would lead to the same conclusion. The Romans retired in 410. Ninian had then been thirteen years in Galloway. He lived for twenty-two years longer. The first thirteen years would not be more than enough for the work he had to effect among his own people. The last twenty-two allow space for the Picts to have come down and occupied the Eastern portion of Valentia, and to have been visited and converted by St. Ninian.

They had overrun and seized on a part, the farthest from his Church, of that wide field which had been committed to his care. He was not then going beyond his measure in endeavouring to win them over. It is an early and a beautiful instance of the power of the Church to reduce under her saving sway, and by the armour of truth, meekness, and righteousness, those whom carnal weapons had in vain opposed—to lead captive the conqueror.

"It deeply grieved the Holy Bishop," St. Aelred proceeds, "that Satan, when he had now been driven from the rest of the world, had found a place in the hearts of the Picts, in a corner of the island, near the ocean. He girt himself accordingly as an energetic athlete to put down his tyranny, taking to himself the shield of faith, the helmet of hope, the breast-plate of love, and the sword of the Spirit, which is the word of God." As associates in his labours, as comforters, and advisers, after the example of St. Paul, he took with him a body of holy brothers, those of his Clergy and religious society, who were most suited for the work. Happily they had not to overcome the hindrance of a different language, for though the dialects of the various portions of the Celtic race were distinguished, there still remained a sufficient similarity to allow of their being mutually understood, even after a much longer and greater separation than had yet taken place; as it is said the people of Brittany and the Welsh now understand each other. They had, however, great difficulties to struggle against, in the antipathy which the free Celts entertained for those who had been under the Roman sway—an antipathy stronger than is felt towards people of quite a different race; and again, from the circumstance that they were themselves the aggressors, who had seized on the territories of the Southern tribes. Still there was something calculated to melt their savage hearts in the presence of one among them so different from any they had known before, preaching the doctrines of purity, humility, and forgiveness; whose graces, notwithstanding, would be recognised and loved by all in whom there was a principle of good. He was one of the people they had attacked, cruelly treated, and displaced, and he was amongst them, not with the tone of complaint, upbraiding, or revenge, but meek and gentle, possessing a sweetness of temper, and a calm and cheerful mind, which he pointed out to them the means of attaining.

Their religion was the same as that of the other tribes of the island had formerly been, though one would suppose, in a more rude state of superstition than the richer portion of the people, among whom the Druids were so superior a caste. St. Ninian called them to forsake their idolatry and superstition, and to turn to that Almighty in Whom, though unknown, they yet believed ; to Him, Who gave them rain from heaven, filling their hearts with food and gladness. He called them from the conscious misery of their present state—from the bondage of vices which galled their very soul, to an obedience and submission, which at once brought relief. He told them of permanent existence, and a future responsibility, of which a voice within testified the truth ; and he professed himself the minister of a gracious dispensation, which would secure those who embraced it in a future dreadful day. This preaching would carry conviction with it to those prepared souls which are found amongst the uncivilised barbarians, as well as among simple rustics or refined philosophers. Wherever man is, there are hearts and consciences which will correspond to the simple doctrines of religion, and be conscious on hearing it of the truth that one thing is needful. But his words, it is said, were not unaccompanied by convincing signs that he was indeed what he professed, a messenger from that great unseen Being in whom they believed. He performed miracles among them. "The blind see," St. Aelred says, "the lame walk, the lepers are cleansed, the deaf hear, the dead are raised up, the possessed are set free from the demons that afflict them." Thus does he apply the description of our Saviour's works to those of His servant. "He that believeth on me the works that I do, shall he do also, and greater things than these shall he do, because I go to the Father."

Perhaps had the evidence for these miracles been asked, the conversion of the people would have been appealed to as a sufficient proof—the effect most distinctly establishing the cause. And had the converts been asked the grounds on which they believed, an appeal to the miracles would probably have been their answer. Indeed, those who profess themselves ready to admit the probability of miracles, where there is an apparently adequate cause for them, must allow it in the case of the Gospel being preached to a barbarous people; since the tangible and obvious evidence of a miracle is best calculated to affect them strongly, and to gain an attention for the preacher, which it would require a long life amongst them, and a long manifestation of the living miracle of a saintly character to obtain.

St. Ninian, it is said, first converted the king of the tribe, whose influence was exerted to further the general acceptance of the Gospel among his people. Such was at this period the usual course of conversion. In the earlier ages, individuals were gained over here and there, unknown to the world, and generally of humble rank, and from them the holy influence spread to relations and neighbours, and those who had the opportunity of seeing what the Gospel had wrought in them; and so the leaven was diffused through the whole mass, and at last affected the rulers of the world. Afterwards the course was generally the reverse. Kings were converted, and brought their subjects over to the profession of Christianity. The early ages gained men by their own individual persuasion, and the work was slow. In the latter period it was more rapid ; and if the converts were now more influenced by earthly motives, their posterity at any rate reaped abundant blessings from being brought into the fold of Christ. Perhaps this change is indicated, when after the lame and blind had not filled the feast, it is said that the last messengers were to compel men to come in.

It is but reasonable to suppose that St. Ninian's preaching was extended to those of the Southern Picts, who still continued in their earlier settlement north of the Frith of Forth. Indeed, as has been said, many writers confine the settlement of this race to the northern districts, and do not suppose them to have had any permanent settlement south of the Roman Wall. The question, however, is not of any importance in its bearing on a history of St. Ninian. Some again have confounded the southern Picts with the British inhabitants of Valentia. Others, with the race called Picts, who came from Ireland, and occupied Galloway in the ninth century, and who alone bore the name in the later period, when the proper Picts were lost among the other nations who occupied Scotland. St. Ninian was ever known as the Apostle of the Southern Picts, and as his proper mission was to the inhabitants of Galloway and Valentia generally, it was not unnatural to imagine these tribes to be those who are meant by the Southern Picts. They were, however, clearly a distinct tribe ; and it is a confirmation of the truth of St. Aelred's history that he does so distinguish them, as Bede had also done, and as the Collect for St. Ninian's day, in the Aberdeen Breviary, "Deus, qui populos Pictorum et Britonum per doctrinam Sancti Niniani Episcopi et Confessoris docuisti."

It was not, however, enough to gain the people to a profession of the Gospel ; St. Ninian also provided for the permanent maintenance of the Church, by the consecration of Bishops and regular establishment of Clergy. His biographer says, " he ordained Priests, consecrated Bishops, arranged the ecclesiastical Orders, and divided the whole country into parishes." The last is noticed as an anachronism, as the system of parochial division did not generally arise till a much later period. It may however very probably mean nothing more than the division of the country, so that the Priests might each have his own definite sphere of labour ; which was very necessary in so wide and thinly peopled a district. In the consecration of Bishops we do not know whether St. Ninian acted alone, as was allowed in cases of necessity ; and would be the more so here, as he was not apparently included in any province, of which the other Bishops might assist in the consecration ; or whether some of the British Bishops joined in the sacred rite. They might still be remaining in their Sees, but were far removed from this country, and the hostilities and dangers which prevailed might hinder them from coming.

We are equally in ignorance as to the succession of the Bishopricks ; of which we know no more than of those of the ancient Britons. It was very possible that they might have been numerous, as those of Ireland were. Of the portion North of the Forth, Abernethy was the Bishoprick, and so continued till later times, the Bishop, or as he was sometimes styled, Archbishop of that See, being called the Bishop of the Picts. In all probability St. Ninian would leave some of his own clergy, as the Priests and Bishops of his new converts. They could not themselves so soon have persons who could be entrusted with the sacred office for preserving the deposit of the truth, and St. Ninian, from his own experience, would be conscious of the value of a long and careful preparation for the sacred ministry. Nor is there any reason why we should not suppose that he revisited the Picts, and from time to time supplied what was wanting for the completeness of their ecclesiastical system. St. Aelred, indeed, speaks as if all had been done in one visit, but he might naturally adopt such a summary mode of narration when he was without any distinct information of the particulars of the visits. He passes on at the conclusion to the tranquillity which characterised the latter days of the Saint. "When he had confirmed the sons whom he had begotten in Christ in faith and good works, and arranged all which seemed necessary for the honour of God and the salvation of souls, the Saint bade farewell to his brethren, and returned to his own Church, where he spent the rest of his life, perfect in holiness, and glorious by his miracles, in great peace and tranquillity of mind."

By the Picts his name was remembered, and the Church he formed among them preserved. It was above a century after when St. Columba came amongst them, and they then professed Christianity, and mentioned St. Ninian as the Bishop by whom they had been converted.

CHAPTER IX

ST. NINIAN'S LATTER DAYS

AND now that we have followed the Saint through the broken incidents of a holy and laborious life, there are few remaining points on which to dwell, but such as they are, they will be interesting to recount.

And first, of the personal habits of St. Ninian. Holy and spotless as he had been through life, it would seem as if he might have been free from penitential austerities, and have spared the hardnesses which others must use with themselves. But such views proceed on erroneous notions, since they contradict the practice of the most eminent saints. The most pure and holy have ever been the most severe in their mortifications. Holy men, such as he was, become, as it would seem, not only indifferent to worldly comforts, but lovers of suffering endured for Christ's sake, and that principally from the love of Him. It seems to them, so to say, unnatural to live at ease, when He endured so much on their account. And they may suffer in a way which corresponds to His sufferings, by suffering for their people, by accompanying their earnest intercessions with those acts of mortification which are natural in deep sorrow. There is ever before them the sight of some, lost to their true interests, passing day by day from a life of folly and forgetfulness into an unchanging state; and yearning for their recovery and salvation, yet unable to effect it, when their words seem to them as idle tales, to weep, to fast, to pray, to endeavour to prevail with God for them is their natural resource. Then again, in a deep humble sense of not having corresponded to the influence of Divine Grace; the consciousness that though they have not wilfully and obstinately continued in sin, yet they have not improved duly the spiritual privileges afforded to them; the knowledge of imperfection and tendencies to sin—all these are so clearly seen, and acutely felt by those who really love God, that the sorrows and afflictions of saints are ever penitential. Let us not then be surprised, if, when we draw near St. Ninian, and learn his secret ways, we do not find contrivances for comfort, or the enjoyment of life.

They show on the coast of Galloway, on the face of a lofty and precipitous line of rocks, against which one of the stormiest of our seas incessantly beats, a damp chilly cave, lying one-third of the way, it may be, from the bottom of the cliff, and accessible only by climbing and springing from rock to rock. It is a deep recess, running back some twenty feet, and gradually narrowing from the mouth, where it may be twelve feet high, and as many wide. There is nothing to screen it from the winds and spray which beat against the rock, no bottom of earth to rest upon, but only bare

uneven stone. Here, the tradition of the country
says, St. Ninian used to come for penitential and
devotional retirement; and it is not improbable.
For a religious person in those days, to retire to
a cave, nay, to live in one all his life, was no strange
thing; it was but to follow in the steps of the confessors of the earlier dispensation, who lived in dens
and caves of the earth. It was the ordinary practice
of good people thus to deprive themselves of every
earthly comfort, and to realise the time when they
should be completely stripped of all which this
world can afford, in the cold and silent tomb. To
practise as it were beforehand, what every one at
some time must actually undergo, silence, and
loneliness, and reflection; without any thing of this
world to occupy the thoughts, or to afford outward
comfort. St. Ciaran, the Apostle of the Scoto-Irish,
had a cave in Kintire; and near St. Andrews, the
place of St. Rule's retirement, there are many caves
which were the retreats of religious men; and he
whom St. Ninian specially reverenced, the Saint
of Tours, as we have seen, lived with his associates
in caves. It has been thought that they were places
of concealment, to which a holy man might retreat
from the persecution his preaching would excite;
and there was need St. Ninian should have such
a protection, for he was not unfrequently in danger
from the attacks of the obstinate and the unbelieving. One would rather, however, view them as
places for religious retirement, and imagine the holy
Ninian going aside to rest awhile, from the many
who were coming and going, to withdraw at seasons
from the hurry and distraction of his office, to con-

sider his own state, to examine his spiritual progress, to mourn over what was evil, to deprecate the Divine displeasure, and to intercede for his people ; and surely it seems more fitting to do so in a lone and cheerless spot, out of the reach of men, in hunger and thirst, in cold and nakedness, with the wild winds howling around, and the sea and the waves roaring, and sea-birds screaming, than surrounded by comforts, and the appliances of luxury. And if it is rather probable antecedently, that St. Ninian should have a place of retreat, and the practice of the times would lead him to choose a cave, we should most naturally believe it to be that which popular tradition has pointed out.

Another instance of his mortified life, not it is presumed uncommon in the histories of saints, is the practice, as it has been reported, of abstaining from all food during the awful season of our blessed Redeemer's sufferings, in sympathy, penitence, and love. It is said he tasted nothing from the evening of Maundy Thursday, till he had partaken of the Holy Sacrament on Easter Day.

There is an old Life of St. Ninian in Ireland, referred to by Archbishop Usher, which reports further acts of self-denial, and withdrawal from all that winds itself around the heart, even the dearest ties of blood. It says that the mother and relations of the Saint were used to visit him, and that to separate himself from all intercourse with them, he went over to Ireland, accompanied by some of his disciples, and there, on a piece of ground given him by the king, founded the monastery of Cluayn Coner, where he spent the rest of his life and died.

The account of his retreat is one of those stories which may illustrate character, and show what it was thought he would do; but, as a matter of fact, it has no authority, and as regards his death, is contrary to the best testimony, which represents him as having died, and been buried in his own Church, at Whithern.

We have one more point in which to view St. Ninian, and then we will take leave of him—that is, as an author; in which character he appears in the ancient collections of our national writers, by Leland, Bale, and Pits. It is by no means improbable, indeed most likely, that he should commit to writing what would be for the good of his clergy and scholars. He had stored up at Rome the lessons of the great teachers of the Church; he had doubtless studied the writings of others, and himself through life meditated on the Holy Scriptures. He was now but perpetuating for the benefit of others, the spontaneous outpourings of his mind, or the solutions of those difficulties which were proposed to him. Such is the character of the writings which are attributed to him — Commentaries on the Holy Scriptures, and in particular, Meditations on the Psalms. These were the Meditations which had been the solace of his travels on the wilds of Galloway, the fruits of a deeply contemplative spirit exercised on those sacred words, which, by their continual repetition, and adaptation to the varying circumstances of the Christian life, are associated with our holiest thoughts. The other work of which the title is handed down, was one composed, doubtless, as a Theological Manual for the Clergy and Students of Whithern.[1] It was a collection of Sentences from the Fathers, of passages expressing their sentiments on points of doctrine and morals ; most probably arranged under heads, and so forming a body of divinity, and giving the most important portions—the very essence of their writings. The value of such a work to St. Ninian's clergy can scarcely be over-rated. They could not afford a large library, and might have read much without obtaining the advantages which such a selection would afford. It might, we may imagine, have been St. Ninian's work at Rome, where he had leisure and free access to libraries, and where such a commonplace book would have proved a useful aid in his own studies, to enter the passages which he would most wish to preserve. For though the most voluminous of the Fathers, as we have them, were only sending out their works during his stay at Rome, there were many remains of older ones which we have lost. And he was now only making that which had been intended for his own reference and perusal, a benefit to others ; and very great was the use of such a selection in instilling and preserving sound doctrine in the minds of those who were to teach others.

Such was St. Ninian, the young and noble Briton, who, for the love of Christ, and the true knowledge of Him, went forth from his country and his father's

[1] " Ex iis autem quæ post se reliquit, aliqua saltem nomine tenus tenemus teste sixto senensi,

Meditationum in Psalmos Davidis librum unum ;

De Sanctorum Sententiis librum unum."

Pitseus de Illustribus Britanniæ Scriptoribus, p. 87.

house. Such was he; a laborious apostle, enduring toil, difficulty, and reproach, in bringing men to Christ; a mortified ascetic, and meditative student; a kind teacher of babes, a humble, gentle, and circumspect governor of a religious society. And great was the fruit of his labours, in the recovery and salvation of souls, great in the glory of which he himself was made a partaker.

His life had been continued till the year 432, that is above seventy years. During the last five-and-thirty, nearly half of the whole, he had laboured in the wild, barbarous, and unsettled country to which he had been appointed as a Missionary Bishop. Worldly honours, comforts, possessions, he had cast behind him. He lived for God, and to do His will. His peaceful days of study and meditation in the sacred city, he might look back upon as sweet and holy days, full of spiritual privileges, and the source of many a blessing; but it would be as one surrounded by the rich fruits of autumn would look back on spring; as very fair, and in its time seeming more pleasant, but chiefly valuable as instrumental towards the true good which he is now enjoying, though it may be, among many labours. But such labours, it has been beautifully said, are sweet— sweet as those of the husbandman, who rejoices in the heavier load of corn by the increased value of his possessions—sweet as to the gatherer of frankincense, by the delights elicited in his toils.

Advanced in years, surrounded by his spiritual children and friends, beholding the effect of his labours, the time is come for him to depart.—To adopt the words of St. Aelred, "To the blessed

Saint himself that day was a day of joy and gladness; to the people over whom he presided, one of tribulation and distress. He rejoiced, for heaven was opening to him. His people grieved at being deprived of such a Father. He rejoiced, for a crown of immortality was preparing for him. They were in sorrow, because their salvation seemed in danger. Nay, even the fulness of his joy was impaired by his love for them; to leave them was a heavy trial, but to be longer separated from Christ appeared beyond endurance.

"But while his soul was thus delaying, Christ consoles him, 'Rise up,' He said, 'my beloved, my dove (in the English Version,[1] 'my love, my fair one'), make haste, and come away.' 'Rise up, my beloved, rise up, my Dove.' Rise up in thought, make haste by desire, come by affection. Suitable, indeed, were these words to this most blessed Saint, as one to whom, as the friend of the Bridegroom, that heavenly Bridegroom had committed his Bride, to whom He had revealed His secrets, and opened His treasures. Deservedly is that soul called beloved, in whom all is made up of love, and there is nothing of fear. 'My beloved,' He says, 'my dove.' My dove — a dove truly taught to mourn, that knew nothing of the gall of bitterness, but wept with those that wept, was weak with the weak, and burned for those that were offended. 'Rise up, my love, my fair one, and come away.'

"'For lo! the winter is past, the rain is over and gone.' Then, O blessed Saint, the winter was indeed past to thee, when, with happy eye, thou didst gain

[1] Cant. i. 10.

the sight of thy heavenly country—that country which the Sun of righteousness illumines by the brightness of His light, which love warms, and a wonderful equality, like the attempering of the springtime, regulates by an ineffable unity. Then the unseasonable winter which fills all on earth with discomfort, which hardens the frozen hearts of men by vices that fall upon them, where neither truth shines, nor love burns to the full—this was past and gone, and thy holy soul, completely triumphant, escaped from the showers of temptations, and the hail-storms of persecutions, into the beauty of perpetual verdure.

"'The flowers,' he says, 'have appeared in our land. For around thee, O blessed Ninian, breathed the odours of the flowers of Paradise, when on thee, as on one most familiar to them, the multitudes of those that are clothed in crimson and white, smiled with placid countenance, and bid thee to their company—they whom chastity has clothed with white, and love with blushing crimson. For though no occasion was afforded thee to give the sign of bodily martyrdom, still that without which martyrdom is nothing, denied not the merit of martyrdom.' For so often as he offered himself to the swords of the perverse, so often as in the cause of righteousness he opposed himself to the arms of tyrants, he was prepared to fall in the cause of truth, and to die for righteousness. Deservedly then is he admitted among the flowers of the roses, and the lilies of the valley—himself clothed in crimson and white, going up from Lebanon to be crowned among the hosts of heaven.

"'For the time of the vintage is come.' For soon, as a full ripe cluster, he must be cut from the stem of the body, from the vineyard of the Church on earth, to be pressed by love, and laid up in the storehouses of heaven.

"Thus the blessed Ninian, perfect in life, mature in years, happily departed from the world, and attended by angelic spirits, was borne to heaven; and there associated with the company of the Apostles, mingling with the ranks of Martyrs, and united to the bands of holy Confessors, adorned with the Virgin's flowers, he ceases not to succour those on earth who hope in him, call on him, and praise him.

"He was buried in the Church of St. Martin, which he had himself built from the foundation, and placed in a stone coffin near the altar, the Clergy and people standing by, and lifting up their heavenly hymns with heart and voice, with sighs and tears. And at this place the power which had shone forth in his life, ceases not in death to manifest itself around his body, so that all the faithful recognise him as living in heaven, because it is evident that he produces effects on earth. At his most sacred tomb, the sick are cured, the lepers are cleansed, the evil ones are affrighted, the blind receive their sight. And by all these things the faith of believers is confirmed to the praise and glory of our Lord Jesus Christ, who liveth and reigneth with God the Father, in the unity of the Holy Ghost, world without end. Amen."

The death of St. Ninian occurred on the 16th of September, A.D. 432; and on that day his memory was celebrated in the Scottish Church, in Catholic ages, with deep veneration, as their chiefest Saint, to whom first they owed it, that they had been brought from darkness to light, and from the power of Satan to God. The service for the day in the Aberdeen Breviary is very beautiful, and in connection with his history, most interesting. It contains nine Lessons, extracted from St. Aelred's life, and throws into devotional form the various events we have been recording. The circumstances of his life and miracles are expressed in hymns and proses, antiphones and responses, which once were chaunted in his praise throughout all the Churches of Scotland. His name and day were noted in the Kalendar prefixed to the Scottish Prayer Book of King Charles the First.

The rest of St. Aelred's work is occupied by a detailed account of miracles wrought at the tomb of St. Ninian, which it is not necessary now to narrate. "When the Saint had been taken up to heaven," he says, "the multitude of the faithful continued to visit, with the deepest devotion, what seemed to be left them of him—his most holy remains, and out of regard to their piety and faith, the Almighty showed, by the evidence of numerous miracles, that, though the common lot of mortality had taken His Saint from the earth, yet he still lived in heaven." A distorted child was first restored; this led many to hasten to bring their varied diseases before his holy relics; in particular, a man covered with a cutaneous disease of a most horrible kind was restored; then a girl, who had lost her sight; and two lepers were made clean by bathing in his

spring. "Through his prayers," to quote a hymn
for his day, "the shipwrecked find a harbour, and
the barren woman is blessed with offspring"; and
St. Aelred says that the power continued to be
manifested even in his own times.

CHAPTER X

CONCLUSION

AND now, that we have followed St. Ninian through his laborious life to his peaceful rest, we may not unnaturally wish to know what became of his Church and people after he was taken from them. On this point, however, our information is very limited, and much is left to be inferred from probabilities.

He had introduced the Ritual and Observances of the Roman Church, which were certainly different from those which the Britons used. Of these, however, no traces can be discovered. It would seem as if they had been lost among the changes which occurred between his death and the time of Bede; for, though that writer carefully sought for instances of conformity with Rome, he makes no mention of this, which would have been marked in itself, and known to the Saxons at Whithern. The Church of St. Ninian may herein have conformed to the practices of the other Britons, under the Episcopate of St. Kentigern, or have quite sunk into obscurity.

We should naturally expect that the instructions he established, would, for a time at least, be maintained; that the religious society would hold together, and continue its work, as a refuge of piety and teacher of religion; and there is some confirmation of this expectation in the statement of Scottish historians, that St. Ninian's monastery was a school which supplied teachers for the people; and that of Bede, that the body of the Saint, with those of many holy men rested in the Church of Whithern, as though there was there a home of Saints.

As regards the succession to his See, we are altogether without information. It is possible that in the troubled state of the country, when the Picts and Scots were so grievously afflicting the Britons, and when there certainly was so great a want of earnestness among the British Bishops, they may have neglected to supply a successor to St. Ninian; and the monastery and country priests may have continued without a pastor, trusting to occasional missionary visits, such as those of Palladius and others. The Church he loved so well was now desolate, and a widow. This seems most probably to have been the case till the time of St. Kentigern, who fixed his See at Glasgow, and included in his diocese the district which had been St. Ninian's care, and, it is said, completed the work of conversion. That diocese, as has been stated before, extended over the south-west of Scotland, and the Cumbrian Britons, as far as Stainmoor; and Whithern, whether it retained its monastery or not, became subordinate.

Meanwhile the Saxons were occupying England; were themselves being converted; and their power rapidly increasing, accompanied by a depth and earnestness of religion, perhaps unequalled in any people. From being the most barbarous, they became the most devout. The nation seemed a really Christian nation, and England was indeed an Isle of Saints. A spirit of piety was diffused through every class. Political measures were in consequence determined by the principles of the Gospel; and Saxon conquests were Christian ones, subordinate to the great objects of extending the privileges of religion, and procuring everlasting good for those whom they subdued.

It was the lot of Galloway in the eighth century to be overcome, and partially occupied by them, as a portion of the kingdom of Bernicia; and they, too, revered St. Ninian; and in the place where he was resting, and where his miracles were recorded to have been wrought, they established a monastery, and introduced a new succession of Bishops, under the metropolitan See of York. Then it was that Bede wrote of St. Ninian, and Alcuin was in correspondence with the brethren of the monastery. This succession continued as long as the Saxons had possession of Galloway; and the names of the Bishops are recorded from 723 to 790.

After this it was again broken; for fresh incursions afflicted the unhappy country. They were now overrun, not by a people who introduced a pure religion and social improvement, but by hordes of Irish, called Cruithne, or Picts, which is said to be a word of the same meaning; a distinct race, be it observed, from all who had previously borne that name. They were an uncivilised and very savage people, who brought their own religion and habits, and established them here.

They were long known as the wild Picts of

Galloway, and continued as a distinct and notoriously barbarous people till after the time of St. Aelred; indeed, Gaelic continued to be spoken here till the time of Mary Stuart. These are the Picts of later times, from whom the Picts' wall is named. During the dreary period which followed their invasion, the Bishop of Man, the nearest See, took charge of the deserted flock. A work of love which may add some little to our interest in that lowly relic of the Celtic Church.

In the twelfth century, however, brighter days beamed on Galloway. The power of the Saxon race who ruled in Scotland increased, and the Lords of Galloway, with their country, became dependent on the sovereign, and enjoyed the dangerous distinction of being the first to make the onset in his battles. David I. was a devotedly religious prince; the perfect example, as historians not disposed to flattery have called him, of a good king, whom St. Aelred loved and mourned over as though he were his father. His great object was to restore religion in Scotland, and with this view he founded Bishopricks and monasteries throughout his dominions, and St. Ninian's See was first restored.[1] But such was the fallen condition of the Scottish Church, that no Bishop was left to consecrate the newly-appointed one. And by the direction of the Pope, Thurstan, the Archbishop of York, performed the office. The Bishop, Gilaldan, from the evidence of ancient custom, as he said, acknowledged the obedience of his See to York; referring

[1] If it had not been, it was earlier; as some think, by Malcolm III., in the preceding century.

to the time of the Saxon succession in the eighth
century. Galloway thus again became part of the
Province of York, which gives the English Church
another claim on St. Ninian; and so continued,
certainly till the fourteenth century, and perhaps
till the establishment of St. Andrew's as a metropolitan Church in the fifteenth. Thus was the
Church again restored in Galloway, and continued
to flourish till the change of religion in the six-
teenth century; her Bishop, out of regard to St.
Ninian, and the antiquity of the See, taking the
first place among the Scottish Bishops.

Soon after this new foundation of the Bishoprick,
the Lord of Galloway, Fergus, followed up the work
of his sovereign and friend, and imitated in Galloway the course he had taken in the rest of Scotland. He is spoken of by the historians of Galloway
as in his sphere, one of the greatest benefactors of
his country. He found his people wild, barbarous,
and irreligious, and to effect a reformation among
them, he established monasteries, as sources from
which flowed forth the blessings of holy example
and Christian teaching, and moral and social improvement, which in time took effect upon the
people.

At Whithern he introduced a body of Præmon-
stratensian canons, an order then recently established, and full of life; it was an offset from Saul-
seat, where he had previously brought a colony
from Cockersand, in Lancashire. These formed the
Chapter (the Prior, during the vacancy of the See,
being Vicar-General), and elected the Bishop, though
with occasional opposition from the secular Clergy.

It was soon after the foundation of the Priory that St. Aelred wrote his Life of St. Ninian, and the chancel of the Church was built not long after; the publication of the Life probably making the virtues of St. Ninian known, and drawing numerous worshippers and offerings to his shrine.

From that time the Saint was held in the highest veneration, and his shrine visited, and his intercession sought by people from every part. Thousands of pilgrims came every year; and a general protection, very necessary in those days of Border warfare, was granted by James the First, in 1425, to all strangers coming into Scotland to visit St. Ninian's tomb; and in 1506 it was renewed for all persons of England, Ireland, and the Isle of Man, coming by sea or land to the Church of Whithern in honour of St. Ninian.

Numerous Churches in every part of Scotland are dedicated to him. In England there is one at Brougham, in the diocese of Carlisle, within the limits of his ancient diocese, the name of which is now corrupted into Ninechurch; and another, it is believed, at a place, called St. Ninian's, in Northumberland, where an annual fair is held on his Day (O. S.), Sept. 27. Many wells too in the Border counties are called by his name, and believed to have special virtues derived from him; never drying in the hottest, or freezing in the coldest weather; and still thought by the people to wash linen whiter than any other water.

The accounts of miracles wrought, and blessings obtained through his prayers, enter largely into the ordinary civil history of Scotland. For instance,

David II. received several wounds from the English archers, at Neville's Cross, before he was taken prisoner; one of the arrow heads could not be extracted, and remained, it is said by the historian of the times, till he went to St. Ninian's, then the flesh opened and the arrow head sprung out.

Besides other kings and nobles who visited the shrine, James IV., on whom the memory of his father's death hung so heavily, made a pilgrimage to St. Ninian's (so Whithern was usually called), once at least every year. The treasurer's books of his reign contain many notices illustrative of the circumstances of his visits and his large almsgivings. One pilgrimage he made on foot to pray for the safety of his Queen on the birth of her first son, and, after her recovery, she came with a great attendance to return thanks for the blessing she had received. This was Margaret, the daughter of Henry VII. and the mother of our Stuarts.

In the next generation, when Whithern was again without a Bishop, these pilgrimages continued so rooted in the habits and affections of the people, that the utmost zeal of the preachers could not put them down, till they were made punishable by law, in 1581. Such was the regard for our holy Saint, and so deeply fixed in the minds of those who had been blessed by him. And doubtless it still lingers in the belief of those who enjoy the fair water of his springs, or show his cave to the passing stranger, or glory in the honour the Saint once gave to their native town.

James I. restored a Bishop to Galloway, who was consecrated in 1610. The succession continued till

1689; when John Gordon, the last Bishop, followed the King to Ireland and France, and continued to perform the offices of the English Church at St. Germains. He died abroad; and St. Ninian's country was again included in the diocese of Glasgow — in name, at least, for throughout the whole district of Galloway, there is no Clergyman or congregation in communion with the Scottish Bishops. So entirely has that portion been swept away, so dreary a region to an Englishman is the country which St. Ninian blessed by his labours and his prayers.

In 1684 the tower of the Church was still standing among the ruins of the aisles, transepts, and extensive monastic buildings. All these are gone; but we may still trace them partly in their foundations, partly as portions of houses, partly as used for building materials, or kept as ornaments. The chancel has been preserved, being used by the Parishioners, till of late years, as their place of worship. It was built upon the site of much more ancient buildings, which had been the crypt, as it would seem, of an extensive Church; for there are large vaults of old and rude masonry around, which rise higher than the level of the chancel floor. They must have been part of the original Church of St. Ninian, of the fourth century; or built by the Saxons in the eighth century, and it would be interesting to ascertain whether they are not really part of a Church, the building and date of which are so marked in the Ecclesiastical History of Scotland. The chancel is a well-proportioned and beautiful specimen of the early English style. The

South-west doorway is round, and elegantly worked, the windows pointed, of single lights. In the north wall, in the usual place near the east end, are two canopied recesses, apparently sepulchral ones, nearly on the level of the floor, in one of which doubtless St. Ninian's body lay.[1] This even is now dismantled; a new building was erected about twenty years ago, which is the place of worship for the Parishioners; and the roof and furniture were removed from the old chancel, and the mere walls left; and that Church—once the most honoured in Scotland, where the holy remains of St. Ninian lay, and crowds of suppliants sought his intercession, where once the chaunt was heard by night and day, where holy men anticipated and prepared for heaven —that Church is now bare and roofless, exposed to the wild winds; grass grows upon the pavement, and ivy and wild flowers ornament its walls. A sad sight indeed; but it is beautiful in its ruins, and more pleasing far thus consecrated by loneliness and desolation, than defaced by incongruities, or applied to uses inconsistent with its spirit. A sad sight indeed, but one which harmonises well with the condition of that system of which it formed a part; a system the fair relics of which we love to trace in history, and complete in imag-

---

[1] The words, north and east are used, though improperly, for the Church stands north and south; a circumstance which we may connect with St. Aelred, for that is the position of his Abbey Church at Rievaux, and persons are sometimes glad to repeat even defects, when they remind them of a place they love. Fergus loved Aelred, and planted a colony of Cistercians from Rievaux at Dundrennan; St. Aelred himself was in Galloway, and probably concerned in founding the Priory.

ination ; which once was, and is no longer. Here St. Ninian laboured to raise a spiritual as well as a material Building, and to frame it in its services and doctrines after the Catholic model. Where is that Church? Where are those services now? There remains but a ruin of what once existed in beauty and honour.

LIVES OF
ST. WALTHEOF
AND
ST. ROBERT OF NEWMINSTER

INTRODUCTION

IT may have been observed that hitherto there have been comparatively few miracles in the Lives of Cistercian Saints. There even seems to be a dislike to looking out for miracles, as arguing a want of faith. Thus St. Aelred, in a passage already referred to, says, " There is also another sort of curiosity, which is the worst, by which, however, those alone are attacked who are conscious within themselves of great virtues, I mean the experimenting on one's own sanctity by the exhibition of miracles, which is tempting God. And if a man consent to this very wicked vice and is disappointed, his anguish of soul will lead him into the straits of despair, or the sacrilege of blasphemy." [1] Again, that is a significant story told of the successor of St. Bernard, at Clairvaux, that he begged of the saint to work no more miracles, as the concourse of people at his tomb distracted the devotion of the monks. In the two lives, however, which close the series of Cistercian Saints in England, there is a marked difference in this respect ; both abound in that class of stories commonly called legends. Many of these are so well fitted to illustrate certain principles which

---

[1] Spec. Car. 2. 24.

should be borne in mind in considering mediæval miracles, that they deserve some attention. Not that anything here said is intended to *prove* that the stories of miracles said to be wrought in the middle ages, are true. Men will always believe or disbelieve their truth, in proportion as they are disposed to admit or reject the antecedent probability of the existence of a perpetual church endowed with unfailing divine powers. And the reason of this is plain. Ecclesiastical miracles presuppose the Catholic faith just as Scripture miracles, and Scripture itself presuppose the existence of God. Men, therefore, who disbelieve the faith, will of course disbelieve the story of the miracles, which, if it is not appealed to as a proof of the faith, at least takes it for granted. For instance, the real reason for rejecting the account of the vision which appeared to St. Waltheof in the Holy Eucharist, must be disbelief of the Catholic doctrine. Without, however, entering on so wide a subject, it will be enough to examine, as it were, the phenomena of the miracles themselves, and to see what can be made out as to their probable truth or falsehood.

First, then, no one can read the legends of the middle ages without observing their highly poetical character. They form in themselves a vast literature of every country in Europe, many of them containing the only contemporary history of the period at which they were written, and many having a beauty and a freshness which has been observed by many who disbelieved them. Besides which, they are the exponents of a well-defined idea, and are formed on a religious type which is clear enough to those who talk most loudly against them. The notion of a saint which they embody is a very definite one, and the writers evidently know what they are talking about. It seems most unphilosophical to suppose that such writers were men who knowingly wrote to deceive; the vast volumes of the Bollandists, illustrated as they are with such astonishing historical and antiquarian learning, would be most extraordinary compositions if this were the case. And, in fact, there are now comparatively few who take this view of the legends of saints. They are generally now opposed on the ground of their poetical character, and not as being intentional fabrications. In fact, the two objections are incompatible; no one would dream of calling a poet dishonest, because his narrative is fictitious. If he believes the stories on which he writes, he may be called superstitious, but that is a very different indictment. To call a tale poetical is, however, by no means to say that it is true; on the contrary, this is the very ground on which legends are commonly said to be false. They are thought to be the natural product of the Christian religion acting upon the vigorous imagination of a youthful people; they are the offspring of the human mind in one stage of its progress, and they come out of it as the acorn out of the oak, and the flower out of the plant. In other words, legends of saints are the creations of the mind of man in the same sense as the Hindoo or Greek mythology; Christianity, indeed, being a purer religion, has substituted some holy virgin as a guardian for the sacred well, instead of the Grecian Naiad, but one being is as much a fiction as the other. And the legends themselves are a proof of this; they are observed to vary in character according to the country which gave them birth. The legends of the sandy Thebais, with their repose and Eastern gravity, contrast strongly with the wild stories of western hermits, which are the genuine products of the forest and the cavern by the sea-shore. Celtic legends also have a savage air peculiar to themselves, with their tales of serpents and monsters, reminding the reader strongly that St. Michael has just succeeded to the holy isles of the Druids; while Saxon stories are of a homely and domestic cast. All these legends, the argument proceeds, show their peculiar origin by their variety, just as the nature of the soil is betrayed by the plants which grow upon it. These legends, therefore, are of the earth, and we need rise no higher for their origin. Secondly, to bring the matter nearer to our subject, not only do these considerations account for the existence of legendary literature, but they account for visions and prodigies of all sorts. The same love of the marvellous which produces fairy tales and ghost stories, will also make the peasant fancy that he sees the elves dancing by moonlight on the mountain-side; and by the same law of our minds, the vivid imagination of a good man, acted upon by his devotion, might produce on his mind a strong impression which might take the shape of a vision. In the case of St. Waltheof, for instance, it may be observed that the visions which he saw occurred always on the feast-days and holy times of the church. Now it may be that a high-wrought state of mind, worked upon by long and exciting services, produced the vision, as the events of a day produce a dream.

This is the way in which men argue, and it is not necessary just now to inquire how far the fact on which the argument is grounded, is true. Few would doubt that many legends of the lives of Saints are strongly tinctured by popular devotion, or it may be by superstition. How, indeed, could it be otherwise? When it is known that many islands on the savage coast of Britanny, for instance, were in a half heathen state, and required missionaries in the seventeenth century, can they be supposed to have been less benighted in the tenth? It may, therefore, very safely be allowed that many legends of the middle ages are but a reflection of the truth rather than the truth itself. Some of them are mere myths, and belong to the same class as the beautiful stories of the Saintgrail, and of King Arthur's knights. And indeed this is the way in which most authors now regard them. The Bollandists are by no means sparing of such epithets as *ineptæ* and *ridiculæ*, applied to many legends which they have published. Time has gone on, and in its course men are altered too; and they can no longer receive indiscriminately what the faith of their ancestors fed upon. We must be men, it is said, and criticism and historic truth must take the place of simple belief.

This is not, however, what we would now dwell upon: our present object is rather to point out that with all the drawbacks that are to be made on the score of the superstition pervading a portion of ancient lives of Saints, the argument drawn out above does not cut the ground from under medieval miracles and visions in general, as it pretends to do. It is quite true that stories of miracles partake of the character of an imaginative age, and are tinctured by the character of particular nations, yet this is no reason for supposing them to be untrue, for individuals partake of the tone of the age and country in which they live, and it is out of the characters of His saints that God produces the wonders which He operates in His church. The human side of events is by no means incompatible with the divine. The inspiration which puts into the heart of a Saint to work a miracle, by no means excludes his will and his temper ; his angelic charity is employed in healing the sick miraculously, as in dressing their wounds or in soothing their sorrows. The undaunted energy, and even the roughness and quaintness of his character, may come out in the midst of the supernatural power imparted to him.

And with respect to visions in particular, there seems no reason why the devotion of a saint should not in a certain sense produce a vision, just as grace implies our habits, and predestination our efforts. And yet, though the intense contemplation of one who is pure in heart may pierce through the veil and see the saints and angels before the throne, this does not exclude the agency of God, whose workmanship we are, though we work out our own salvation. It is a wide-spread error by which men suppose that when they have classified all that they know of a subject, they have got to the bottom of the whole matter, and have a right to exclude whatever does not necessarily come within their system, even though it may not be incompatible with it. They think that they have discovered all that is to be known, when they have but found out the formal cause, that is, when they have analysed their own idea, forgetting that the real cause still remains as far off from them as ever. Some philosophers have argued, that because the idea of God in the human mind is the creation of the soul of man, imagining to itself the supreme good, therefore God Himself is nothing more than the ideal standard of good dwelling naturally within us. But such men forget that, although the thought of God may come into the heart of man by a natural process, this is not incompatible with the fact of His existence as our Everlasting Creator and Master. And in like manner visions might be real, that is, come from God, though they were ever so much the effect of the intense devotion of the Saint.

And to carry these remarks further, in matters of physical science it is often said that men now-adays have no superstitious views of such pheno-mena as earthquakes, eclipses, and thunder, because their causes have been discovered. Now it may or may not be superstitious to be afraid of thunder, but to say that it is caused by electricity removes none of those reasons for fear which affected men in the dark ages. What is meant by a law is only the human way of viewing in succession, what to Almighty God, and it may be even to the angels, is one and undivided. So it is quite true that "the glorious God maketh the thunder," though it is also true that electricity is the cause of it, and that it proceeds on a natural law. So also the dark ages might be right in ascribing certain extraordinary events to divine agency, even though men had discovered, which they have not, the psychological law on which such effects are produced. They might be connected with the imaginativeness of the human heart, for imagination raised by Christianity above its natural powers becomes intense devotion.

To go to another branch of the same subject, it is often said that what was called diabolical possession was only a natural disease called epilepsy, and therefore had nothing to do with devils. But evil spirits might have power over the body, and might always act in a particular way, so as to constitute a law. Or else they might bring to pass, in a supernatural way, effects which also happen from natural causes, so that exorcism may be a supernatural power, even though natural means can in time remove what may be done miraculously in an instant. Again, in the present day, strange effects of mind over matter have been discovered, and in some cases mesmerism seems to make an approach to what would formerly have been ascribed and rightly to supernatural causes. But this, so far from telling against medieval miracles, only proves that human souls and bodies possess mysterious powers on which the Holy Spirit may have deigned to work, and that things are possible which men have long denied on the score of their impossibility. Nay, supposing that Satan could thus in certain false systems of religion imitate some Christian miracles by signs and wonders, it would throw no discredit upon them. Natural philosophers have been said to draw down lightning from heaven and to make diamonds, but they do not make the slightest approach to the power of God, nor bridge over the infinite gulf which divides causation from creation.

It appears, then, that to talk of the power of imagination is nothing to the purpose, if it is meant to show that such visions as those with which St. Waltheof was favoured did not really come from heaven. Imagination, translated into the language of the Church, means devotion; and no one can tell how far Almighty God may have made use of the Saint's own devotion in framing the vision before the eyes of his soul. And what has been said on similar subjects by great writers in the Church falls in with this notion of the influence of the soul in such matters. St. Augustine discusses whether the cloven tongues of fire, seen on the first Whitsunday, were seen in the spirit within, as though they were without, or really without before the eyes of the flesh. In another place, he touches upon "the power of the soul in changing and influencing bodily matter,"[1] though, at the same time, he says, that it cannot be called the creator of the body, who is God alone. So also St. Thomas discusses the very case which, as will be seen, happened to St. Waltheof, of a child appearing at the time of the elevation of the Host. He thus determines that what was there seen was not the body of our Lord, but that an effect was produced upon the eyes of the Saint, "as though it were seen externally." "And yet," he continues, "this had nothing to do with deception, as in the case of magic charms, for such an appearance is formed by divine influence on the eye to

[1] St. Aug. de Trin. 3. 8.

figure a truth—viz. to show that the body of the
Lord is really under the Sacrament; as also Christ,
without deception, appeared to the disciples going
to Emmaus."[1] Again, in an instance which brings
us close to St. Robert of Newminster, St. Godric,
who does not at first seem likely to reason on what
he saw, is recorded to have said, after seeing a vision
of a departed soul, that he saw not the soul itself,
for it was invisible, but that what he saw was a
form which signified its presence.

And if it be asked, why should these visions be
real, and alleged appearances of false gods and of
beings created by superstition be untrue?—the answer
is, that, as has been said before, the visions in the
lives of Saints presuppose the truth of the Catholic
faith, and are real because the faith is true. We
believe Christian visions to be real because Christianity is real, and the portents of heathen mythology
are false because they are part of a false religion.
And here, as in many other respects, the analogy
between the natural and the spiritual sight is perfect;
for all our senses, and sight among the rest, require
it to be taken for granted that the sensations which
we feel are produced by an object without us; and
philosophers have been found who reason very
plausibly, that all that we see and touch is merely
ourselves touching and feeling, just as faithless men
argue that the visions of the Saints are mere creations
of their own minds. Substance is taken for granted
in our bodily vision, as the faith is presupposed in
supernatural visions.

And in distinguishing what are most commonly

[1] Summa Theol. 3. qu. 76, 8.

called legends from what is historical in the lives of
Saints, it should be borne in mind, that though the
prevalence of a certain tone, which may be called
poetical or romantic, does not throw discredit on
miracles in general; yet it is quite true that, in
many particular instances, the strange stories in
medieval narratives are strongly tinctured by the
spirit of the age, call it poetic, superstitious, or
faithful, as you will. The proof of it is, that a love
of the marvellous evidently affects the narratives
of historians as well as hagiologists; and this both
makes it likely that the same tone should appear
in accounts of what is confessedly supernatural, and
also shows that truth and falsehood may be blended
together without destroying each other. In the
grave chronicles of the age, most of them proceeding from the lonely cell of some religious man,
accounts of marvellous portents, of bright colours
and strange figures seen in the sun and moon, are
mingled with just as much of the news of the outer
world, of the victories and defeats of kings, as was
drifted into the monastery. If it were not for the
undeniably life-like energy of the barons and kings
who make their appearance, the reader would be
tempted to put down the whole for a production
of the vivid fancy of some solitary monk, so much
does the whole scene savour of the romantic. Sometimes the list of portents reminds us of the marvels
which appear in the pages of Livy. Even the
shrewd William of Newbridge, though by no means
without his tinge of private judgment, is overcome
by his love of the marvellous, and some accounts
very like fairy tales appear in the midst of his facts.

As a specimen of his narrations, in one place, among many other marvels, it is said that near Winchester some quarrymen found embedded in stone a live toad, with a gold chain and collar round his neck. In the same way, at a time when men were not given to patient investigation on any point, it is not wonderful that the lives of Saints should present manifold exaggerations, and that the convent traditions should in some cases grow, like any other narratives. The objections commonly urged that man is liable to error, and that inspiration alone is infallible, are in place here, however senseless they may be when they would sap the foundations of all history, by rejecting any amount of evidence. There is a good substratum of truth in the medieval lives of Saints, which will stand the attack of any philosophy which would reduce them to the state of myths; while at the same time the busy, romantic element of the human heart has naturally exercised itself on Christian Saints as it did on the champions of Christendom in the Holy Land. Evidence, internal and external, must be the criterion here, as in every other kind of history.

These remarks are the more apposite, because there are instances in Josceline's life of St. Waltheof which will illustrate what is meant. One of them is as follows: On a certain day, when one of the canons of Kirkham was celebrating mass in the presence of St. Waltheof, a spider fell into the sacred chalice about the time that the words Agnus Dei are sung; the celebrant, not knowing what to do, managed to attract St. Waltheof's attention, and asked him what course ought to be taken. He could not drink the contents of the chalice, because the spider was a poisonous insect, and he could not take it out for fear of profanation. St. Waltheof, making a short prayer and signing the chalice with the cross, bade the canon boldly drink, in the Lord's name. Then Josceline, after detailing his admiration that the canon received no hurt, goes on to say: "When dinner was over and the canons were sitting in the cloister, the priest who had celebrated mass sat rubbing his finger, and after a short time a lump appeared on it, and lo! the spider, breaking the skin, came out alive, to the wonder of all who were sitting round, and by the command of the prior was committed to the flames. Now there is no reason to doubt that the spider did fall into the chalice, and that the canon felt the difficulty and drank its contents, for spiders were then believed to be poisonous. As for the story of the reappearance of the insect, as the whole goes on the assumption that spiders are poisonous, and that there was a miracle in the case, it may fairly be concluded to be an excrescence on the original story, and that it had been appended to it in conventual tradition, just as any other narrative "vires acquirit eundo." It, however, no more implies fraud, than the addition of this gold chain and collar to the neck of the unfortunate toad, which, doubtless, was found in the quarry near Winchester. Many more instances might be taken from this source, but enough has been said to show how truth and fiction may lie together, blended in the same narrative. If it be impossible to separate them, that is a reason either for neglecting the whole, or for receiving the whole.

Religious minds would probably take the latter alternative, not thinking it after all so very great a misfortune to believe a few miracles too much. They would rather venture a little than lose one record of God's dealings with His Saints. However, we do not believe it to be in all cases impossible to make the separation. In the present instance, some attempt has been made to do so. Josceline, the monk of Furness, who is the author of the life in the Bollandists, wrote about sixty years after the death of St. Waltheof. He professes to draw his narrative from some aged monks of the abbey of Melrose. It seemed therefore lawful to give as much of his narrative as would be interesting, without relating every circumstance which it contains.[1]

In conclusion, it will be well to see in what light such visions and miracles as are here related are considered by spiritual writers in the Catholic Church, that it may be seen how far they are from laying stress upon them, though they will not faithlessly set limits to God's grace in His dealings with His saints. "There are some," says an author whom most men would call foolishly credulous,[2] "whom the devil deceives; but there are others, too, who are deceived by the weakness of their imagination, fancying that they see and hear extraordinary objects and voices, though in effect they see and hear nothing. There are some also who not only are

[1] The precise date of his work cannot now be easily ascertained. It appears that he began it at the request of Patrick, Abbot of Melrose, and finished it after his death. Patrick succeeded William as Abbot in 1206, and died the year after. Josceline, therefore, probably finished his work shortly after 1207.

[2] Boudon, L'Amour de Dieu seul; discours préliminaire.

deceived by the devil, or by themselves, but seek to deceive others by voluntary and diabolical wickedness. So we repeat what we have said; we must be on our guard, not easily to put faith in extraordinary things. Spiritual directors should take care to guide souls put under them in the ways of pure faith, which is the immediate union of the soul with God. This is the teaching of the great doctor of mystical theology, the blessed John of the Cross; he gives it as a rule in his books, that such things as visions and revelations should be left to the judgment of God, and that we should remain in quiet faith, without dwelling upon them. This teaching shields us from all illusions of the devil; for by resting in pure faith, a man cannot err. He walks by a sure path, and the light which guides him is infallible; besides which, since these unmerited graces which God gives us, such as visions and revelations, come externally to us, and are independent of us, we therefore are safe in not examining them. I do not mean that directors should not make use of such marks as holy doctors have given us to discern the true Spirit of God in such extraordinary things from the evil spirit; but I mean that, after all, we must suspend our judgment, and lay no great stress on such things, and lean entirely on faith. With respect to those persons who are the subjects of such extraordinary occurrences, they should not let their minds dwell upon them at all, but leave them to the judgment of God, whatever value they may have in His sight. Thus, if they are the work of the devil, he will be confounded; if they come from the Holy Spirit, He will increase His blessings."

LIFE OF

ST. WALTHEOF

THE lives of the Saints of the middle ages are like the ruins of their own monasteries, lovely and melancholy fragments, which are but indications of a beauty which has passed away from the earth. Not indeed as though the Church were dead, and there were no Saints now in Christendom, but a Saint of the nineteenth century will never be precisely like one of the twelfth. The beautiful infancy and youth of Christianity are past, and even Saints may partake something of the acuteness and activity of the age with which they have to contend. If Melrose could be roofed afresh, and the vaulted ceiling restored, the painted glass replaced in the east oriel, and the niches filled again, it would certainly not be a facsimile of the Melrose of six hundred years ago. But the building would not be so unlike its predecessor as the new members would differ from their brethren of old, though they wore the same habit and kept the same rule. But it is wrong to mourn over what must be ; and perhaps the new brethren would in some respects surpass the old. So we must just take Melrose as it is, a beautiful ruin; and we will try to write the life of its holy Abbot Waltheof, imperfect as the attempt must be. We will do our best to put into shape the scanty records left by brother Josceline, just as a man standing on the Eildon Hill on an autumn evening would fill up the outline formed against the glowing sky by the ruined abbey.

I. HOW WALTHEOF LIVED IN THE WORLD

There are some persons who, from their birth, appear destined to take part in the roughest scenes of the world's politics, and to this class Waltheof seemed to belong. He was apparently born to inherit the strongest prejudices, and to be placed amidst conflicting interests, in which he was unavoidably to take his part. He was of one of the most illustrious families of England, descended from the old kings and earls of Northumbria, from Ida, the bearer of flame, and from Siward, who had defeated the tyrant Macbeth, and set Malcolm Canmore on the throne. His grandfather, whose name he bore, was that Waltheof whom the Conqueror had first, as he thought, won to himself, by bestowing on him the hand of his niece Judith, but whom he had afterwards ruthlessly beheaded at Winchester. His body was taken to the Abbey of Croyland, where the affectionate remembrance of the poor Saxon canonised the victim of the Conqueror's revenge, and pilgrims often knelt at the tomb of the English martyr. The daughter of this Waltheof, Matilda, was given in marriage to Simon of St. Liz, a Norman noble, as if to obliterate the remembrance of her Saxon blood ; and of this union were born two children, Simon and Waltheof. Not long after their birth, their father incurred the displeasure of Henry I., and he assumed the cross and went to the Holy Land. He left England, never to return ; news soon came to his wife that she was a widow, for her husband had perished as a good soldier of the Cross in Palestine. Matilda was still young when this happened, and her cousin, King Henry, afterwards gave her in marriage to David of Scotland, and with her bestowed on him the possessions of her first husband. When David inherited the throne of Scotland, his step-sons followed him, and were brought up in the palace of Dunfermline with his own children.

The course of Waltheof's life seemed thus to be marked out for him : he was to be a staunch defender of the Saxon line, and a hater of the Normans, who had slain his grandfather and caused the exile of his father ; and he was to be a staunch partisan of the succession of the Empress Matilda. But there are men who apparently come across their destiny—some for good, and others for bad—and of these was Waltheof. It was evident, however, from his infancy, that he was not made for the world which was moving around him. Their mother, Matilda, used to smile at the contrast between her two boys, when they were mere children, playing at her feet. While Simon, the elder, the future earl and warrior, was building castles of wood and charging, at a mock tournament, astride on a cane, Waltheof would be raising churches of sticks and pebbles, making the sign of the Cross like a priest, and imitating the chants which he had heard in church. As he advanced in years he seemed hardly to change, so naturally and evenly did his character grow in strength and beauty, without losing its childlike freshness. It was, as says the Scripture, the righteous man blossoming as the lily. When he came to David's court, he showed the same purity and the same unearthly character; and so little did he seem to belong to the scenes which were passing about him, that the nobles of Scotland did not know what to make of him; and he puzzled them the more, from the striking difference between him and his two companions, Prince Henry and Aelred. The high-spirited Henry was an indefatigable hunter, and marked out for a soldier from his birth; and even Aelred, who, from his bookish propensities might be classified with Waltheof, still showed some marked differences from his friend: he was more easily understood, from his frank and sociable temper. But Waltheof, without any appearance of moroseness, was fond of solitude; he had but few friends, while Aelred had many. Again, Aelred was very cheerful, and took interest in all about him; but Waltheof might have seemed apathetic. Though none could look on his bright countenance and think him gloomy, yet it was evident that the scenes which passed around him affected him but little: he was an unworldly character, and such always are incomprehensible to men of the world. King David alone saw through his step-son; he used to take Waltheof with him into the noble forests which surrounded

Dunfermline to hunt the wild deer; and would give him his bow to carry, in order to keep him near himself. But the young lord soon grew weary of the chase, and giving up the care of the king's bow to some one else, he used to plunge deep into the woods; and finding a level spot of green sward under the shade of some broad oak, he would read a book or kneel down to pray. One day David, who used to wonder at his periodical disappearance, came upon him in his retirement, and though the whole chase swept rapidly past him, David's quick eye had time to spy him out in his hiding-place; and when he came home, he said to his queen, "That son of thine is not of our stamp; he is nothing to the world, nor the world to him; depend upon it, he will either die young, or else fly away to the cloister."

The nobles about the court, however, did not take this view, and Waltheof still remained a mystery to them. They even made experiments upon him, as philosophers would on some strange phenomenon. As far as they durst, by covert insinuations, they put evil before him, but his imperturbable simplicity baffled them. Waltheof probably did not know himself any more than they. It often happens that those whom God is leading on to perfection, are unconscious of the end to which they are tending. Those about them often think them incapable of anything very great, and they themselves have often not made up their mind what course of life is to be theirs. The notion of choice does not come before them, till something external forces them to election, and they choose at once the better part. So in the case of Waltheof, an event occurred which opened the eyes of all parties, both his own and those of the nobles, who were looking on to see how this would end. A young and noble lady fell in love with Waltheof, and the courtiers used with delight to watch them speaking together, hoping that at last the lord Waltheof was becoming like his neighbours, and was human after all. Soon after, some one spied glittering on Waltheof's finger a gold ring with a sparkling gem, which the lady had given him. The news soon spread that he was in a fair way of being a confessed lover; there was joy in the gay circles of the court that day, for they thought that Waltheof had fallen from his high estate, and had thus become like an ordinary mortal. They were, however, mistaken, for when this report reached him, it opened his eyes at once to his situation. He must either make up his mind to marry or to go into religion. The children of this world are in their generation wiser than the children of light, and they taught Waltheof a lesson, that such attachments are dangerous. There can be no half measures, and the crucifixion must be complete. So Waltheof took the shining jewel off his finger and threw it into the fire. From that moment, he looked upon himself as destined for the priesthood.

2. HOW WALTHEOF QUITTED THE WORLD

He was now considered as certain of a bishoprick either in England or Scotland; and when the King of Scotland was his step-father, and the King of

England his mother's cousin, it was no unreasonable conjecture. Waltheof, had, however, by no means the same views for himself; his only wish was to serve God in the lowest station in His Church. While he was revolving these thoughts in his mind, Aelred announced his intention of becoming a monk and of quitting Scotland. It seemed much less likely that the gay and open-hearted Aelred should be the first to go, but so it was;[1] and Waltheof must have felt very solitary, when the only friend who understood his feelings and character had gone into religion and had left him in the world. He was not one who could make new friends in a day, and he had still some time to remain in solitude after Aelred had left him. He found more external obstacles than Aelred had met with, in his way from the world to the cloister. He was an important political personage; and in times when the north of England was a debatable ground, it was of the utmost consequence to put the great sees into the hands of friendly churchmen, as not long after Henry II. saw when he created the bishoprick of Carlisle to counteract the see of Glasgow. Waltheof, as David's step-son, would have been a more respectable personage to fill St. Cuthbert's chair than William Comyn, who was put in by Matilda's party. He was not therefore his own master. His brother Simon, too, whose warlike propensities made him look upon his brother's love for the cloister as fanaticism, had early in Stephen's reign become

---

[1] Waltheof did not leave Scotland till his brother was an earl—*i.e.* probably not till Stephen's reign.

Earl of Northampton;[1] and he as well as King
David opposed Waltheof's wish. At length he
stole away from David's court, and took refuge in
Yorkshire, at a priory of Austin canons, dedicated
to St. Oswald, one of the ancestors of his family.
Here Waltheof hoped that the world would forget
him. "Here," says brother Josceline, "he determined to lie hid and die, as, says the blessed Job,
in his little nest; and to grow up noiselessly as
a palm-tree, hidden from the provoking of all men
in the secret place of God's countenance, forgotten
by all his kith and kin, like a useless vessel flung
aside, like a dead man in the hearts of his friends."
Such was Waltheof's wish. "But the Lord of all,"
continues Josceline, "had decreed far otherwise."
First of all, he was made sacristan of St. Oswald's,
and then the canons of Kirkham chose him for
their prior. And here at last he seemed to have
obtained the rest for which his soul longed; and
indeed many men might envy him the place in
which his lot was cast. It was in a beautiful valley
in Yorkshire, not far from the spot where the waters
of the Rye, after passing under the walls of the
abbey of Rievaux, joined the broader stream of
the Derwent. He was therefore now a near neighbour to Aelred; the abbey and the priory had a
common founder, and their possessions touched
each other, and the monks had frequent intercourse
with the canons. Among their visitors at some
time or other was certainly Aelred, for he mentions

[1] v. Knyghton ap. Twysden, 2386, and Brompton, 1030. Brompton
says, Earl of Huntingdon, p. 975, which he was not till afterwards,
as appears from John of Hexham, p. 258.

Kirkham, and calls it a most lovely spot.   His
friends in Scotland evidently bore no ill-will to
him for his flight from them, for his half-brother,
Prince Henry, loved Kirkham for its prior's sake,
and bestowed many lands upon it.   His canons, too,
loved Waltheof for all his virtues, but specially for
his humility ; for he did not rule over them with a
high hand, but treated them as brethren.

He might have quitted them, if he had pleased,
for a much higher station.   In 1140, Thurstan,
archbishop of York, died, and there were great
deliberations in the court of Westminster.   The
question was, who would make a respectable archbishop, and at the same time a good partisan of
King Stephen.   From Waltheof's noble birth and
reputation for sanctity, he would have been an
obvious person to fix upon ; and though, from his
connection with King David, he was not at first
sight likely to fulfil Stephen's conditions, yet it
seems that his brother Simon had taken the side
of the king against Matilda, so that there were
hopes that he might follow his example.   Many
nobles urged Stephen to appoint him, but the
king was afraid of him.   With all Waltheof's
sweetness and humility, there was a certain unmanageable element in his character which did not
suit Stephen.   It is a dangerous experiment to
place on an episcopal throne a man who could
neither be bribed nor frightened. In fact, what
could Waltheof be bribed with ? He had already
given up everything on earth.   He had no earthly
wishes ; so what could be done with such a man ?
Again, if he did wish for anything, it was to suffer

humiliation with his Lord; force, therefore, would have been equally unavailing. So, on the whole, King Stephen thought that Waltheof was not the man to be Archbishop of York. All this while the Prior of Kirkham was very quietly in the wilds of Yorkshire, utterly ignorant that he was the subject of grave deliberation in high places, till one day he received intimation that the puissant Earl of Albemarle[1] had arrived at Kirkham, and wished to see him. After some conversation, the noble earl said, " How long dost thou mean to bring dishonour on our house, by burying thyself in this dungeon of a cloister? Why not show thyself in public oftener? If thou wouldest but take the trouble to gain the favour of the king and his counsellors by gifts and promises, thou wouldest win any bishoprick thou mightest affect. If thou wilt but promise to give me the township of Shirburn, to be held by me during my lifetime, I will undertake to get thee the archbishoprick of York." His lordship of Albemarle certainly knew very little with what sort of man he had to deal; he was therefore, probably, not a little surprised to see the pale cheek of the gentle monk suffused with red, and his eye kindle for a moment with something like anger. It, however, passed away as quickly as it came; and Waltheof calmly said, " Be thou quite sure that thou wilt never see me seated in a bishop's throne, nor

---

[1] William, this Earl of Albemarle, was son of Stephen, who was the brother of Judith, St. Waltheof's grandmother. Stephen and Judith were the children of Odo, Earl of Albemarle, by Adeliza, sister of the Conqueror. William was first cousin to St. Waltheof's mother.

thyself in possession of the township of Shirburn."

It was not, however, surprising that a worldly-
minded man, like the earl, should not be able to
penetrate the depth of Waltheof's character. It
would have been a hard matter for any one who
saw the lowly prior abasing himself beneath the
lowest lay - brother of the community, to tell how
highly favoured was this humble soul. It would
have been difficult to suppose that this humble
man, who busied himself so noiselessly and regularly
with the rule of his convent, and threw his mind
into all the wants and desires of his brethren, was
all the while wrapped up in the contemplation of
heavenly things, in a way which none but those
who are dead to earth can know. Sometimes
our blessed Lord would, as it were, break through
the cloud ; and as after His resurrection He would
appear suddenly in the midst of His disciples, so
now and then in Waltheof's life, He all at once
converted contemplation into vision, and gave His
servant sensible indications of His presence. One
of these visions appears to have occurred at Kirkham. One Christmas - day, while the convent was
celebrating the Nativity of the Lord, as the Prior
was elevating the Host, in the blessed sacrifice
of the mass, he saw in his hands a child fairer
than the children of men, having on his head
a crown of gold, studded with jewels. His eyes
beamed with light, and his face was more radiant
than the whitest snow ; and so ineffably sweet
was his countenance, that the prior kissed the
feet and the hands of the heavenly child. After

this the divine vision disappeared, and Waltheof found in his hands the consecrated wafer.

The servants of Christ are, however, never suffered by Him to dwell on the joys which He vouchsafes to give them. When the Apostles were, after our Lord's ascension, straining their eyes to penetrate the cloud which carried Him out of their sight, two angels appeared, to ask them why they stood gazing up into heaven. So the vision which Waltheof saw was but for a moment, or rather it hardly could be measured by time at all; and when it disappeared, and he came down from the altar and went back into the monastery to set about his business, all looked as it did before. The cloisters echoed to his footsteps as if nothing had happened, and the canons, bowing in silence to their prior as they passed him, reminded him that he must go on with his work. And sad work he soon had upon his hands; that same archbishoprick of York which he had rejected was now a bone of contention in the north; and news arrived at Kirkham that William, the treasurer, Stephen's nephew, had been elected, but that the presence of the Earl of York at the election made men suspect that undue influence had been exerted, if not by William, at least by his friends. William's character was not such as to please Waltheof's Cistercian friends; he was amiable indeed, and none accused him of immorality; but he was at that time indolent and magnificent. They were unsparing in their censures, these Cistercian monks; popes, cardinals, and bishops equally came under their lash, and in this case they determined to oppose William's election as being uncanonical. Waltheof was already a Cistercian in heart, and he joined himself to his neighbours, William, abbot of Rievaux, and Richard, abbot of Fountains, in their efforts to obtain a sentence against the election. The parties in opposition to each other in the diocese of York were, on the whole, regulars against seculars, that is, at least in this case, strictness against laxity; and Waltheof did not hesitate which side to choose. In 1142 he appealed against the election with the abbots of Fountains and of Rievaux, and others of the regular as well as some of the cathedral clergy. In 1144 we find him at Rome with his colleagues in the appeal. No particulars appear of his journey across the Alps; but doubtless the tombs of the Apostles saw more of Waltheof than the papal court. How they sped in their cause has been too well narrated elsewhere to require notice in this place; besides which, it has little to do with Waltheof's history. He brought back to Kirkham a heart not a whit more in love with the great world on account of the glimpse which he had seen of it. All that he had seen on his way to and from the great city remained on his mind like a bewildered dream; and neither the snowy Alps, nor the blue lakes and sunny sky of Italy, seemed to him half so beautiful as the rugged outline of the Blackmoor hills, and the first sight of the green banks of the winding Derwent and the tower of his own church at Kirkham, from which the bells were ringing to welcome his arrival; and the brethren issuing out of the church with cross and banner to meet their prior.

scion of their stock should be a novice in a poor
Cistercian monastery. A mitred abbacy he would
not have quarrelled with, but that his brother should
be the lowest monk in a low convent was intolerable;
and he sent a message to the brethren of Wardon
that he would burn the abbey over their heads if
they allowed his brother to remain amongst them.
The poor monks trembled, for they well knew Simon
was a man to keep his word, and amidst the general
license of the period, burning an abbey was not so
very rare as to make it remarkable. Waltheof,
therefore, was again a fugitive, cast out on the
wide world by his own mother's son. But our
Lord has promised to give us an hundred fold that
which we give up for His sake; and so when Waltheof's own brother turned against him, Aelred,
who was more to him than his unnatural brother,
was given back to him. The monks of Wardon,
when they found themselves obliged to send their
novice away, transferred him to Rievaux, where he
was out of the reach of his brother.

Henceforth Waltheof's external trials are over;
yet our Lord, who never will leave His Saints to
be without the cross, now prepared for him an
interior trial, which was harder to bear than any
other. Hitherto he had walked in the light of
God's countenance in spiritual joy; but now the
countenance of the Lord no longer shone upon
him, and there had succeeded a cold and dreary
state of darkness, in which he seemed to have lost
sight of the object of his faith. He felt neither joy
nor sorrow; he had no feeling at all. When he
thought on the Passion, he did not weep; and when

he meditated on the Resurrection, there was the same dull blank in his soul. Formerly, fasts and vigils, and bodily suffering of all sorts, were a joy to him, because they were a means of partaking in the crucifixion of his Lord ; but now all the various actions of his monastic life were gone through mechanically, as a daily task. The doctrines of the Mirror of Charity were exactly suited to his case ; but, as generally happens in such temptations, he fancied that his state had something peculiar in it, which exactly excepted it from the consolations which Aelred held out. He thought that he had done wrong in leaving his priory, and he was sorely tempted to quit the Cistercian order before he finally took the vows. The devil, who knows well that obedience and patience are the proper means of escaping, in God's own time, from such spiritual depression as then weighed down his heart, was anxious to make him by a definite act break away from Rievaux, and take the law in his own hands. But it is best to give the whole in Josceline's words : —" When Waltheof had spent some time in the cell of the novices, by a temptation of the Evil one, the observance of the rule became loathsome to him ; the food appeared to him tasteless, the clothing rough and vile, the manual labour hard, the psalms and night-watches wearisome, the whole course of the order too austere. When he thought on the former years which he had spent as a prior, it grew upon him that the rule of the canons, though less austere, was more in accordance with Christian discretion, and more fit for the saving of souls. As soon, however, as he felt this suggestion creep into his heart, he sought, in constant and earnest prayer, an antidote for its poison. After, however, the temptation, far from diminishing, had only increased, so that he debated whether he should quit the Cistercian order and go back to his canons, he was at length relieved by the Lord, and blushed at his own weakness. For, one day after the bell had sounded for the office, at one of the canonical hours, and all the novices had gone out in seemly order, he alone remained behind in the cell. Led by the impulse of the Spirit, he threw himself across the threshold, half in and half out of the cell, and praying, with many tears, he said, 'O God Almighty, Creator of all, who knowest and dispensest all things, whether it be thy good pleasure that I remain a monk, or that I become again a canon shew me, O Lord; and take away from me this temptation which afflicts my soul.' And our Lord heard his prayer, and soon, almost without feeling, the mourner felt 'the dull hard stone within him' disappear. He never knew what happened to him in that hour, or how it happened, but he felt himself raised off the ground, and found himself in the seat which belonged to him in the cell, and where he used to read and meditate. Nothing can express so well what he then felt as the words of an English poet, whom we have almost unconsciously quoted :—

These are thy wonders, hourly wrought,
 Thou Lord of time and thought,
Lifting and lowering souls at will,
Crowding a world of good or ill

Into a moment's vision ; even as light
Mounts o'er a cloudy ridge, and all is bright,
From west to east, one thrilling ray
Turning a wintry world to May.

Waltheof never felt the temptation after this ; and
in due course, at the end of the year, he received
the white habit at the hands of Aelred. Great
must have been the joy of both in that hour when
Aelred put the habit upon his friend with the usual
words, " The Lord put off thee the old man with his
deeds," and the convent responded, " Amen."

4. HOW WALTHEOF BECAME AN ABBOT

Waltheof and Aelred had been, as it were, drifted
together for a little time, probably that Waltheof
might be strengthened for the work which was now
before him. This was the reason that the temptation above-mentioned was sent to him, according to
brother Josceline. " By a wondrous providence," he
says, " our God, in His wondrous mercy, permitted
him whom He destined for the government of souls
to be tried by this temptation, for the increase of
his crown, and that by his own experience he might
have compassion on others." And he proceeds to
tell us what was this government of souls. In the
year 1147, the monks of Melrose elected him their
Abbot, and sent to Rievaux to beg of Aelred to
give him permission to accept the office. Again,
therefore, the two friends were separated, though not
for ever, for the abbot of Rievaux was the regular
visitor of the community of Melrose. It was Wal-

theof's lot to win back all his old friends in the
course of his life; after many years, he now found
again his step-father King David, and his brother
Prince Henry. How his whole former life must
have rushed upon him as he re-crossed the border,
after so many years of monastic trials! His life, as
a courtier in Scotland, must have appeared a very
point in his existence, and the adventure of the
ring and the lady at that distance almost ludicrous.
When he reached his abbey, he found himself lord
of an extensive domain; for though the abbot of
Melrose was not the mitred prelate that he afterwards became, yet the whole countryside was in his
hands. The people had been all but converted by
St. Cuthbert, as prior of the monastery; and King
David had endowed the community with extensive
lands, so that the abbot of Melrose, by a double
title, was spiritual and temporal lord of a large
part of Tweeddale. Waltheof found his abbey in
a delicate state. Richard, the first abbot of New
Melrose, had just been deposed for harsh conduct
towards the monks; the new abbot had, therefore,
to recover the authority lost by his predecessor,
without irritating the brethren, who, of course, were
exceedingly sensitive to any exertion of discipline
on the part of their spiritual ruler.

As Melrose was, in point of fact, a new abbey,
this state of things might have ruined it. The
abbey had seen strange vicissitudes: first, it had
come under St. Columban's rule,[1] with all its minute

---

[1] Mr. Michelet thinks that St. Columban's rule differed from that
of St. Benedict, in that it was mystical to such an extent as to make
light of the grossest sins of the flesh. If he had construed the passage

and severe penances, and its uncompromising severity. It seems hard to say precisely when it became
Benedictine, for the rules of St. Columban and of
St. Benedict were not so far opposed to each other
that they were incapable of existing side by side.
Some communities observed both together, till at
length St. Benedict's rule got the day, as being the
wisest legislation for monks, considering the average
capabilities of man. While St. Columban's monks
fasted every day till evening, St. Benedict varied
the hour at different times of the year. Again,
there is a special provision for difference of climate
in the Benedictine habit, which is not the case in
that of St. Columban. On the whole, the Benedictine rule was found on experience the better.
It was framed in that mild Italian spirit which
was needed to temper the fierceness of our northern
blood; and probably the rejection of the Scottish
usages about Easter, and the Benedictine rule, came
hand-in-hand into Melrose. Certainly St. Cuthbert,
who was himself a convert from the Scottish mode
of keeping Easter, was also the first to introduce
St. Benedict's rule into Lindisfarne. This is bringing the matter very near Melrose, and seems to
point to him as the person under whom the abbey
first became Benedictine. In the time of Waltheof's

on which he founds his opinion, he would have seen that it has no
reference to actual guilt, but was a provision to exclude the very sus-
picion of it. Si quis monachus dormierit in una *domo* cum muliere,
duos dies in pane et aqua. What he translates, S'il ignorait que ce
fut une faute, means Si nescierit mulierem esse in domo. It would
be invidious to point out a blunder however gross in so long and so
able a history, if so monstrous a conclusion had not been founded upon
it.—Histoire de France, tom. i. 277.

predecessor it underwent another change, for King
David had made it Cistercian, and put it under
the jurisdiction of Rievaux. The convent seems to
have been entirely removed from its old spot, for,
about half-a-mile from the present ruins of the
abbey, is a place which tradition assigns as the site
of old Melrose, on a promontory, stretching so far
into the Tweed that the waters all but convert it
into an island. The convent did not at first flourish in its new locality, owing to the harshness of
abbot Richard, and perhaps to the impatience of
the community under their new rule. The monks
were very anxious to get rid of their abbot, but
they were afraid to take any steps to get him
deposed, as he was an intimate friend of the king.
At last, they hit upon the expedient of electing
Waltheof in his room. This effectually disarmed
David's anger, and Waltheof was joyfully welcomed
by him back to his dominions.

Waltheof thus found himself again a man in
authority. During the rest of his life he was now
to be everything for other people, and nothing for
himself. Of the many years which he spent at
Melrose but little is known ; how they passed, however, we may judge by the kind of idea which was
still preserved of him in the abbey at the time when
Josceline wrote his life. Every tradition points to
the paternal kindness and sweetness of his rule.
The old monks still told of him, that when a monk,
who had fallen into a grievous fault, had once confessed it publicly and done penance, he would always
punish severely any one who reproached the offender,
or made any allusion to his fault. "Often he had

in his mouth," says Josceline, "that saying of the blessed Hugh of Cluny, 'If either happened to me, I would rather be punished for showing too much mercy, than for too much severity.' In the secret of the confessional, he showed himself so mild and soothing a physician, that, however stubborn was the breast of the sinner, the droppings of his words of holy consolation would soften it to a true and fruitful penitence ; and, by smiting it with the rod of the Lord's Cross, he would cleave the hard rock, till it burst forth into a fount of tears ; and then, when he saw him weep, tears of compassion used to flow from his eyes." A tradition still remained of the beauty of his countenance ; and it was said that, notwithstanding his austerities, his face had still a delicate colour in the midst of its paleness. Besides this, the earnestness of his preaching was remembered, as well as his eloquent and lucid speech, whether he spoke in French, English, or Latin, of all which languages he was perfect master. With these qualities and acquirements, it is not wonderful that he should be said to have gained an immediate influence on all who came in his way, by his persuasive words and kindness of manner. And this overflowing love extended itself even to animals. Stories were told of his affection for the old grey horse which he constantly rode, and which he used playfully to call his brother Grizzle.[1] He was even known to punish himself severely with the discipline used in the order for having killed an insect, saying that he had taken away the life of a creature of God, which he could not restore.

[1] Frater Ferrandus, v. Ducange in voc.

It was, however, not only within the walls of the abbey that his kindness of heart was known. The abbot of Melrose, as head of the Cistercian order in Scotland, was not a man who could always remain within the cloisters of his monastery. He had to go up into the Highlands as far as Elgin to found the abbey of Kinloss; and at another time down among the Cumberland hills, to lead a colony from Melrose to Holmcultram. In his time, too, an abbey was projected by his half-brother, Prince Henry, and the site was fixed upon near the town of Cupar-Angus, not far from the banks of the river Isla; it was not, however, put into execution till the time of his successor. His greatest sphere of action was in the wild country around Melrose itself. The abbot's grey horse and his truly apostolic retinue were well known in the valley of the Tweed, and among the many winding glens, which each sends its tributary stream into the broad river, along the banks of which lay the possessions of the abbey. This was the very ground which had witnessed St. Cuthbert's labours before he was made bishop of Lindisfarne, and the Saint had never a worthier successor than abbot Waltheof. His retinue was not of the kind which brother Josceline regrets was becoming in fashion among the Cistercian abbots of his time. They could not sleep, he says, for a night in a grange of the abbey without a train of servants and numerous sumpter-horses with pack-saddles containing mantles of the finest cloth, lined with lamb's-wool. His train consisted of a monk and a lay-brother, with three boys to look after the horses. The abbot was so little solicitous about his personal appearance, and travelled with so little luggage himself, that he used to ride with the boots and other apparel of his attendants slung on in front, to save them the trouble of carrying them.

He was, however, not the less beloved by the vassals of the abbey because he travelled about in the guise of a poor man. Melrose was the regular refuge of the whole countryside, in the midst of the many physical sufferings which came upon the peasantry in those hard times. Sometimes grievous famines come upon the land, and the whole population from a great distance round used to assemble about the abbey. It required faith to undertake to feed these multitudes, and God rewarded the faith of the abbot, by working miracles to enable him to do what he had undertaken. At one time it is said, a sore distress afflicted the country, and no one knew what to do. It was yet three months to the harvest, and the last year's provision was all spent. The corn was still green in the valleys and on the hill-sides ; and what was to be done in the meanwhile, before autumn came? Melrose was the only resource, and so all trooped off to the Tweed side with their wives and children, and thronged the abbey gates. It was hardly possible that the granaries of the monks could supply them ; but at least it would be better to die under the abbey walls, where the brethren would administer the rites of the church to the dying, than to lie down and perish in detachments in their lonely glens. A vast crowd, therefore, collected together, and, as it were, besieged the gates of Melrose. Waltheof went out with Thomas the cellarer and some of the brethren to learn how large was the multitude. He found that they had regularly encamped about the abbey, under the trees of the many woods, and on the level grounds by the side of the Tweed, for two miles around ; four thousand men were said to be assembled on the spot. Waltheof turned to Thomas, and asked him how this number of men were to be nourished till the autumn. Thomas was called in the country the good cellarer, on account of his kindness to the poor; he said that the numerous flocks and herds of the abbey might be slain to feed them ; but, he added, all the corn of the abbey was consumed except what remained in the two granges of Gattonside and Eildon. The abbot, on hearing this, took his crosier in his hand and crossed the Tweed to Gattonside, then a grange belonging to the abbey, now a village smiling amongst its orchards opposite to Melrose. He then went into the granary, and striking his crosier into the corn, knelt down and prayed with many tears. He remained a long time on his knees, and, when he rose, he made the sign of the cross, and went away; he also proceeded to an upland farm called the Eildon grange, and did the same thing there; then he turned to Thomas and said, " Now disperse boldly, and give to the poor and to ourselves, for God will give the increase, and multiply enough for the use of both." The monk did so, and the abbot's faith was rewarded, for the granaries of the two granges lasted out the three months which intervened to the harvest.

It was not, however, only among the poor of the land that Waltheof obtained influence ; his noble birth, and his brother's high station, made him a

conspicuous character ; and whenever the business
of the abbey for a moment brought him in contact
with his lofty kindred, the contrast between his
poverty and the station to which he was born
acted as a practical homily in a place where the
voice of religion was seldom heard. He once had
occasion to go to King Stephen, who, as well as
the King of Scotland, was his kinsman. This meeting with Stephen took place in the open air, and
he found him standing with Simon, the Earl of
Northampton, his own brother. The abbot had
not altered his apparel or increased the number of
his attendants, though he was going into the king's
presence. He appeared as usual on his old grey
horse, with the boots of the grooms slung on before
him instead of costly trappings ; and altogether he
was a very uncouth figure to appear among the
nobles, who were round the king, dressed in their
burnished armour, it could not be denied. His
brother felt ashamed of him as he approached, and
said : " See, my lord king, how my brother and
thy kinsman does honour to his lineage." Stephen
fixed his eyes on the abbot, and said with his
usual oath, " By God's birth, if thou and I had only
the grace to see it, he is an honour to us ; he is an
ornament to our race, even as the gem adorns the
gold in which it is set." Then he came forward
and kissed the abbot's hand, and asked for his
blessing, and bent his head to receive it. He granted
Waltheof all that he wanted, and took leave of him.
After he was gone, Stephen remembered his own
troubled life, how he had to fight for his crown,
and how little it profited him. He was a merciful

prince, and of much good feeling, and was affected
by this encounter. He was no friend to churchmen, on bad terms with the Pope and with both
English archbishops ; but his religious feelings were
roused, and he burst into tears, and said, " This
man has put all worldly things under his feet, but
we are in chase after this fleeting world, and are
losing body and soul in the pursuit." Such was
the effect of the sight of Waltheof on Stephen ;
his prayers for his brother had a more lasting result,
though he had to wait long to see the fruit of
them. Simon listened at last to his brother's ex-
hortations, and repented sincerely of his irregular
life. He founded the abbey of St. Andrew at
Northampton, in which house St. Thomas afterwards took refuge, as well as a nunnery dedicated
to St. Mary without the same town, and the Cistercian abbey of Saltrey, dependent on the house
of Wardon.

The favour of God was manifested to Waltheof
in other ways besides this answer to his prayers.
Our blessed Lord rewarded the crucified soul of
his servant with a foretaste of those joys which He
will give to His blessed ones in heaven. Sometimes, at long intervals, when the abbot was keeping
his Christmas or Easter festival in the church at
Melrose, Christ was pleased to manifest Himself to
His Saint in visions, one of which we will give in the
words of Josceline :—" Once when on Easter-night he
celebrated the vigil, and the convent was chaunting
psalms and hymns, the Saint saw in the Spirit the
whole course of the Lord's Passion, as though it
were going on before his eyes. It seemed to him

that he saw the Lord, after the scourging and mocking, bearing the crown of thorns upon His head, crucified on the tree, His hands and feet distended by the nails. He thought that he saw him giving up the ghost, and commending His soul into the hands of the Father, and afterwards pouring forth from His pierced side blood and water, to be our bath and our chalice, the price and the reward of man's salvation. He looked upon his soul, separated from the body, spoiling hell, and, followed by a numberless multitude of souls, coming out from the pit, resuming the body, bringing joy to the Angels by His resurrection, and by His appearance prostrating the soldiers, who were set to watch lest the Life should arise from the dead. Then in a vision he saw Him beautiful, in His robes of glory, going forth in the greatness of His strength, bringing into paradise the spoils of captivity."

5. HOW WALTHEOF WAS TAKEN TO HIS REST

This was the way in which the Lord recompensed him for the austerities with which he crucified his flesh, for his intense devotion, and for the many nights spent on the cold stones in the church, after the brethren had retired to rest, when compline was over. But he further rewarded him, by taking him to his rest from the cares of the world, and by calling him away while he was still at Melrose in the midst of his monks.

Waltheof had been many years abbot of Melrose,

and there seemed but little likelihood of his being
disturbed by attempts to remove him. He was,
however, to have another trial before he died. In
the year 1159, when St. Aelred happened to be
at Melrose, the brethren were one day surprised to
see a large and glittering cavalcade approach the
abbey; it was composed partly of ecclesiastics,
partly of men whose dress and bearing showed them
to be of high rank. They proved to be several of
the canons, accompanied by the great men of the
realm, come to offer Waltheof the vacant bishopric
of St. Andrew's. The abbot, as they had expected,
refused the see; but they had recourse to St. Aelred,
as his superior, to force him to accept it. The
Saint enjoined him on his obedience to accept it.
Waltheof, however, begged his friend to hear him
in private; and, when they were together, he
informed him that God had revealed to him that
he had now not long to remain in the world, and
that the charge was too much for one who was
soon to sicken and die. St. Aelred looked mourn-
fully at his friend, and saw that, from his emaciated
features and wasted frame, death could never be
looked upon as unlikely: but he would not believe
the message which Waltheof gave him; he shut his
eyes to the notion that his friend was to go to
his rest before him, and leave him alone upon earth;
he therefore persisted in his command. Then they
returned together to the chapter - house, where the
assembly was anxiously waiting for their return.
All were glad to hear St. Aelred's decision; but
Waltheof stood up and said, " I have put off my
old garment, how should I put it on again ? I have

washed my feet clean, how should I stain them again with the dust of the world's business?" Then he added, solemnly, with the tone and manner of a prophet, "Believe me, ye will elect another man, and have him for your bishop." Then he pointed with his finger to a stone in the pavement of the chapter-house, and said, "There is the place of my rest; here will be my habitation, among my children, as long as the Lord wills." All who were present saw that he was resolved, and the assembly retired, saying that they would let the matter rest for a time.

Waltheof was right; soon after this he was taken violently ill; his body was racked with pains. About the time of the dog-days, says Josceline, he grew very much worse, and all men thought that he must die at once. Nevertheless he lived for three weeks after this in dreadful pain of body, but perfectly collected in mind, so that in the intervals of his agonies he used to call the brethren around him, and exhort them to love and concord amongst each other, and charity to the poor. During the last nine days he seemed to be dying every moment, and the attendants wondered how it was possible that a frame so exhausted and so racked with pain could hold together. Then it was remembered that he had been used to pray that in his last sickness he might suffer pain as a penance for his sins, so that his life seemed to be prolonged in these fiery pains, in answer to his own prayers. As soon as a fit of pain had passed away and a short breathing time was allowed him, he would smile faintly, and lift up his hands, as if to thank God. Once he said to those about him,

"Oh! if I could but speak, I could tell you of wondrous things which I have seen." It is probable that God, who had so often favoured him with visions, now deigned to console him with a foretaste of heavenly joys, even while he was lying in agony. On Lammas-day, when the Church celebrates the memory of St. Peter's miraculous delivery from prison, he was so visibly dying that he received the Body and Blood of Christ and the rite of extreme Unction. Yet for two days and two nights he lay in pain, hourly expecting death, and yet kept alive to suffer. About the dawn of day on the 3rd of August, the convent was summoned to be present at the death of their father, and he was placed on sackcloth to die, according to the rule of the order. When he heard the low chaunt of the psalms and litanies around him, he opened his eyes and looked round upon them as if to thank them. He seemed so much revived that they retired; once again this scene had been renewed, when after sext, as the convent was sitting down to its mid-day meal, they were summoned for the last time. "There," says Josceline, "with the chaunts of his brethren sounding about him, this holy soul, after being tried as in a fiery furnace with fevers and manifold pains, and purified as gold in the fire, quitted the mortal tabernacle of its spotless body. Thus did the holy father pass from the world to the Father, from faith to sight, from hope to joy, from the shadow to the reality, from darkness to light, from the toilsome race to the hard-won crown, from the misery of this present life to the everlasting glory of a life never to pass away."

Thirteen years after the death of the Saint, the stone under which his body lay, in the very place which he had pointed out, was raised by abbot Josceline, and his remains were found uncorrupt. Again the same thing was found forty-eight years after his death. Many miracles were done at his tomb, which now lies neglected and unknown among the ruins of his abbey. A stone, indeed, is pointed out by tradition in the choir, to which his remains may have been translated. Nothing, however, certain is known, except that his body will rise gloriously in the resurrection of the just.

LIFE OF
ST. ROBERT [1]

WHAT is meant by the word obedience, as applied
to our blessed Lord, we cannot tell, still less can we
conceive how, in consequence of His humiliation, He
could be exalted. All that we know is, that for us
He bowed Himself down to the death of the cross,
in obedience to the will of the Father; and that for
our sakes He, in His human nature, was received up
into glory, though His everlasting glory could neither
grow nor decrease. His glory is represented as being
the reward of His voluntary sufferings; and yet,
incomprehensible as it is, this is not a mere representation, but both the glory and the sufferings are
real. And this, again, is the case with all members
of His Church; as His merits are imparted to them
not by a nominal imputation, but by a real and
ineffable union, so also the cross which they bear is

[1] This life of St. Robert is principally taken from a manuscript life of
him in the British Museum, which contains a few particulars not in the
Bollandists. It speaks of having heard things spoken of him by the
old men in the Abbey, and also of a book preserved there called
Collectaneus Sti. Roberti, containing his meditations and prayers, and
also of the book of his miracles. Many miraculous stories are told of
him in the life in the Bollandists.

not figurative, but a very crucifixion of body and soul. In proportion, too, as Christians are more saintly, that is, more Christian, they also partake more of the cross. They are not content with the narrow bounds of natural suffering, but they seek out for themselves, as it were, a supernatural cross, that they may learn to live above the flesh and to crucify it with their Lord. It is this inseparable connection between glory and suffering which makes the most contemplative Saints to be also the most austere. It is this which has driven holy monks and hermits into the wilderness; they durst not, without crucifying their bodies, give themselves up to the holy joys into which their love for Christ threw them, when they contemplated His mysteries. "There is no Thabor without Calvary," as it has been expressed; and "this is a fundamental law of Christian mysticism."

The first Cistercians were no exceptions to this rule, which is, in fact, the principle which gave life to all monastic orders, and which connects together ascetics in all ages, St. Anthony and St. Bruno, St. Benedict and St. Romuald. On the low, vine-clad plains of Burgundy St. Bernard renewed what St. Basil had begun in the solitudes of Pontus. In the wild forests and on the lonely mountains of the north of England the same scenes appeared as in the first ages were witnessed in the deserts of Egypt. And this was especially the case with the first generation of English Cistercians; from peculiar circumstances, they were distinguished by sterner features than those of France. There is little enough of sternness in the idea which we

form of St. Bernard writing his sermons on the
Canticles in the arbour of twisted flowers,[1] in the
garden of Clairvaux; or in St. Basil's description
of his solitude, and of the clear river sweeping
round his woody mountains, which collected its
waters into a clear basin like a lake, and then
again narrowed into a river. But our first English
Cistercians had little leisure for scenery. The colony
sent to Rievaux came over from France and found
a home ready for them; but the first monks who
broke away from a Benedictine abbey, as St. Stephen
did from Molesme, had to endure a trial which it
required superhuman energy to bear. Their history
forms the principal portion of the very brief life of
Robert of Newminster which remains to us.

Few, indeed, are the particulars which are related
of him, except as far as he is connected with Fountains Abbey. He was born in the district of Craven,
apparently at the village of Gargrave.[2] He went to
the university of Paris, and his biographer appeals
to a book on the Psalms, which he is said to have
composed, as a proof of his progress in theology.
He then was ordained priest to his native village
of Gargrave. He next appears as a monk at
Whitby. In the year 1132, however, news reached
the monastery of a movement in the Benedictine
order, which entirely altered Robert's plan of life;
and we must transport the reader into the chapter-
house of St. Mary's Abbey at York, that he may

---

[1] Pisatiis floribus intextum. Vita Sti. Bern.

[2] Ex provincia Eboracensi quæ Craven dicitur. Gargrave ubi natus
fuerat. MS. The Church of St. Andrew of Gargrave was given in
1321 to the Abbey of Sallay by William Percy. Vide Dugdale.

see how the voice from Citeaux found an echo in
England.

The abbey was rich and magnificent, but any
one who entered it soon perceived that St. Benedict would hardly have known it for his. It was
not that the monks were men of scandalous lives.
"On the contrary," says the chronicle of Fountains,
"they lived honestly, but they fell far short of the
perfection enjoined by the rule." The abbot was
a kind-hearted man, but he was old and ignorant,
and the monks led an easy life. A noise of chat-
tering and laughing might be heard all over the
abbey ; some, indeed, kept aloof, and would go into
the church to pray while others were idle. The
greater part, after compline, instead of going to
the dormitory, walked about, and, dividing into
knots, talked about the news of the day. Thus
there were two parties in the community ; but the
strict party were a very small minority, only thirteen
monks. However, they had at their head Richard,
the prior, and Gervase, the sub-prior, so they hoped
that something might be done through them ; and,
on the eve of the feast of St. Peter and St. Paul,
he went, with the sub-prior, to Godfrey, the abbot,
and propounded to him his thoughts as to the lax
state of the abbey. But the poor abbot trembled
at the very notion of innovation. He said that the
convent would have an ill name, that all the world
lived as they lived, and that he did not see why
they should affect singularity ; in fine, it was impossible. Richard, however, stood his ground manfully ;
as for innovation, it was only going back to the rule
of St. Benedict ; and, as for impossibility, the monks

of Clairvaux and Citeaux found it possible enough. The abbot put off his decision, and begged him to put down in writing what he wanted. By the time, however, that this was done, the other monks had heard of what was rumoured; "and," says the chronicle, "there arose a great tumult in the monastery." Richard, seeing that the case was hopeless, applied to Thurstan, Archbishop of York, saying that they were threatened with excommunication by their brethren. They protested that all that they wanted was "to follow Christ, who was a poor man, in His voluntary poverty, and to bear Christ's cross on their bodies." The archbishop applied to Abbot Godfrey; and the old abbot wept, and said that he would not oppose their holy resolution, but could do nothing without the chapter. So the archbishop promised to meet the chapter.

On the appointed day, Thurstan, with several grave and reverend ecclesiastics connected with the cathedral, went to St. Mary's Abbey, to try to pacify it. When, however, they reached as far as the door of the chapter-house, they were met by the abbot, who protested that the archbishop alone should enter, without the secular clerks who attended him. When Thurstan remonstrated, out rushed from the chapter-house the whole convent, and with them a number of strange monks, Cluniacs and Benedictines, assembled for the occasion. Such an uproar ensued as St. Mary's Abbey has never witnessed before or since. They roared, they bellowed, and they declared that they would rather suffer an interdict for an hundred years than yield an inch. Suddenly they shouted, "Seize them, seize them!" and then they attacked Richard and his friends, and would have torn them to pieces, if they had not clasped the archbishop's knees for shelter. Then they drove archbishop, monks, and clerks, altogether, pell-mell into the church, with cries of "Seize the rebels! seize the traitors!" So the archbishop quitted the monastery, and took with him the brethren thus forcibly ejected, being twelve priests and one sub-deacon, and lodged them in his house. Here they remained till Christmas-day, when the archbishop took them with him to Ripon Minster, and, in the midst of the solemn services of the festival, he assigned them their habitation, of which they set out to take possession, after having elected Richard for their abbot.

This was what Robert heard at Whitby; he must also have been told that nothing could equal the desolation of the place, or the hardships which, in that rugged season, they endured. We know nothing of the previous workings of his mind, but that this did not deter him is quite clear, for he obtained leave from his abbot to join them, and set out to find their habitation, and a more desolate scene could hardly be imagined. It was on the banks of the Skeld, under a ridge of rocks, and surrounded by pathless woods, then in all the nakedness of winter. And where were the monks themselves? Under a broad elm, in the midst of the belt of rocks, they had made a hut with hurdles roofed with turf. Here they lived, in the midst of the terrible cold of winter; their very existence was a miracle, but it was still more wonderful how medita-tion, and the chaunting of psalms by night, and the regular hours, and the holy sacrifice of the mass, could go on regularly, almost in the open air, to the sound of the wind howling about them through the leafless trees, and of the hoarse roaring of the swollen Skeld. Robert's must have been a resolute heart, not to be appalled by such a scene as this; but he was supported by his resolution to suffer with Christ, so that the bitter cold, and the long fasts, and coarse food of the little community were a source of joy to him, because they united him to his Lord.

He found the brethren employed in hewing down trees to build a chapel. As for tilling their ground, that was out of the question at that time of the year; and they were supported solely by supplies which they obtained from the Archbishop of York. It seems wonderful how human bodies could manage to pass the winter in such a solitude, and with so little shelter, but the grace of God supported them. "No sign of sadness," says the Chronicle, "was seen among them; not a sound of murmuring, but all blessed God with entire fervour, poor in worldly goods, but strong in faith." After the winter was over, and the voice of spring was heard in their woods, they determined to send to Clairvaux that they might be affiliated to the Cistercian order. We may suppose with what joy the Blessed St. Bernard received the two brethren whom they sent, and wrote to them a letter with his own hand, sending them an aged monk called Godfrey, to teach them Cistercian discipline. According to Godfrey's directions, they built their house, and ordered their whole life according to the institutes

of Clairvaux. Very soon the spark which they had
kindled spread in England, and ten novices appeared
to share their hard life with them. Abbot Richard
received them joyfully; but it was a great act of
faith to receive them, for still they had no possessions of their own but what the Archbishop of York
gave them. For two years they struggled on, sometimes obliged to live on roots and on the leaves of
trees, till they almost despaired, and Richard set
out for Clairvaux to expose their distress to its holy
abbot. St. Bernard assigned them a grange belonging to his abbey, for their support, but Richard on
his return found that God had had compassion upon
them, and had rewarded their faith by moving the
heart of Hugh, the Dean of York, to become a
novice of the poor house of Fountains, and to give
them all his wealth, so that the abbot when he
returned, found plenty reigning in his monastery.
He found also a library, and the books of the Holy
Scripture, which Hugh had given them.

Years went on, and the community flourished
more and more, till in the fifth year after their
foundation, a noble baron, called Ralph de Merlay,
offered to endow a Cistercian house if they would
send a colony of White monks into his lands.
Abbot Richard joyfully assented, and he appointed
Robert to be the leader of the twelve brethren of
the new house. " It was a beautiful place, pleasant
with water, and very fair wood about it," and was
called Newminster.

Of Robert's government of his abbey, such scanty
records remain that it is impossible to form a connected history of it. As a proof of its flourishing

condition, three colonies were sent from his abbey during his lifetime, Pipewell in 1143, Sallay and Roche about 1147. Further than this, only scattered notices are inserted, two of which are here put down, because they help to give a faint idea of the abbot, and because they have never been published elsewhere. One day, Abbot Robert wished to return from a grange, where he had been visiting the lay brethren of the abbey; a great festival was approaching, and he wished to hurry back to Newminster. He had no palfrey to convey him back, so he called for a pack-horse, which used to carry bread to the granges. He mounted his sorry steed and pulled his cowl over his face, and began to pray and meditate as he was wont to do wherever he went. As he was riding along, he was roused from his meditation by a voice rudely asking him whether he had seen the lord abbot in the place which he had left. This was a nobleman who had come to the abbey on business, and had been directed to seek him at the grange. Seeing this shabby figure, the nobleman thought that it was some lay-brother. Robert did not choose to undeceive him, for he wished still to pass for a poor lay-brother, and so he shrewdly said, "When I was last at the grange, the abbot was there." But the nobleman when he had looked further at the speaker's features, knew at once from his saintly face that the abbot himself was speaking to him, so he humbly got down from his fine horse, and made the abbot mount it, and when he had finished his business with him, he begged for his blessing and went away.

At another time a great trial befell Robert, one probably more harassing than all his bodily mortifications. He was accused to St. Bernard of misconduct in the government of his abbey, and it appears that the saint so far believed it that Robert was obliged to take a journey into France to clear himself. But when St. Bernard saw him and marked the angelic temper with which the abbot bore the humiliation, without speaking harshly of his accusers, he felt sure that he was innocent, and from that time loved him the more. During this journey he also saw Pope Eugenius,[1] and returned back to Newminster full of joy, for good had come out of evil; and it is especially recorded that he did not speak a word of reproach to his accusers when he returned.

It was in 1159 that this saint passed to his rest. He had been to visit his great friend, St. Godric, the holy hermit of Finchale, whom he used to consult in all spiritual matters. It was now fifty years since St. Godric had entered his hermitage; and though he was lying in extreme weakness on his bed from which he never rose, yet his mind rose above his body, and he was endowed with many supernatural gifts so that he often knew of events which happened a great distance off as though he were present. It was a little before the feast of the Lord's Ascension that he quitted St. Godric to hasten back to his monastery, and the holy hermit told him at parting, that he should see his face no

[1] This fixes the date to 1147-8. William, Bishop of Durham, who is said in the MS. to have given the lands of Walsingham to the abbey, is William of St. Barbara.

more. On the Saturday after the festival, he fell ill, and knew that he was to die. When he had received the Holy Sacrament, and was visibly dying, the older brethren of the monastery came to him, begging of him to name as his successor the man whom he thought most fit. But the saint said, "I know well that ye will not follow my advice, but elect brother Walter," and so indeed it befell after his death. Soon after this he raised his hands to heaven, and prayed for his spiritual sons, and for his monastery, and then he passed away to the joys of heaven on the 7th of June 1159. At the time that he gave up his soul into the hands of God, a vision appeared to St. Godric, which we will give in the words of the chronicle. " The man of God, Godric, saw while he was praying, an intense light penetrating into the darkness of the night and two walls of brightness reaching from earth to heaven. Between these walls angels were flying up to heaven, bearing with songs of joy, the soul of Abbot Robert, one on the right hand, the other on the left. The soul, as far as it could be seen, was like a globe of fire. As they were ascending, the enemy of the human race met them, but went back in confusion, for he could find nothing to lay hold of in him. And the servant of God saw the soul of his dear friend thus ascend to heaven, of which the gates were opened for him. And, lo! a voice was heard, repeating twice, ' Enter now, my friends.' "

The body of St. Robert was buried first in the chapter, and afterwards translated to the choir in consequence of the miracles which took place at his tomb.

THE RIVERSIDE PRESS LIMITED
ST BERNARD'S ROW, EDINBURGH